TO MOVE WITH THE TIMES

TO MOVE WITH THE TIMES

THE TIMES

The Story of Transport and Travel in Scotland

Anne Gordon

ABERDEEN UNIVERSITY PRESS

First published 1988
Aberdeen University Press
A member of the Pergamon Group

© Anne Gordon 1988

British Library Cataloguing in Publication Data

Gordon, Anne
    To move with the times: the story of
    transport and travel in Scotland.
    1. Transportation—Scotland—History
    I. Title
    380.5′09411   HE245

    ISBN 0–08–035080–1
    ISBN 0–08–036398–9 (Pbk)

PRINTED IN GREAT BRITAIN
THE UNIVERSITY PRESS
ABERDEEN

CONTENTS

ILLUSTRATIONS

ACKNOWLEDGEMENTS

I am very grateful for all the help given by Mrs Rosemary Mackenzie, Tain; Mrs Jessie Macdonald, Balintore; Dr Michael Robson, Newcastleton; Miss I Robb, Newton St Boswells; the staff of the National Library of Scotland and the Map Room; Aberdeen City Library; Aberdeen Art Gallery; Grampian Regional Transport; Borders Regional Library Headquarters, and Mr J Luby of Duns Library, Berwickshire. Particular thanks are due to Mr H Mackay of Hawick Library, Roxburghshire, Mrs Anne Carrick who did the drawings on pp. 63, 104, 109, 120 and 181, Jim McDonald who did the drawing on p. 218, Miss J Lawrie for proof-reading, and to my daughter, Venetia Thomson, for much generous help.

A NOTE ON THE TEXT

This book is concerned with the social effects of transport, or the lack of it, on the everyday life of the people. It omits sea transport except in so far as it affected something closely involved with land transport, such as ferries.

Scots currency went out of use officially in 1707 but, in spite of that, it continued to be used for a long time thereafter and certainly into the 1760s, and in some cases accounts appear in both Scots money and in sterling. Scots money equalled one-twelfth of sterling.

It may be helpful to give a rough idea of people's wages:

	1790s	1830–40
Farm worker with food	£6–£8 per annum	£12–£14 per annum
Female	£3–£5 per annum	£6 per annum
Day labourer with food	10d.–1s. 0d. per day	1s. 6d. per day
Wrights, masons with food	1s. 6d.–1s. 8d. per day	2s. 6d. per day

1 THE EARLY HIGHWAYS OF SCOTLAND

From early times Scotland, at least in the south, has had a road system of a sort, starting with the three main lines of roads made between AD 178 and 185 by the Romans. One of these was over the Cheviot Hills and on to the River Forth via Melrose; another was from the Solway Firth to the Lower Clyde via Annandale; and the third was from the Roman wall at Camelon via Stirling to the Tay, with connecting roads between them. Parts of these roads still survive and show how wide and how well constructed they were.[1]

Apart from the remains of Roman roads there appear to have been roads, or at least suitable routes, in southern Scotland during mediaeval times. Professor Barrow, in an article on the evidence concerning mediaeval roads in Scotland[2] makes a strong case for there having been roads capable of taking wheeled traffic in those days because, for one thing, it is known that army supplies were often carried in horse-drawn carts and ox wagons which on occasion managed to cover the ground at a surprising speed. In 1296 Edward I of England set out to conquer Scotland, with baggage trains and siege engines, and got as far north as Elgin and, because there are very few references to his spending money on repairing or making roads during this advance, it is inferred that in the north too there was a road system capable of coping with an army on the move. Even allowing for the fact that Edward went by the east coast route which was the easiest, and presumably made use of a bridge which crossed the Spey a few miles below Rothes, a bridge which has long since gone, it was a remarkable achievement. Church establishments such as abbeys also used wheeled vehicles in late mediaeval times for carrying their produce and obtaining supplies, including stone and wood for building, but this was obviously a limited traffic.

From early times there are references to the King's Highway, the high road and the gait or gate, these roads often being known by the name of the place to which they led. Professor Barrow doubts that they were merely tracks for pedestrians or horses although it is said[3] that the word 'road' originally referred to riding and that it was only about the end of the sixteenth century that it was used to refer to a road for other forms of travel. These roads may have served as rights of way as much as anything else: in 1555 an Act of the

Scottish Parliament said that highways, especially those from burghs and seaports, should be kept open and that anyone stopping them up would be punished as an oppressor, which gives an impression that the highway's primary role was to give access; it does not necessarily seem to have been a word denoting the condition of a road.[4]

Pilgrimage is one of the oldest reasons for travel and between 1493 and 1513, James IV visited widely separate sacred sites in Scotland, including eighteen visits to the Shrine of St Duthac at Tain, Ross-shire, usually travelling by the same coastal route to Elgin which had been used by Edward I, and then crossing over the ferries of Ardersier and Cromarty, or else continuing along the coast by Inverness and Dingwall and round the head of the Beauly and Cromarty Firths. One year he brought his wife, Margaret Tudor, with him which must have increased his travelling difficulties and his baggage train considerably.[5] There still exists, a little south of Tain, a small section of what is called the King's Causeway, said to have been built by the people of the town when they heard that the king was coming barefoot on one particular pilgrimage, which implies that previously there was no proper road, just a beaten track. This causeway was probably very similar to several

1   The King's Causeway. Children from Tain Academy working to clear it, c.1967. King's Causeway is said to have been built by the people of Tain, Ross-shire, for James IV when they heard he was coming barefoot on a pilgrimage to the shrine of St Duthac.

2   Old Roman bridge at Bothwell. Source: Scottish Ethnological Archive, Royal Museum of Scotland.

old ones in the parish of Campsie, Stirlingshire, on the line of the road to the church, which according to tradition were made as a penance by offenders, and in particular, by seven McDonald brothers.[6]

'Beaten track' is how Joseph Mitchell, General Inspector of Highland Roads and Bridges under Thomas Telford, described the road which ran along the coast from Aberdeen to Inverness prior to the eighteenth century.[7] It was also interrupted by deep rivers, for both the Findhorn and Nairn were unbridged and by then the Spey was too, as were other smaller but also formidable rivers. This makes the journeys of Edward I and James IV all the more impressive; but it was one thing for an army or a king to travel, with their financial strength and powers of obtaining local back-up services, it was quite another for ordinary people to do so. James IV was an exceptional traveller anyway as not only did he also make annual pilgrimages to Whithorn in the south-west of the country, but he is said to have sometimes come north alone and travelling lightly and to have ridden on one occasion the 130-mile journey from Stirling via Perth and Aberdeen to Elgin in one day.[8] This feat was reported by a Bishop of Ross, but even coming from a churchman it is hard to believe.

An idea of how the path of early royal travellers was smoothed by calling on local services can be seen from what happened in the Coldingham area of Berwickshire in 1616. That year the Privy Council began making preparations for the expected Scottish visit the following year of James VI, the only one he made after he went south. They ordered that part of the way in the parish of Coldingham should be enlarged and mended by the people of Coldingham and Oldcambus, and later on decreed that horses and carts from every Berwickshire parish should be made available for the royal progress. But orders were one thing and carrying them out another, and the work was still not begun a month before the king was expected and threats of being held to be rebels had to be made against the people to hurry them up.[9]

However, ordinary people most certainly did not travel nor move goods in the way that kings, armies or abbeys could. Scotland's physical features militated against easy communications. Ranges of hills and mountains could prove almost insuperable obstacles — in spite of James IV's 130-mile ride — and although unbridged rivers could be crossed by ferry at a price or by ford at some risk, this could be impossible when there were heavy rains or spates, what the writer of the *Statistical Account for Roxburgh* in the county of that name called 'the accidental magnitude of the rivers'. Firths ran far inland and many routes were made extra long because of the need to find safe water crossings.[10] There were great areas of boggy ground, far more in pre-drainage days than now, and these made travelling very dangerous.

Some of the hazards of early journeys were graphically described by Taylor the Water Poet in 1618; on leaving Brechin, Angus, he

> tooke another guide which brought me such strange wayes over mountaines and rockes that I thinke my horse never went the like ... I did go through a countrey called Glaneske [Glenesk] where passing by the side of a hill, so steepe as the ridge of a house, where the way was rocky, and not above a yard broad in some places ... if either horse or man had slipt, he had fallen a good mile downeright. ...[11]

It is possible that James VI on his journey of 1617 did not think much of the facilities either, as that year an Act was passed requiring all highways and routes between market towns and seaports to be at least 20 feet wide, and these roads along with those from towns to parish churches were put in the charge of Justices of the Peace.[12]

The Scottish Parliament continued to try to improve roads in the mid seventeenth century with various Acts. One of 1641 ratified earlier Acts of 1555 and 1592 and required JPs to inform the Privy Council about any new road that might be needed from a town to a parish church and also referred to keeping open roads to market towns.[13]

One of the Instructions for the Justices of the Peace in Scotland required them to order highways and bridges to be repaired, as well as ferries to be regulated.[14]

These Acts did little good and there are so many eighteenth century references to the need for roads and to those that existed being very bad, that one wonders what happened to the mediaeval ones. Certainly old place names often indicate travelling routes — paths, fords and so on — but apart from the accounts of a few travellers which are necessarily subjective, the main reports of road conditions and of bridges in the mid eighteenth century, apart from those in the Highlands, appear in the *Statistical Accounts* of the 1790s, by which time, however, improvements had begun, especially in southern Scotland. A typical *Statistical Account* report for the state of things in the middle of that century in eastern Scotland said that the King's Highway which passed through the parish was until about 1750 'very insufficient and in winter almost impassable'[15] while on the other side of the country, in Ayrshire about the same date, the roads were described as 'merely horse paths'.[16] Even in Jedburgh, an abbey town in southern Scotland which lies almost on the Roman road of Dere Street, the roads prior to 1750 were described as very bad, with those to church and other market towns — such as the Act of 1617 had sought to provide for — unfit for wheeled traffic and in winter almost impractical.[17]

The further north one went, the poorer the roads were. The records of military surveyors after 1726 provide good descriptions of Highland roads[18] which were classified by how uneven, wet or steep they were. Thomas Telford, the great engineer, making his first report to the Commissioners for Highland Roads and Bridges in 1803 said of Highland roads that before 1742 they were 'merely the tracks of black cattle and horses, intersected by numerous rapid streams, which being frequently swollen into torrents by heavy rains, rendered them dangerous or impassable'.[19] Matthew Paris's map of thirteenth-century Scotland showed the far north and west as 'marshy and impassable, fit for cattle and shepherds',[20] and that continued to be the situation for many years, none of the mediaeval roads apparently having penetrated to these parts. Thomas Pennant did not see a single road in Caithness when he visited it in 1769 and described the county as little better than an immense morass, though with what he called some 'fruitful spots'.[21]

One writer said of travel in the mid eighteenth century, 'A journey in those days was a challenge to one's nerve — a veritable campaign against weather, distance, time and inconveniencies innumerable. Nothing tamer than undeniable necessity would commit one to it'.[22] When necessity required Dr John Kemp to travel north in 1796 in his capacity as Secretary of the Society for the Propagation of Christian Knowledge, he found not even a beaten track on the way to the very north-west coast. He had to follow a guide over large rocks among loose stones or over the tough surface of the moss which was 10–12 feet deep in some places, or through the beds of burns which had washed away the moss and made a firm bottom. In order to follow a straight line they had to ride very much in water and crossed one burn twenty-four

times in an hour. In the whole of that county of Sutherland, which stretches
from coast to coast, there was only one bridge in the 1790s.[23]

Not unnaturally the position in the Northern Isles was as bad. Of the
parish of Delting, Shetland, it was said,

> 'There are no bridges, nor so much as the form of a road through the island. The
> traveller goes on his way with caution, through the hills and deep mosses; and by
> turning sometimes to the one hand and sometimes to the other, endeavours in the
> best manner he can, to get clear of the mires and ditches and peat-banks that fall
> in his way'.[24]

In common with many of the *Statistical Accounts*, this quotation ended with
the suggestion that roads could be made there, but nothing much was done for
many years — fifty years later Sandsting and Aithsting, Shetland, still had no
roads;[25] neither had the island of Westray in Orkney;[26] and the *Account* for
Fetlar and North Yell, Shetland, sounded quite pathetic as it said 'We have no
roads of any kind, not even sheep tracks, and must make our way by meaths
(landmarks) from hill to hill and from toon to toon'.[27]

Even in the nineteenth century there were no roads in large parts of the
Western Isles, but in places like Tiree the fine sandy beaches provided easy
access,[28] and North Uist could boast that Nature had provided the parish with
the best possible road when the tide was out but not when it was in.[29] On the
mainland also beaches could be used as roads — in 1650 when the Duke of
Montrose was defeated at Carbisdale in Ross-shire, he had been surprised by
troops marching along the southern shore of the Dornoch Firth.[30] About
the mid eighteenth century the Greenock to Gourock road was 'by the
shoreside, and if strong gales produced a high tide, an embargo was placed on
all travellers till the weather moderated'.[31] In a rather similar way, people
going from Selkirkshire to Edinburgh used the bed of the Gala Water as a
road when it was sufficiently dry to do so, a dry water course being better than
a bad road.[32]

The question is, what happened to mediaeval roads? Were they as good as
their reported use implies? Certainly the *Statistical Account* for Swinton and
Simprim in Berwickshire referred to an earlier perfection in the art of
road-making which had by then died out.[33] Was movement on mediaeval
roads largely achieved by the brute force of all the king's men, whether in
military or civilian life? Were road surfaces made at all? Such surfaces are,
after all, not necessary for wheeled traffic so long as the ground is firm[34] and
the traffic amount limited. Water crossings presented problems but they
could be overcome by using fords and ferries. Did these early roads fall into
disuse and disrepair during the turbulent times of the Reformation, the
Covenanting troubles, the Restoration and the Revolution, as well as the
Stuart risings? Or was it that roads were just not necessary to a population
living at subsistence level, wanting little and unable to supply very much?[35]

Such travelling as was done by ordinary people was on foot; only the well-off rode, while goods were transported on pack horses and the great Highland export of black cattle could be moved alive along such tracks as there were.[36] Whatever the truth about early roads, progress really began in the eighteenth century and has never looked back.

2 ROADWAYS OF THE HIGHLANDS

Slightly pre-dating the main road-making being carried out elsewhere and then running concurrently with it, great things began to happen in the Highlands in the eighteenth and nineteenth centuries. These included the building of the military roads between 1726 and the 1760s by General Wade and his successor, Major Caulfield; of the parliamentary roads of Thomas Telford in the first decades of the nineteenth century; and of the destitution roads which were built as relief works after the potato famine of 1846. These have all been well described in other works but nevertheless they must be mentioned here.

After the Jacobite rising of 1715, the Highlands were in a state of turmoil. English troops were stationed at the garrisons of Inverlochy (Fort William), Fort Augustus and Fort George, as well as at Ruthven Barracks near Kingussie. But something more than garrisons was needed and in 1725 General Wade, who had been effective in suppressing Jacobite support in south-west England, was sent to Scotland to see what could be done to pacify the Highlanders. He came as a soldier, commander of the troops in North Britain, training men and confiscating forbidden arms; but he left with the reputation of a road builder because he was given the task of carrying out one of his own recommendations, that of linking up these garrisons by roads so that troops could be easily moved between them and also joining them to the Lowlands. Although Wade had no experience of road-building he obviously had a natural flair for it and a pioneering spirit and between 1725 and 1732 he completed some 250 miles of roads. To do so, he had about five hundred soldiers, based in different places in detachments and receiving a little over the normal army pay. All they had to work with were the basic road-making tools of the time, along with barrows and explosives for stubborn rocky sections. As they did not work on these roads in the five or so winter months, their achievements are all the more remarkable; but they were perhaps helped by the fact that roads went just where Wade decided they should, without consultation with or compensation to proprietors, and fords were made rather than bridges, for which skilled civilians were called in later on. After the main road works were finished, Wade had forty or so bridges built, of which the main ones were over the Spean, Tummel, the Perthshire Garry and the Tay at Aberfeldy.[1]

Following it seems, Roman ideas, military roads ran as straight as possible, up hill and down dale, with little attention paid to gradient.[2] One writer said of the military road which ran from Carlisle to Portpatrick — not one built by Wade — that its line was 'so preposterous that mere folly could hardly have stumbled upon it . . .'.[3] In fact, going high had its sensible points for a military road as it gave an opportunity of reconnoitring for rebel movements and Wade himself did not shirk road-building at a height as is shown by the Corrieyairack Pass at 2,500 feet on the Dalwhinnie–Fort Augustus road which he built in 1731. It was a courageous route to attempt but not a wise one because for much of the winter it was blocked with snow and therefore of no use.[4]

The Highlanders' initial reaction to what Wade was doing was unappreciative. They had been humiliated by their defeat in the Jacobite rising of 1715, then suffered the indignity of being disarmed and of having English soldiers garrisoned at the various forts, and Wade's road-making was a further cause of discontent, bringing southern soldiers into their communities. Highland chieftains complained that military roads opened up the country and deprived them of security from invasion;[5] and in places such

3   Old Military Road, Glenshiel. Source: Scottish Ethnological Archive, Royal Museum of Scotland.

as Kintail, Ross-shire, the people had for a long time had a great aversion to roads: 'The more inaccessible, the more secure, was their maxim.'[6] There were also complaints that the building of bridges made their people effeminate and less fit to undertake the crossing of rivers.[7]

But people gradually got over these objections. The public were always allowed to use military roads, including the earlier ones from Carlisle to Portpatrick and Stirling to Dumbarton,[8] and to many they were their first eye-opener to the benefits that could accrue from improved conditions. Several *Statistical Accounts* reported improved access to markets, thanks to these roads.[9] The military road in the south-west, from England to Portpatrick, though not a Highland one, was described in glowing terms, which could well apply to any other military road: 'By means of it, mountains which formerly appeared impervious are now no longer formidable. The stranger passes with ease to give and receive information; and articles of trade are transported with facility'.[10] It is little wonder that aversion to them soon changed to gratitude.

There was occasional co-operation between military and civil authorities in road maintenance if not in road-building, as in parts of Perthshire,[11] and where this happened it must have been very welcome.

General Wade left Scotland in 1740, ultimately became a Field Marshal, died in 1748 and was buried in Westminster Abbey. Major Caulfield, who had been his assistant, became his successor and between 1740 and 1767 constructed some 830 miles of road, including the notorious Devil's Staircase, built under terrible weather conditions in 1750; the road over Mam Ratagan from Fort Augustus to the barracks at Bernera which had been constructed in 1715; and the Contin to Ullapool road whose 38 miles, including bridges, cost £4,500, a remarkably modest £118 or so per mile. So associated are military roads with Wade's name that the last two roads mentioned are often referred to locally as Wade roads, with Wade bridges upon them, although they should really be called Caulfield roads. (During this time, some of the income from estates forfeited after the Stuart rising of 1745 was used for, among other things, building roads and bridges.)

Some military roads or parts of them not surprisingly soon fell into disrepair once they ceased to be needed after the pacification of the Highlands, and when they ran through very wild country. The Fort Augustus to Bernera road was only kept up until 1776 and from then on both it and its bridges were neglected.[12] Otherwise, military roads were maintained by the work of soldiers until 1790 and from then until 1814 by contractors paid by the Government, after which it was officially decided that none of them had any further military role to play.

There were those, however, who thought that the roads still had a possible part to play in army life. One of these was William Aiton who thought that road-building would be an ideal occupation for troops in peacetime.

It would tend greatly to preserve their health, vigour and morals from contamination, to keep them employed on the public roads rather than to have them lounging half-idle in towns and cities, debauching the inhabitants and being debauched by them. The Romans very wisely employed their soldiers in making and repairing the highways in time of peace and I trust our Government will follow the same course.[13]

But the Government did not do this. They handed the military roads over to the care of the Parliamentary Commissioners for Highland Roads and Bridges, the establishment of which may not have employed the army but which did untold good in the Highlands.

This Commission was established in the earliest years of the nineteenth century to take steps to arrest the emigration and depopulation which followed Scotland's eighteenth-century history. After the Jacobite risings were quelled and clans disarmed, chieftains no longer had their private armies available to them and when they lost their power of heritable jurisdictions — the power of pit and gallows — chiefs and lairds by the late eighteenth century saw little benefit in having clansmen and found it more profitable to let their land to southerners as sheep farms. So began the Highland Clearances and the drift from the Highlands to coastal holdings, to large cities to join in the progress of the Industrial Revolution which began about 1783, and abroad. During this time Highland soldiers had been giving distinguished service to Great Britain abroad, service which could not be disregarded, and the problems of the Highlands became a matter of concern once again to the Government. They were alarmed at the extent to which depopulation was going on and decided that something must be done for these people. To this end, Thomas Telford (1757–1834) was engaged in 1802 to report on the state of the Highlands and to suggest ways of improving them and opening them up.[14]

One of the subjects of Telford's first Report was 'The cause of emigration, and the means of preventing it'. This Report was submitted to a committee of the House of Commons which took evidence and issued four reports, advising that roads, bridges and fishing harbours should be built with half the cost borne by the Government; and that the Caledonian Canal should be constructed totally at Government expense.[15]

These preliminaries completed, two Parliamentary Commissions for Highland Roads and Bridges, which consisted of the same people, were appointed to carry out the programme although the actual work was done by Telford, for whom no praise can be too high. As General Wade had done before him, he rode miles in all weathers, without waterproof clothing, through areas where obviously enough there were no roads nor decent accommodation for the night. He saw what was needed, he produced business-like reports for Parliament and then saw to the carrying out of his proposals. Construction work began in 1804 and went on into the 1820s and, under Telford, Highland roads had the great benefit of being engineered by skilled men. Some 875 miles of road and about 1,300 bridges of all sizes were built, costing in total £540,000 of which £257,000 came from the Government.[16] The balance came from the counties themselves, through assessments on proprietors of land and houses of a certain value. This meant in practice that proprietors were receiving 50 per cent grants and they were not slow to take advantage of them although they were not keen to do repairs which were not grant-aided.

Telford had a knack of choosing good men to help him with his work. To start with he had as assistant and Chief Inspector of Highlands Roads and Bridges, John Mitchell, who when he died in 1824 was succeeded by his son Joseph, whom Telford appointed to this very responsible job in spite of the fact that he was only twenty-one. Between them their achievements were remarkable and nowhere more so than in Sutherland. Describing this in 1828, Telford wrote,

> In no part of the Highlands is the progress of improvement so evident as from Bonar Bridge along the coast of Sutherland to Helmsdale. Previous to the commencement of the Dunrobin road, the Bonar and Helmsdale bridges, in 1808, when I travelled into that quarter, in surveying for the future roads, it was with difficulty and not without danger that I could scramble along a rugged, broken, sandy shore, or by narrow tracks on the edge of precipices, frequently interrupted by rude and inconvenient ferries; and having for lodgings only miserable huts ... while the adjacent country had scarcely the marks of cultivation.[17]

He reported that things had improved so much that a mail coach ran from Tain to Thurso without being interrupted by a single ferry. Along the Sutherland coast there were good inns, the one at Golspie equal to any to be found in England. Helmsdale had become an important fishing station, with two decent inns and a number of herring houses, while at Brora and at Bonar Bridge new villages had developed. The spin-off benefits included a rise in the value of land, the building of better and more comfortable houses, along with churches, manses, schools and further inns; but even Telford, in spite of all that he did, could not do everything and inevitably there were outlying districts unaffected by his works.

Road-making was a valuable source of employment to local people and to the soldiers and sailors returning after 1815 from the Napoleonic wars with no work to go home to. In the same way, much further south, in Lanarkshire, work on improving the Glasgow–Carlisle road in 1819–20 'afforded seasonable employment to the manufacturing population in these troublesome years'.[18] But in the Highlands, when most of Telford's road programmes were completed about 1828, they left a legacy of unemployment at a time when the price of wool and cattle had fallen, fishing was not being

4   Road-building, Braemore. Source: Scottish Ethnological Archive, Royal Museum of Scotland.

successful and the kelp trade had collapsed. This last particularly affected the west coast. During the wars, barilla from Spain was unobtainable for the manufacture of glass and soap, and kelp, the product of burnt seaweed, provided an alternative and such a profitable one that in Lewis alone between four and five thousand people were employed making it, and crofters found it paid so well that many of them felt that they could subdivide their crofts among members of their families and still have an adequate income. But once Spanish barilla was obtainable again, that was the end of kelp-burning which, along with other factors, caused great hardship which occurred at a time when, in spite of the Clearances, the population was increasing due to various reasons,[19] one of which was the success of smallpox vaccination.

All this was serious enough but in 1846 the potato famine began. From about the mid to late 1700s the potato had become the staple food of the common people of Scotland. It was a most obliging crop, capable of feeding a family for nine months of the year and until that disastrous year never failing. When this happened it caused utter destitution, and relief from outside the Highlands was required. In December 1846 a meeting was called in Edinburgh under the auspices of the Lord Provost and another in Glasgow the following month to call for subscriptions for the Highlands and an astonishing amount of money was raised at home and abroad, including well over £50,000 from the British Association. A Central Relief Committee was formed and divided into two sections, the Edinburgh one being responsible for the north-west Highlands and Shetland, the Glasgow one for the rest, with county committees to organise relief in the first instance.[20]

The Boards provided help by giving meal in return for work on useful projects such as the building of piers and the making of roads which, sadly, came to be known as destitution roads. In some areas, they split the cost of road-works equally with proprietors and/or county authorities and, one way or another, people were fed and public works completed. Sometimes landed proprietors were paid to handle relief work on their own estates but whether this happened or not, many landowners came out of this tragic time very well because, although their tenants could not afford to pay rent, so that they had no income, they went to endless efforts to see to their people's welfare without thought for their own circumstances.[21] The earlier efforts of two Lords Macdonald in Skye who after 1828 did excellent work for their people there, deserve a special mention. Some of them however, were less concerned with the plight of the people, and their attempts to send grain away by sea for sale in the south resulted in the meal mobs of 1847, to which there are many references in the local press of the time.

Because relief was provided in return for work, there was a lot of grumbling because of the 'work test' for the able-bodied — if they would not work, then they were not in need, seemed to be the maxim. This was made very clear by Captain Elliot, the Inspector General of the Edinburgh Destitution Committee, in 1848 when he stated that the object of the Committee was 'to prevent starvation — not to advance public works, of however greatly

5   Stone-breaker in Glenesk. Source: Scottish Ethnological Archive, Royal Museum of Scotland.

preponderating general advantage they may be. The primary objective in exacting work is to test the destitution: and next to avoid the obvious evils of eleemosynary [charitable] relief'. He sounds as unpleasant as his language was pompous.[22] In 1848 the Editor of the *Inverness Courier* wrote an article about the work test, starting with a disclaimer of something which must have become general opinion: 'A whole day's hard labour', he wrote, 'is not exacted for a pound of meal.' He went on:

> The rule practically acted upon is to give the maximum allowance of $1\frac{1}{2}$ lbs meal for eight hours fair labour; the relief officer having it in his power to give only one pound when the working time is idled away. But a day's honest work also entitled the labourer to half-a-pound of meal per day for every child too young for employment; while the wives by spinning, or in certain cases by attention to personal and household cleanliness, can earn three-quarters of a pound or a pound per day, Sunday included.[23]

The Glasgow Committee raised a lot of money to provide for children under twelve, to give further allowances to mothers for knitting as well as spinning and to give older children a full allowance for such work as they could do.[24]

In spite of this the people thought themselves hard done by and there is an impression that the destitution roads were created out of people's misery which in a sense is true but it was sincerely meant to be a humane and practical method of coping with a situation which had primarily resulted from the people's over-dependence on one form of food.

The final reports of both Boards closed on a note of disappointment. At the end of 1850 the Glasgow Board confessed that the majority of the inhabitants in its area were in a worse condition than when destitution began in 1846; while in 1852 the Editor of the *Inverness Courier* wrote, 'The result of this splendid fund has altogether been so unpopular and unproductive generally proportioned to its amount, that we are convinced no such subscription will ever again be raised in the Highlands'.[25] Surprisingly enough, within only ten years of that comment, the annual grant of £5,000 for Highland roads and bridges — the money which was used to maintain the roads and bridges built by Telford — was stopped on the grounds that the Highlands were now very prosperous thanks to Government help in opening up the country and by the Highland Roads and Bridges Act 1862 the roads built by Telford and his team were transferred to the several Highland counties.[26]

3 STATUTE LABOUR

In spite of the various Acts which had been passed in the sixteenth and early seventeenth centuries to do with roads, they were described in 1669 as having 'yet for the most part proven ineffectual'.[1] This was largely because Justices of the Peace, who had been given the task of seeing to road care, did not control finance and were in any case largely ineffective. The office of Justice of the Peace had been instituted in 1609 by James VI with the intention that they would represent him, but the existing courts and the nobility, jealous of their own powers, ensured that this did not happen and although these Justices were revived at the time of the Union of the Parliaments in 1707 they ended up as just an adjunct of Sheriffs.[2]

An Act for Repairing Highways and Bridges,[3] which provided for statute labour, had been passed in 1669 but was not used at that time; another Act of 1718 gave the Lords of Justiciary authority to keep an eye on road works and to fine counties which failed to carry out their duties in this respect but this Act had little effect except in the area immediately around Glasgow.[4] But as Scotland became more settled after 1745, as wheeled traffic came into more general use making the hill paths of pack horse days no longer suitable and as things moved towards the Industrial Revolution, so better roads were needed and statute labour was, or seemed to be, the answer to the problem and thus in about the 1730–40s the old Act of 1669 was at last brought into play.

This Act first of all required roads to be at least 20 feet wide, as had the 1617 Act already referred to, so that horses and carts might 'travel summer and winter thereon'. The care of highways and bridges was placed in the hands of the Sheriff of each county, a Deputy Sheriff who had to be a heritor and the JPs, and heritors in both county and in burghs were to be taxed for road works at a rate of not more than 10s. Scots in every £100 Scots of valued rent. The decision on how much this tax or assessment should be was fixed by the Commissioners of Supply, a body started in 1667 specifically for collecting land tax at county level. Apart from a few burgh officials, these Commissioners were all landowners, representing only themselves and much involved in the eighteenth century and into the nineteenth century with everything to do with roads, bridges and ferries. They existed until 1930 although all their functions of any importance were taken over by the establishment of County Councils in 1889.[5]

So far as ordinary people were concerned, the feature of the 1669 Act that mattered to them was statute labour. This was compulsory unpaid labour on roads and bridges. All tenants, cottars and their servants between the ages of fifteen and sixty were required to give six days labour a year — the 'parish road days' as they were called — between seed time and harvest. This was slightly changed by an Act of 1670[6] to any time of the year except seed time and harvest and came to be three days in summer and three in autumn or a total of five days in summer.[7] The 1718 Act which brought the Lords of Justiciary into the picture required townspeople to do statute labour too, something they strongly opposed when it was enforced, with some employers preferring to pay fines rather than have their workers taken off to the roads.

When statute labour was needed, the Act required notification in whatever was the most convenient way — in practice, an intimation was usually made by the precentor at the parish church immediately after morning worship, telling the people to come the following week to whatever was the appointed place.[8] They had to bring sleds, spades, shovels, picks, mattocks and any other suitable tools, and those owning horses and carts had to bring them too. The Act gave JPs the authority to appoint overseers — 'power to appoint the most skilful to attend and direct the rest and to appoint them fitting wages for attendance', wages which unfortunately were not enough to encourage them to do their work properly. It also provided for the punishment of absentees by giving JPs and overseers the power to poind their goods for 20s. Scots for each day of absence and 30s. Scots for a man and a horse 'and in case the said absents shall have no poindable goods to punish them in their persons as they shall see cause'.

Life was already difficult enough for ordinary people without additional burdens like statute labour. In some places, tenants were still at that date being required to give services at hay and harvest time to their landlords and they had little enough time left for growing and gathering their own crops and for getting in a supply of winter firing, especially if the latter was at a distance. Even without giving these services, people could ill spare six days a year without payment and for the elderly and unfit statute labour was a severe imposition. The Sheriff and JPs were required to meet on the first Tuesday of May annually to arrange for the carrying out of the Act and in view of the penalties laid down for ordinary people, it is interesting that it was ordered in an Act of 1686 that any of them missing these May meetings was to be fined 20 merks for each day's absence, this money to be used for repair of the highways.[9]

At the outset, statute labour was performed, parish by parish, a bit here and a bit there. It was a haphazard, patchwork method of road-making, with detached sections of road and possibly a bridge or two made one year and then these allowed to fall into disrepair while something else was tackled the following year.[10] Worse still, these sections of road were not necessarily linked up within the parish or outside it, whereas military roads had the great advantage of linking not just parishes but counties. In very isolated areas and large parishes, statute labour was beyond the capacity of the people due to the distance to be covered and the scarcity of population to do the work, and in such places it quickly fell into disuse. Unless road-making benefited people directly, which meant that roads were made in the vicinity of their homes or places of work, they could see little reason for it[11] and although statute labour was a good idea in theory, in practice it was never really satisfactory, as was reported again and again, as for instance at Grange in Banffshire:

> Roads are in wretched repair, statute labour being mainly used in autumn when the day is short and the land is soaked by autumn rains. The different passes are rendered still worse by having loose clay thrown into them for proper materials were never sought or obtained but the mire from the ditches is thrown into the middle of the road so that a piece of new made or mended road is generally impassable. Statute labour is done with very great reluctance. A poor labourer, who has neither horse nor cart and perhaps little or no crop, and whose labour cannot maintain a large family of young children, so that he is supplied by the poors' funds, is obliged to work six days on the roads, while a farmer who pays £40–£50 rent, works four carts, and needs only one servant beside boys for herding, is liable only for twice as much as the poor labourer; and servants are entirely exempted from this heavy tax, though they are much better able to bear it than many householders.[12]

Some of the physical conditions under which statute labour was performed were described thus in 1786:

> At this time, the inhabitants of Skye were mostly engaged upon the roads in different parts of the island, under the inspection of the gentlemen and tacksmen, and accompanied each party by the bagpiper. Many of these people had to travel eight miles from home, and the greatest part of them were at a loss for lodgings, excepting that which the cold earth and the open sky afforded.[13]

Working a ten-hour day under these conditions, with no time allowed for travelling, it is no wonder that statute labour was very deeply resented and therefore badly done. Many *Statistical Accounts* refer to this. It is described as 'very ill performed';[14] 'the people deem it a great hardship';[15] 'it is performed here with as much reluctance and as imperfectly as anywhere';[16] 'it was always too superficially performed because too much was attempted in one year and soon the roads were bad again. This made the people averse and awkward in performing statute labour'.[17] Lack of know-how is also apparent in these *Accounts*: 'The people have seldom sufficient skill for this kind of work and always perform it with reluctance. The roads are not likely to be well made but by sufficient undertakers',[18] or 'The people turn out to this work with reluctance because they do not experience the benefit of it; for by unskilful management the roads are often worse rather than better for all they do'.[19] One writer said that statute labour 'required a great deal of supervision, at the best was only indifferently done and was a source of great annoyance'.[20] It seems surprising that no one realised that work without pay cannot be relied on.

The relationship between workers and overseers was also a source of discontent. It was said of overseers that '. . . unless they are uncommonly unbiassed, there is scope to relax in the demand of labour from some men and to be too rigorous in exacting it from others'.[21] That this was only too true appears also in various *Statistical Accounts*. One said, '. . . the overseer, loth to impose a hardship on those who are generally his neighbours, or to offend them, is too easy in his duty',[22] while another said they were often 'partial' as well as negligent.[23] This problem became sufficiently serious for overseers in Dumbarton in 1737 to be required to take an oath that their reports were true.[24]

While the men appointed overseers might be 'the most skilful to attend and direct the rest' as the 1669 Act required, that did not make them experienced road-makers. How could it, when there had been no way for them to learn? But that did not stop there being far too many of them and one of the faults of statute labour was the number of grieves, overseers and inspectors in every district, all of whom had to be paid with money that could otherwise be spent on the roads. Unless these people were uncommonly upright, there was great scope for embezzlement and Dr James Robertson, writing about Perthshire in 1799, said in a cleverly worded paragraph:

> Without saying that these overseers are not always chosen according to their experience of or knowledge of road-making; without saying that they neglect their business or that there are too many of them; without saying that it is impossible for the Commissioners of Supply when auditing their accounts to know whether the money raised can be fairly accounted for, unless every individual in the district is called before them, to learn who has paid money and who has performed labour; the thing itself is an error'. (Here he was referring to the commutation of statute labour into money.) He suggested that a proper road-maker should be employed which would prevent, among other things 'all the teasing applications, employed in soliciting these little posts, which are never fought for but with a view to influence or emolument, or both.'[25]

In some areas, lack of leadership was one of the problems. One of these areas was Rogart, Sutherland, where the people were averse to statute labour 'and their superiors give themselves little trouble about the matter'.[26] It was the same in Keith, Banffshire, where the roads in the 1780s were very bad because no one had bothered to see to it that statute labour was regularly used.[27] In one area of Stirlingshire, where the roads were very bad and in wet weather impassable, farmers constantly complained and when asked individually seemed anxious to help with repairs but no one would set about the work alone. What time suited one did not suit another and, of course, when good weather came the road dried up and became firm and the matter dropped.[28] The writer of the *Statistical Account for Peterculter, Aberdeenshire*, also expressed the wish for someone to take a lead. No one, he said, could help being annoyed at seeing stones gathered off fields and thrown into pits or ditches at the roadside, when they could have been used to fill up parts of the middle of the road. 'I am of the opinion that farmers would readily do this if any gentleman who takes a concern in the public roads, would express a wish for it to be done'.[29] A real leader in a community could achieve a great deal and this *Account* goes on to say, 'Within these last few years Lord Findlater's factor has exerted himself in a very laudable manner, has introduced a better mode of repair, and is more regular and strict about exacting statute labour. Though the inhabitants murmur a little, they should thank him'.

One of the most progressive men in Scotland in the eighteenth century was Sir John Sinclair, the Caithness improver of *Statistical Account* fame, who between 1776 and 1785 was largely instrumental in using statute labour to make a number of roads in that county. On one day he assembled 1,200 men to make a road in the parish of Latheron which opened up communications from Dunbeath on the east coast directly through the interior of the county to Thurso in the north. On another day, he collected a further large number of men to make a road through the Causeway-mire in the parish of Halkirk, a road which went through a bog.[30] The logistics of such an undertaking in those days are almost unimaginable.

There were so many difficulties with statute labour that it was gradually realised that it would be far better to commute the six days' labour into money and to use this money to employ proper workmen under a competent man to make and repair roads during the summer months. The usual commutation or conversion rate was 3*d.* a day or 1*s.* 6*d.* to cover the year's total of six days and certainly by the 1770s this was beginning to be used. Until 1845, when commutation was permitted without a private Parliamentary bill, permission to commute labour into money had to be given by a private Act of Parliament, county by county or area by area, so that there was considerable variation around the country. These private Acts lifted the care of the roads to which they applied out of the hands of JPs and Commissioners of Supply and put them into the charge of trustees who, of course, tended to be more or less the same people. Permission to commute statute labour often, but not always, went hand in hand with permission to build turnpike roads and levy tolls upon them, but that will be dealt with in another chapter. Parishes could elect to be excluded from commutation[31] and people, in theory anyway, had the choice of working or paying, which must have made the organisation of road works very difficult, with part of the workforce reluctant, unskilled and unpaid, while the others, more experienced, received wages for their work.

Although this commutation system was better, it presented problems to those in charge. Commutation money was difficult to collect because of a casual attitude to registrations of births which meant that it was difficult to establish people's ages at the lower and upper limits and whether they were liable for statute labour in either form. It was only in 1855 that births, along with marriages and deaths, had to be registered properly; prior to that it was pure chance if the parish records were up to date or even existed. On top of that, short of calling all the relevant men before them to discover who had worked and who had paid, it was virtually impossible to know if the accounts were accurate.

The people's attitudes to paying commutation money varied. 'It is not to be imagined that a man will work for a day on the roads when he may redeem his labour for 3d.', said one Aberdeenshire minister,[32] while another pointed out that elderly people in particular grudged having to pay for failure to work, implying that their health might have excused them if the only option was work.[33] There is an implication of 'no choice' in the *Statistical Account for Avoch, Ross-shire*, which pointed out that 1s. 6d. a year was a lot for some poor people to pay, when they had little ready money, and would rather give their work in the moderate way it used to be exacted[34] and because people were unwilling, or more probably unable to pay, 'recourse must sometimes be had to the taking of pledges',[35] with the inevitable result of a build-up of debt.

Under the commutation system, landowners were more highly assessed than before. All those owning land of £100 Scots in value had to pay so much per £100 Scots valuation — but not more than £3 stg per £100 Scots — as well as something for horses, oxen, coaches, gigs, chaises and similar vehicles. A proportion of their yearly assessments was passed on to their tenants according to the real rent, which was higher than the valued rent. This proportion varied round the country; in Selkirkshire, for instance, it was a half when the assessment was not over £2 but if above that, £1,[36] while in Argyllshire it was two-thirds.[37] This assessment appears in rent books as an additional charge, as in that of John Ross, tacksman on the farm of Pitmaduthy, on Balnagown Estate, Ross-shire, in 1833:

Rent	£98.	5s. 2d.
Proportion of school salary	1.	17s. 3¼d.
Road assessment	2.	2s. 6d.
Cholera assessment	−.	13s. 3¼d.

The tenantry also varied in their attitude to commutation and assessments. Some farmers were said to like the new system[38] while others found it burdensome.[39] In Selkirkshire and Roxburghshire the application for an Act of Parliament to allow commutation of statute labour was opposed by several farmers on the grounds that it would make a material alteration to the terms of their leases by subjecting them to a heavy tax, fixed and unavoidable, assessed on highly valued land, instead of on their horses and servants which they had the option of reducing.[40] In addition, in the late eighteenth century when all this was taking place, farm workers were in great demand and farmers were 'pinched by the high wages' they had to pay[41] and so any extra costs were unwelcome.

The opposition of the farmers of Selkirkshire and Roxburghshire was in keeping with what went on in many parts of the country. When a bill to commute statute labour was proposed in Angus 'the whole country was in a flame. There were many meetings and much speechifying and much writifying upon the subject and the people in the towns were crying loudly against its injustice and oppression'.[42] In 1842, there was a remarkably peaceable demonstration at Fort William, Inverness-shire, by some five hundred tenants and small farmers against an attempt to enforce payment of these assessments. They came into the town from various districts, each group led by a piper, and marched through the streets until they learnt that their case was bound to fail on legal grounds when, it was reported, they all 'dispersed in a happy temper'.[43]

In fact, townspeople came off quite well in spite of their initial fears. In Angus, for instance, occupiers of houses in towns and villages, with a garden, had to pay 1s. for a house rented at between £1. 10s. and £3; 1s. 6d. where the rent was between £3 and £5; and for houses rented at £5 and over, 2½ per cent per annum of the annual rent, or of the valued rent if the house was occupied by the proprietor. Inn-keepers with horses for hire, and carters who kept them for carrying goods, had to pay 4s. 6d. for each beast. Everyone owning carriage or riding horses had to pay 6s. for each animal, exclusive of what they paid for coaches, chaises and so on. Ministers and schoolmasters were exempt unless they owned land or houses in addition to those associated with their work; and those really unable to pay, such as people on the poors' roll, could be exempted too. Loud though the complaints had been, this worked out very favourably for town dwellers. It meant that occupiers of houses with less than 30s. rent to pay, did not pay at all towards roads, while those with houses below £5 in rent did not even have to pay what would provide a man for one day's labour; for working horses, not half's a day's labour, and even for other horses, the charge would not hire a man, with a horse and cart, for one day.[44]

Charges elsewhere were similar, though not necessarily identical, as in Jedburgh, Roxburghshire, where occupiers of houses and tenants and possessors of burgh roods and acres had to pay 1s. 6d. for each house with an annual rent of between 10s. and £1, and 3d. additionally when the rent was over £1, while carters and carriers with horses for hire were required to pay 2s. 6d. for each beast and 1s. 6d. for each man employed with them.[45] Although the average town dweller did not suffer with these charges, they could be very hard on widows, especially in seaport towns where there was often a high proportion of young women who had lost their husbands at sea and were left with young children to support.[46]

Under the commutation Acts, the money raised went to employ men paid at the rate of about 6d. to 9d. a day and the trade of road contractor gradually developed. Overseers were in some cases 'respectable farmers', appointed to inspect roads, manage funds and see them properly applied,[47] a post which might be rewarded with some £15 per annum. In some places, the schoolmaster was engaged to collect commutation money. The parish-on-its-own system of using statute labour was altered and counties were divided into districts with several parishes in each, under the management of trustees, who always included the landed proprietors, all the JPs, the Sheriff or his Substitute and in some cases, should there be towns in the district, some of their officials, as well as tenants paying £300 yearly rent or more.[48] In practice, however, the proprietors and JPs seem to have been the trustees who influenced and ran things.

The trustees met every April or May to fix the commutation rate and then met again to decide how it should be used, as one press notice of a meeting said, 'to lay on and appropriate the current year's conversion money'. This notice went on, 'Applications for money for the making or repairing of roads must be signed by a Heritor of the parish where the roads lie, and be lodged with the Clerk before the day of the meeting'.[49] There could be great variation in the assessment of different parishes even within one district, depending on local conditions, availability of road-making materials, whether trees overhung the roads and spoilt them with their dripping and so on. At the Annual General Meeting of the Kelso District in Roxburghshire in 1854 the trustees suggested assessments varying from 15s. per £100 Scots in the parish of Hownam, to 20s. in Ednam, 25s. in Morebattle, several of 30s., while Kelso landward was 35s. and Linton 50s.

Although General Wade and Major Caulfield had done such impressive work in the Highlands and although Thomas Telford was doing very skilled work there in the early years of the nineteenth century, the ability and determination of these men were not shared by those who had to do with road-making elsewhere in the country. To be fair to them, dirt roads were suitable where wheeled traffic was light but as it increased, so did road damage from it. A cart-wheel under a heavy load acted like a plough, rutting the road so that on the level, wet weather turned it into a swamp and on a slope the rut became a drain.[50]

Often enough, a hole in a road was repaired by putting a large stone into it, after which vehicles had to heave up over it and then come down with a thud on the other side and very soon the original hole became a small mountain sitting in a pit of mud.[51] One writer said

> ... from the inexperience of the trustees, they have been deceived by some of the contractors and a few errors have escaped them ... No contractors should be employed but those who bring undoubted certificates for their fidelity and knowledge in their profession. Ignorant or designing men often give in estimates at a low price but such generally turn out most expensive in the end and the road made by them never gives satisfaction to the trustees or the public. Skilful inspectors are absolutely necessary to superintend the making of a given quantity of road; or broad parts of it, when completed, should be dug up and examined.[52]

Trustees also tended to follow the line of old roads, however bad those lines might be, because it saved making new ones through the by then enclosed fields of their fellow landowners and because it enabled existing bridges to continue in use and so saved money. A sage piece of basic advice on this subject was given by Dr Bryce Johnston of Dumfries in 1794: 'The best line is not always the shortest. It is best to choose a line on which the same horses will travel in the shortest space of time and draw the greatest weight with them'.[53]

The 1669 Act required all cultivated land on either side of roads to be fenced with dyke, ditch or hedge and if this was not done by 1671 JPs could poind occupiers of the land for 4s. Scots for every ell left unfenced and use this money for that purpose.[54] Enclosures were a genuine agricultural improvement even though they had unfortunate social consequences. They could also make practical difficulties for the traveller. For instance, about 1750 when fields were still unenclosed, the road to Dalkeith was a mile nearer Inveresk than thereafter. Once the fields were fenced off, people on foot had to go between two walls or hedges, over their feet in mud if it was wet or else they had to break over the fences[55] and the *Statistical Account for Coldingham, Berwickshire*, suggests that one of the main motives for proper road-making was because landowners — and it was they who applied for the necessary Acts of Parliament — realised that unless roads were passable there would be continual damage to their enclosures.[56] The minutes of the Statute Labour Conversion District of Melrose, Roxburghshire, refer to numerous occasions when landowners planning enclosures which would affect the line of public roads, asked for a committee of trustees to inspect and advise before any decision was taken, and this was common practice.

Whatever the trustees' lack of experience at the outset, they learnt fast. Although surveyors and inspectors were employed, the trustees had the right to inspect road-works too and the Ross-shire 1st District Roads Committee, for one, required the collector to notify any of them living in the neighbourhood of any new road which was ready at least three or four days ahead of the surveyor's inspection 'so as to give such trustees an opportunity

Melrose 3 April 1824

Sederunt General Meeting of Trustees for the Statute
Labour Roads within the District of Melrose.

Present

Charles Riddell Esq. Muislee
James Pringle of Torwoodlee
John Murray of Uplaw
Charles Simson of Threepwood
William Scott younger of Raeburn
John Ormiston of Hayburn
Adam Walker yor of Meirhouselaw
Alex. Kay of Charlesfield
Robert Mercer of Blainslie
James Stedman of Broomhill
William Smail of Calshawhill
Thomas Wilson of Seanfield
John Simson younger of Blainslie

Charles Riddell Esq. Preses

The Clerk states that under authority and as di-
=rected by the Sederunt of the Trustees, of date the
sixth of March last, he had advertised this Meeting
in the Kelso mail Newspaper, specifying the purposes
of it to be 1st For the purpose of appropriating the
several sums necessary to be expended on the Roads in
the District the ensuing year – 2d. For assessing the
several Parishes in the District for Statute Labour
year payable June and December 1824 – 3d to fix
a day for annually holding the General Meeting for the
purposes above mentioned and 4th to consider any
other business that may occur –

The

6   Minutes of Statute Labour Conversion District of Melrose, 1824.

of attending and giving their assistance to the surveyor' and the minutes state clearly that no road would be accepted unless such notice had been given to the trustees. These particular trustees found that roads which had been made for some little time became 'very much rutted and cut up . . . where the gravel is completely worn off' and they insisted that if poor quality gravel was used the contractor should remove it and put on 'good binding gravel' instead.[57]

These inspections had a real value because contractors could be a tricky lot and would readily try to pull the wool over the eyes of the trustees. When some road-works were begun in 1814 in the Melrose District of Roxburghshire, and completed not long afterwards, the surveyor, David Sinclair, reported that the work was so badly done that the trustees refused to pay for it. The contractor, a Mr Middlemass, complained that Sinclair was an enemy of his and he had known all along what his report would be. At this, one of the trustees, a Mr Adam Walker, asked Middlemass to bring a man he could trust and who knew something about road-making, to inspect the road along with the surveyor of a different district. Middlemass's man, a Mr Kinghorne, and the independent surveyor produced an even worse report than Sinclair's and Middlemass was ordered to lay a further layer of stones on the whole line of road at 4s. per rood. This he refused to do and the work had to be done by others. In 1825 Middlemass petitioned the trustees for payment for the work done in 1814, by which time he must have felt safe to do so as Mr Erskine, who had originally ordered the work, had died, Sinclair had gone to America and Mr Kinghorne to New South Wales. But he did not bargain for Mr Walker who, although eleven years had passed, had an excellent memory and also had kept the original reports and described Middlemass's attempt to obtain payment as 'a bare-faced attempt at imposition'.[58]

Many trustees did excellent work, for instance the JP who lived in the parish of Barrie, Angus, who was reported as having 'faithfully and judiciously' used the amount of money allotted to that parish,[59] while in Arbirlot, in the same county, it was said that '. . . the conversion money raised in this parish has been laid out by the gentlemen of the district to great advantage. Being furnished with every qualification requisite for the improvement of the roads, we may justly be confident that they will take the most effectual measures in order to complete a scheme so consonant to friendly intercourse, sympathetic aid and sound policy'.[60] This was perhaps overdoing the praise but such sycophancy may be explained by the fact that the writer was the parish minister and parish ministers were very dependent on the attitude of heritors. The truth is that there were also trustees who did not carry out their obligations properly and this is referred to in many Statistical Accounts and New Statistical Accounts, and the fact that these were almost always written by parish ministers is surely strong condemnation. The Statistical Account for Crimond,[61] Aberdeenshire, said that ten, twelve or twenty years previously the then resident heritors often repaired their own private roads with statute labour. Was the writer's careful reference to this having happened in the past so as not to get into trouble with the existing heritors? But worse still was reported in the *Account for Peterculter, Aberdeenshire*, when the writer said, '... if what I have heard is true, some years the commutation money has been collected through the whole district and none of it applied to the making or repairing of roads'.[62]

Under the commutation system, with several parishes in a district trustees had the power to use money in any part of their district they thought necessary. Parishes were not always equally represented on district committees and very often one parish's commutation money went outside it, possibly for sound reasons but also because of an overweighting of trustees from elsewhere. This is illustrated in the work of the 1st District Roads Committee in Ross-shire, which consisted of the three parishes of Tarbat, Fearn and Nigg. Nigg had only one representative on the committee which explains the complaint made in 1841 that '... the roads have been much neglected. Thousands of pounds have been taken from the parish of Nigg to make and repair roads in the parishes of Tarbat and Fearn, the three parishes being constituted into one district, and the heritors of Tarbat and Fearn taking care of their own interests to the neglect of the parish of Nigg'.[63] In Glensheil, Ross-shire, the area of Letterfearn suffered very much from the lack of a road and the people complained, reasonably enough, that although they had had to pay road money like everyone else, their area had not shared in the benefit of its outlay and it was difficult for them to get to church and school.[64] On the island of Iona, there were no proper roads for years and the use of vehicles was impossible, so that it was said, 'It is not to be wondered at that Ionians should grumble at the way their interests are neglected by the powers that be'.[65]

There was another great grievance: not just the money but the labour of a parish might be 'carried out of it to make a road in another when their own roads were exceedingly bad'.[66] In Argyllshire roads were bad because statute labour had been allowed to be used on roads that were more immediately necessary, outside the parish, for many years.[67] In parts of Aberdeenshire, it was said that 'the management of the roads throughout the district is grossly defective',[68] and in Morayshire that the proprietors had for many years been in the practice of using the statute labour of their own tenants only for roads on their own estates. 'Of the smallest interference of each in the appropriation of this labour, they were all equally and extremely jealous'.[69] Reverend James Headrick, writing on the agriculture of Angus, said 'Everyone struggles for what he conceives to be his own interest. Some people think there should be a Board of Roads and Bridges. Some think that, because men see more clearly what may promote their neighbour's advantage than what will help their own, that it might be advantageous to the public were the trustees of one district charged with roads of a contiguous district, where they have no personal interest, and vice versa'.[70]

Towns, as has already been said, did not come off badly money-wise. Commutation of statute labour and the money raised, if well laid out, resulted in great improvements but towns too could suffer from the self-interest of the landed trustees who were in the majority on road committees. The towns had no control over expenditure of road money and its use was 'at the discretion of a certain class of proprietor of land, who naturally enough directs its application to their own farm roads'.[71] (This obviously applies only to small country towns.) There was wide variation in application of road funds, partly because each county had a different Act for commutation to every other county; partly due to the calibre of road trustees; and partly due to faults on both sides. People who complained among themselves did not take the proper steps to have things put right, such as telling non-resident heritors or their factors of local conditions so that these could be put forward at meetings of trustees and perhaps too they expected too high a standard on little-used by-roads.[72]

A tragic side to the practice of commutation was reported in the parish of Kirkmichael and Cullicudden, Ross-shire. With the exception of a few hundred yards of road at the east end of the parish, there was about the 1840s not an inch of what might be strictly called 'made' road. What there was had never been properly formed or metalled but was patched by men employed by the District Committee who kept the trenches open on either side and threw what came out of them on to the surface.

> And yet notwithstanding this wretched state of the public roads, the commutation money for statute labour has been, year after year, most punctually and even rigidly exacted. The blankets have been often taken off the beds of old bed-ridden people by the merciless exactors. This state of things evidently arises from mismanagement as well as from a want of public spirit.[73]

The removal of blankets was in fact the poinding of goods which trustees were empowered to do where there were arrears of money due, although uncovering the bed-ridden was surely carrying things too far. In 1816 the 1st District Roads Committee in Ross-shire had arrears of £400 and declared that it was

> indispensably necessary that the Collector should immediately set about the Collection thereof and in order to show the Necessity of that Measure, they prepared a paper for him to show to the Principal Tenants, of the absolute necessity of their making immediate payment of their full arrears, otherwise they will be under the disagreeable necessity of proceeding with legal measures to compel payment.

Reading the prepared paper did not apparently have the desired effect and
shortly afterwards the trustees instructed the collector 'to use the most
vigorous measures for its [arrears] recovery by poinding such as will not pay
without that necessary step'. Getting in the money continued to be a problem
and in 1819 the collector was ordered to collect not only arrears but the whole
assessment of the district up to the previous May. This does not appear to
have been successful either as in 1820 the trustees ordered him to 'apply for
a warrant for poinding and sale of the readiest goods and effects of the persons
in the lists now given in whose arrears exceed £2 stg . . . and when a day of Sale
is appointed of the Poinded effects, authorise him to advertise the same at the
different churches of the District that the same is to be sold at the Cross of
Tain on the appointed day to the Highest offerer'.[74] A list of inhabitants of this
district poinded by Hugh Fraser, the constable, in 1824 for not paying their
commutation money includes the following:

Alexander Ross, cabinet maker, 3 chairs, 12s.
Daniel Mitchell, saddler, 3 chairs, 12s.
Donald Munro, mason, 5 chairs, 1 large press, 1 cupboard, for 9 years, £2. 14s.
William McGrigor, cartwright, 2 harrows, £1. 6s. 6d.
Donald Tayne, 1 green chest, 2 chairs, 1 fir table, for 5 years, £1. 10s.
Charles Macdonald, mason, 2 green chests, for 5 years, £1. 10s.
David Sutherland, 1 dresser and 1 vessel board, 6s.
Duncan Roy, pair of wheels, for 2 years, 12s.
Lachlan Gallie, pair of wheels, for 2 years balance, £1. 3s. 9d.
Munro Ross, a coup with wheels and iron axle, a pair of wheels on a rung cart, for
3 years, £3.
James Fridge, 1 pair wheels with iron axle, £1. 4s. 9d.[75]

Comparisons of prices show that the value of poinded goods was very low
which made this process even harder on people with little enough of this
world's goods. The domestic tragedy of losing household articles like chairs,
dressers and cupboards, vital items of a sparsely furnished home, must have
been very hard to bear. Trustees could exempt people on the grounds of
poverty — and in those days poverty really meant what it said — and in 1821
these particular trustees drew up a list of those considered unable to pay and
in all £135. 5s. 9d. of arrears in the three parishes was regarded as 'perfectly
irrecoverable'. As twenty-one people were ordered to work for their arrears,
one feels that ill-health had to be added to poverty to qualify for exemption.
No wonder that statute labour, in kind or in cash, was resented and that very
strict supervision was used when people worked in lieu of payment, as this
Ross-shire entry shows: '1817, By Wm. Duff, constable, his account for
attending the people at work, £7. 5s. 0d.'[76]

Too great a number of roads seems a surprising thing to find at the end of
the eighteenth century, yet the *Statistical Account for Baldernock, Stirlingshire,*

says, 'Multiplicity of roads makes it impossible to keep them all up, therefore masters and tenants, for the improvement of the country and their own interest, might pay attention to shutting off some of the least useful roads and making an extraordinary exertion to get the rest into repair'.[77] Closing of roads had long been provided for: an Act of 1661 said that 'for the encouragement of planting and policy' power was granted to heritors at the sight of Sheriffs, stewards, lords of regality, barons and JPs to 'cast about the highways according to their convenience' provided they did not remove them further than 200 ells — about 250 yards — on their whole ground.[78] The Scottish Parliament gave permission for highway-moving before that time however: in 1607 James Durham of Pitarro received a warrant to alter the highway through his policies;[79] in 1645 John Malcolm of Balbidie was allowed to alter a road which passed near to his house;[80] and in 1661 Sir Andrew Ramsay was granted permission to alter the course of the highway to Kirkcaldy near his house of Abbotshall;[81] and there were a considerable number of similar cases. It seems that in each case these 'roads' were old rights of way passing inconveniently close to heritors' houses or properties. As road-making developed, old roads continued to be closed and although this was often sensible, one is left with a suspicion that in a good many cases it was done for the convenience and amenity of the trustees rather than for the benefit of the community.

Examples of this happening occur in the minutes of the 1st District Roads Committee in Ross-shire, which have already been freely quoted. In 1821, Mr Macleod of Geanies, one of the trustees, told his fellow trustees that the Ross-shire County Act of 1810 had been extended so that it might be

> lawful for the trustees ... with consent of any two trustees ... to shut up and suppress public roads of every description which may appear useless or of little importance to the public. Provided always that notice ... be given by advertisement at the churches of the parishes through which the road passes and at the parishes at either extremity of the road for two successive Sundays, one month at least before the said road shall actually be shut up.

He went on to say that anyone feeling aggrieved about this might apply for redress to the Sheriff Depute. Having given this piece of information to the meeting, Mr Macleod was himself the first to take advantage of the new provisions. An old road passed through the lawn in front of his house and he thought it should now be closed as a 'new road had been built and was open to all travellers from the eastern part of Tarbat parish to Milton of New Tarbat, to the Ferry of Cromarty, and to Tain by Fearn'. He asked permission to advertise closure of the road through his lawn at the appropriate churches and, if there were no objections, he would request the trustees to 'give authority to suppress the same as a public road in all time coming'. The trustees agreed. It was much easier for a road to be closed by the agreement of the trustees than it was for anyone objecting to the closure to apply to the Sheriff Depute — especially as Mr Macleod of Cadboll, also a trustee, was himself the Sheriff. At the same meeting, hard on Mr Macleod's heels, Mr Ross of Nigg asked for the old road running through his land from the church to Nigg Ferry to be closed. He pointed out that a new road had been made and as it was the only one to qualify for repairs by the committee he 'humbly requested authority from the trustees to put gates on the said old road, but leaving an opening for foot passengers on weekdays and leaving the gates open on Sundays for those going to church'. To this the trustees also agreed, provided that there were no objections after advertisement.[82]

Part of this old road ran through the lands of Westfield and although the minutes of the committee are not available after 1821, information on the closure of a further section of it appears in the Kirk Session records of Nigg Old Church. Trouble began in April 1831 when two fishermen, James and David Skinner, who lived nearby, came before the Session to ask for certificates of poverty to enable them to sue Mr Murray of Westfield *in forma pauperis*. 'They stated that they had been served with summonses on Saturday last at the motion of William Murray Esq of Westfield to appear before a justice of the peace in Tain on Thursday 6th May to be fined for travelling by their ordinary road to the church, a road that had been used from time immemorial as a county, church, funeral, ferry and market road.' Mr Murray alleged that the road had been closed by the trustees but for some reason it was considered that they had no power to close this particular road, and even if they had, the steps prescribed by Act of Parliament had not been adhered to. In any event Mr Murray had jumped the gun as he had ploughed up the road and ditched across it the previous autumn or winter, well before any official closure by the trustees. The local people had continued to use the road even so, with Mr Murray harassing them as they did so. One of his men had threatened 'to shoot with a gun which he had in his hand' three people using the road; and two young women had had their umbrellas, very valued possessions, forcibly taken from them either by Mr Murray himself or one of his servants, and all this although the closure had never ever been advertised. This road closure affected people from a particular part of the parish very badly and a further six men then came to the Kirk Session to ask for certificates to enable them to sue Mr Murray as paupers before the Supreme Court for the way in which he was oppressing them by illegally closing their road to church, what the Session records described as 'shutting up, ploughing and rendering impassable in the most oppressive and unwarrantable manner' the road from the church to the ferry. The fact that the minister and Kirk Session had become involved in the affair obviously angered Mr Murray, who was supported by the other heritors; this explains the entry in the Session minutes which says that celebration of the Lord's Supper had to be put off because of the 'harassing persecutions of the Minister, Elders and Session

Clerk and many others by some of the Heritors'. Even so, the Kirk Session were unbowed. At their next meeting, they not only granted the necessary certificates but also decided to petition the Lord Advocate 'as the conservator of the public peace and the guardian of civil and religious liberty' because Mr Murray's action was preventing many people of the parish from attending church. Furthermore, the Session agreed to petition the General Assembly to grant aid to the oppressed people of the parish by maintaining their right to the road. The heritors counter-attacked and a rumpus ensued. The story is fully told in Rev J R Martin's *Church Chronicles of Nigg* and shows how high-handed heritors could be over the matter of roads and also how determined the ordinary people could be too. The trouble caused by this road closure only ended with the devastating cholera outbreak of 1832 when everyone had to pull together for the general good and thus the breach was healed.[83]

Another instance of moving a road occurred at Kiltearn, also in Ross-shire. The old road over Struie Hill used to run closely in front of Foulis Castle, home of Sir Hugh Munro. It is said that a line of trees, some of which are still visible at each end, marked this early route. When road improvements began, the laird induced the authorities to adopt the present line of road which is a wide 'U' carrying the road away from the castle. Perhaps as an expression of gratitude for the removal of the thoroughfare from his front door, he built at his own expense the bridge to carry the new road over a burn below the castle.[84] There is an inscription on the outer face of the bridge, towards the castle, in a most inaccessible spot, almost as if it is not meant to be read by the public. This piece of self-interest was described in the *Statistical Account for Kiltearn* thus: 'The chief heritor has at considerable expense carried off the road in a sweep or curve, about a quarter of a mile further south than it was formerly. By this means, travellers will not only pass through the middle of rich fields and fine plantations of trees, but will also have a full view of that ancient and elegant mansion, Foulis Castle.' The *Account* does not say that by the former route they had a much closer look at the castle.[85] Ross-shire's experience in this connection was by no means unusual as roads were elsewhere also said to be routed 'to accommodate country gentlemen with regard to their parks, policies and gardens'. To avoid these, roads would go in a semi-circle or off at a right-angle 'causing a loss to the public and a delay to the traveller'.[86] In fact, Quarter Sessions had final control of all petitions to close roads, but reading minutes of road trustees, it does not seem as if all applications were referred to them although those that were, were usually granted.[87]

Having said all that, it must also be said that there were many cases where trustees stood up manfully for the rights of the general public over road clos-ures, even when it meant opposing the nobility. There was a case of this in 1812 when the Earl of Buchan 'unwarrantably made' what was obviously a new piece of road in order to close an existing one at Monksford in Roxburghshire, only to find that the trustees ordered their surveyor to have the old one re-opened. That same year, another proprietor illegally closed a road in the same area and after a site inspection, the trustees ordered their surveyor to make the road again on the old track.[88] Trustees were also called in to make decisions in cases where enclosures encroached on the width of old drove roads.

Road trustees were empowered to borrow money so as to be able to get on with road-making and to use the commutation money for repaying loans. Very often they advanced the necessary money themselves, to be repaid with or without interest as they saw fit. Unfortunately, this could mean that a considerable debt might arise. In Buittle, Kirkcudbright, about 1824 there was a debt of £549 stg. To reduce this, the heritors decided to assess themselves with an extra sum of £17. 6s. 1d. annually and by 1844 the debt had fallen to £136.[89] Presumably a proportion of this assessment was passed on in the usual way to the tenants. Certainly in another Kirkcudbright parish, Borgue, it was reported that, 'Funds for keeping roads have been burdened with a considerable debt which makes the present assessment somewhat oppressive to the tenantry on whom it has been laid'.[90] Although heritors who advanced money might never be repaid in full, they could see very well what furthered their own interests, because the roads for which any heritor advanced money usually ran through or gave access to his own property, which increased his amenity and meant that he stood to receive higher rents from tenants who would pay more when there was good access to markets, where good roads allowed heavier loads to be carried or drawn, and all with a reduction of wear and tear on beasts, harness and carts. Ironically, the increased assessments paid by tenants helped to raise their rents.

The *New Statistical Accounts* of the mid nineteenth century make clear how much road work was done between then and the earlier *Statistical Accounts* of the late eighteenth century. Between 1790 and 1840 approximately was a time of great development generally and in spite of some self-interested landowners, there were many who made roads at their own expense or else subsidised statute labour money to make them, leaving their maintenance thereafter to the appropriate bodies. Even before 1790 this was happening — about 1777 General Grant made a road for wheeled traffic in the parish of Inveravon, Banffshire, which was continued thereafter with statute labour, as well as making a two-arched bridge.[91] About 1775 the Duke of Buccleuch decided to do something about the roads in the parish of Canonbie, Dumfries-shire, where anywhere out of the course of the River Esk was almost inaccessible except in a dry summer. To make roads and repair them, he appropriated 5 per cent of the whole land rent of the parish and added £50 himself. A ½d. was levied on every horse load at the various coal pits, equal to

2*d*. a cart load, and to all this was added commutation money, and so the work was done.[92]

Although not strictly appropriate to this chapter, one cannot overlook the private efforts of landowners which involved neither statute labour nor commutation money. One of these was the road built by the Marquis of Stafford in 1830 over the wild moorland area of Sutherland known as The Moin. He also built a house to serve as a shelter for any benighted travellers, a house which though derelict is still standing and which bears a now rather defaced plaque which shows that philanthropic though the Marquis may have been, he did not believe in hiding his light. The plaque reads,

> This House erected for the refuge of the traveller serves to commemorate the construction of the road across the deep and dangerous morass of the Moin, impracticable to all but the hardy and active native, to him even it was a day of toil and of labour. This road was made in the year 1830 and at the sole expense of the Marquis of Stafford. Those who feel not the delay nor experience the fatigue nor suffer from the risks and interruptions incident to the former state of the country can but slightly estimate the advantages of its present improved condition or what it cost to procure them. To mark this change — to note these facts — to record this date, this inscription is put up and dedicated by James Loch Esq, MP Auditor and Commissioner upon his Lordship's Estates and John Horsburgh Esq, Factor for the Reay country, Strathnaver, Strathalladale and Assynt, under whose directions this work was executed and who alone know the difficulties that occurred in its execution and the liberality and perseverance by which they were overcome. Peter Lawson, Surveyor.

Elsewhere others were doing road works privately too, such as Mr Pultney who built 8 miles of road from Langholm to Annan in Dumfries-shire at his own expense in the 1760s. All the other roads in that area were made or being made at the end of the eighteenth century at the expense of Sir William Maxwell and what were called the 'voluntary contributions' of his tenants.[93] Successful private fund-raising depended on having enough well-off and interested people in an area who could see a genuine need for a road and where this was so, subscriptions for this purpose came to be quite common. In 1809 a road from the north side of Inverness to Glenelg was built with the Inverness-shire assessment as far as Aonach, but beyond that point it had to be undertaken privately. The amounts subscribed included £1,000 from Lord Macdonald, £500 from Lord Seaforth, £400 from Macleod of Macleod, £300 from Hugh Innes of Lochalsh, £200 from Sir James Grant of Grant, James Murray Grant of Glenmoriston and R G Macdonald of Clanranald and £100 each from Charles Grant MP and Alexander Howe of Harris, as well as many smaller subscriptions.[94] In Tough, Aberdeenshire, landowners subscribed 50 per cent of their valued rents to pay for a road to Aberdeen in the 1790s[95] while in the parish of Knapdale, Argyllshire, the Llaibh Gaoil road was made by Sheriff Campbell. Initially he got an English surveyor to advise on what should be done but this unfortunate man found the rocks so precipitous, the ferns so gigantic and was himself so unwieldy and so unused to rough ground that, after much tumbling and grumbling he finished his survey by boat and declared that to make a road there was impossible. At that point Sheriff Campbell paid him off and himself successfully set about making a road which was of great use to the area.[96]

But something more was needed if road-making was to progress and that something was turnpike roads, the making of which in most cases overlapped with commutation. Nevertheless the importance of statute labour and the role it played, especially after commutation was allowed, must not be disparaged. The *Statistical Account for Humbie, East Lothian*, makes plain what practical results followed from it — before commutation, at no time of the year could more than 5 bolls of grain be sent to market in a two-horse cart but after 1770, when it was introduced there, 10 bolls became the usual load;[97] and from all around the country *New Statistical Accounts* repeatedly tell of improvements resulting from it.

4 TURNPIKE ROADS

In spite of the rather ambiguous comment by the writer of one *Statistical Account* that 'the country has for some time past been amused with schemes for turnpike roads',[1] a number of writers of these *Accounts* were unequivocal in their desire for them, sharing the opinion of one who said, 'I despair of seeing them [roads] much altered for the better till a proper turnpike is established'.[2]

Turnpike roads were main roads on which tolls were levied to pay for their building and maintenance. Along these roads, at intervals of a few miles, there were gates or 'turnpikes' — counter-balanced bars — from which they took their name, as well as a toll-house where the toll-keeper lived. A relic of these days is the word 'toll' appearing in place names. A few toll-houses still survive, and it is possible to recall some of them which had the scale of charges written up outside even into the 1940s, although they had long since gone out of use.

Turnpike Acts which established Turnpike Trusts to deal with these new roads were usually but not always associated with the commutation of statute labour. Landowners applied to Parliament for these Acts and each one referred to a specific area and lasted for only a limited time, say twenty years, after which further Acts had to be obtained as the need for them arose. The 1669 Act which introduced statute labour gave powers to the Privy Council to order tolls to be levied on roads[3] but this was first put into practice in an Act of 1750 obtained on the initiative of proprietors in East Lothian primarily to repair a section of road between Dunglass and Ravensheugh and, from that date to 1844, some three hundred and fifty Acts were passed in Scotland.[4] The right to manage Turnpike Trusts was, like statute labour, vested in the country gentlemen whose property valuation was high enough to allow them to assume this role but, in general, those who served as trustees were those through whose land a particular turnpike ran.[5]

Turnpike roads had to be of a certain standard before tolls could be imposed and so their building encouraged the introduction of better techniques. To start with, roads had been made by making a ridge, laying it with the biggest stones that could be got and putting clay on top. John Loudon

MacAdam (1756–1836) contributed greatly to improved roads by making them on a level surface topped with a layer about 3 inches deep of small stones of not more than $2\frac{1}{2}$ inches diameter. Although his system was not accepted by the British Government until 1823, it was being used before that and an enthusiast for his principles was John Erskine of Mar who suggested in 1795 that road contracts should specify the size of stones to be used on roads, all of which should be small enough to go through an oval ring or iron, $1\frac{1}{2}$ inches at its smallest diameter. 'This method', he said,

> is perfectly easy as the trustees as well as the inspector of roads could carry the ring in their pocket and the proof of the size of the stones is ready and expeditious; whereas the common practice in Scotland is to ascertain the size of the stone by its weight, which is extremely troublesome as well as fallacious. All the stones ought to be broken to their proper size at the quarry or if the stones are picked off the land, the heaps should be broken before any are allowed to be carried to the roads, otherwise the contractors may easily deceive their employers by laying on larger stones than the size specified in the contract and covering them with the smaller stones.[6]

The preparation of this road metal, as it was called, led to the occupation of stone-breaker, the tap-tap of whose hammer was still being heard this century as he worked away in roadside recesses. Sometimes stone-breakers wore goggles to protect their eyes — there is a pair of these in Tain Museum, Ross-shire, made like spectacles but in place of glass there is the finest of wire mesh, mesh which bulges out in a very alarming way and must have made any stone-breaker who wore them a frightening figure. Among many ancient healing skills which used to be practised in the countryside was the ability to lick foreign bodies out of eyes with the tongue. Such a talent was invaluable to a stone-breaker and there is a living memory of a child who spent all his spare time with a stone-breaker, having this done for him by the old man when he got a chip in his eye.[7] But not all stone-breakers had companions and it could be a lonely job which made them vulnerable to trouble-makers, possibly travellers who had taken drink, and various press reports tell of assaults on these men, including one case when the offender already had three convictions for similar offences.[8]

Stone-breaking by the roadside was necessary but it could cause problems, as is apparent from this report.

> The new roads are everywhere encumbered with little heaps of broken stones deposited in waiting for any necessary repair. Although a traveller may keep the road in the dark, his horse often stumbles and sometimes falls over these heaps. When the ground is covered with snow, it is dangerous for a carriage even in the day time; in the dark, it is by chance alone, by no skill or care of the postilion, that being overset is avoided. It is said that by these nuisances the mail coach is occasionally overturned. It has been imagined that the trustees might be found liable in a court of justice for any injury caused.[9]

7   Road-building in Angus. Source: Scottish Ethnological Archive, Royal Museum of Scotland.

Maintenance of turnpike roads worked out at about 50s. a mile[10] while the cost of building them varied considerably, depending on the availability of materials and such factors. In Caithness a road 24 feet broad with 12 feet of the centre metalled to a depth of 9–12 inches cost £240 per mile in the early nineteenth century.[11] In one eastern part of Ross-shire about a mile of road was built at a cost of £367. 13s. 5d. in 1816 while in 1819 a nearby road cost approximately £128 per mile.[12] (An 'S' bend on the latter road was straightened in 1978 at an estimated cost of £22,000 and the former road was remade for industrial purposes at a cost of about £166,000 a mile in the early 1970s, although admittedly to a very different standard.)

The money for turnpike roads was raised, as was also done with statute labour ones, by the trustees borrowing capital, but now it was borrowed against the expected income from tolls and not against commutation money. In general this worked well although sometimes a road turned out to be more expensive to make and less used than anticipated, as happened in the case of the Perth–Crieff road. It was 35 feet wide all the way and due to denes and ravines on one part of it, that section cost £260 per mile, including bridges, and the rest £239 per mile, which was so expensive and 'the resort of travellers so small' that the tolls were insufficient to pay for it.[13]

The right of collecting tolls or public dues of any kind, be it on turnpike roads, bridges, in the market place or anywhere else, was always let annually to a tacksman — a tenant — thus giving the public authority a known income and leaving the business of collection and profit to the tacksman. In the case of turnpikes, the right of collecting tolls and pontage (bridge tolls) was let annually, from May to May, and every spring newspapers carried advertisements for the roup of the tolls. The trustees tried to avoid letting to bad payers and advertisements frequently said that security must be provided, that applicants 'must immediately find caution for payment of their rents, otherwise they will not be preferred'. To make absolutely sure, an advertisement might say that those intending to offer for toll-bars were 'requested to bring their cautioners to the roup as no person will be preferred who does not find immediate security for the punctual payment of the rent'.[14]

An idea of the rents paid appears in the report of a roup of tolls in Kelso Town Hall in April 1854 (see Table 1).[15]

'Neither a lender nor a cautioner be' is wise advice. It is surprising that all the would-be toll-keepers in the country could find people willing to stand surety for them, especially when the rents came to large sums and even though they were paid in instalments. A toll-keeper had to gauge carefully what income from tolls should be before he offered for them, and if he got it wrong he was in trouble. This happened to David Baird, tacksman of Stonyford Bar on the Lauder–Kelso road in 1824. His arrears of rent were such that the trustees had to take out a caption — a formal warrant to apprehend a debtor or similar defaulter — against both Baird and his cautioner, John Hislop,

TABLE 1

	Present rent £ per annum	New rent £ per annum
Kelso Bridge	1,225	715 (for ½ year)
Ednam	230	212
Rosebank	196	170
Teviot Bridge	146	177
Maxton	80	52
Sprouston	40	50
Carham and Learmonth	86	89
Cowbog	76	80
Yetholm Mains	112	130
Loanhead	389	355
Maxwellheugh	610	750
Crooked House	69	44

tenant of Earlston Mill. Poor John Hislop was threatened with imprisonment unless he paid something and he managed to produce £20 on condition that he should be molested no further until as much as possible was recovered from Baird. Ultimately the debt was reduced to £16. 12s. 10d., exclusive of interest and expenses, at which point the trustees had Baird arrested and imprisoned in the jail at the Castle in Jedburgh. There he immediately applied to the Magistrates of the burgh for aliment under the Act of Grace as an indigent person and was awarded 1s. per day to be paid by the trustees. A minute at this point shows the trustees' cashier asking them whether to pay this or to allow Baird to be freed and to try to recover the debt from the unfortunate John Hislop. Unfortunately the end of the story is not known.[16]

Toll-keepers' financial calculations about rent could be upset by prolonged snow-storms which closed the roads. After one 'unprecedented stoppage' in 1823 in the Borders, toll-keepers appealed for, and got, a 5 per cent reduction of rents on condition that this should not be regarded as a precedent.[17]

As each county had its own Act or Acts for turnpikes, there was variation in toll-gathering and what was or was not exempt from toll. Pedestrians rarely paid toll on roads[18] and for anyone carrying goods there was no charge for the return journey unless they had a fresh load. Tickets for return journeys were not transferable, under threat of a penalty. With agriculture developing fast, lime was in great demand but while it was exempt in certain places, in others it was not and in fact the *Statistical Account for Kincardine* said that it would hardly be worth collecting tolls at all were lime excluded. In some areas there were reduced rates not only for lime but also for coal and manures, although in fact the carriage of these was particularly heavy on roads. Road-making materials were always exempt and parish ministers, military traffic and vagrants went free too and there were special arrangements for mail. Should a landowner gift land for a turnpike road, then he could be granted a limited

8   Artafallie Toll-house, Ross-shire.

exemption as well. Under the Scottish Turnpike Act of 1831 'for amending and making more effectual the laws concerning turnpike roads in Scotland' any parishioner attending the funeral of anyone who died and was buried in that parish was exempt from paying at any turnpike in the parish; this funeral exemption was extended by an Act of Parliament in the early 1850s which removed all tolls on funeral processions: '. . . no funeral procession or carriage in such procession and no foot passenger while going or returning from the place of interment, shall be liable to any toll or pontage.'[19] The *Kelso Mail* which reported this provision said that it believed few toll-keepers were yet aware of the alteration and were liable to a penalty if they exacted tolls from those attending funerals, no matter whether in their own parishes or not. One cannot help wondering how many 'funerals' people gave as their destination at toll-bars. Just one or two examples give an idea of what these charges were about the 1790s: horse or mule 1½d.; saddle horse 6d.; wheeled vehicles were charged according to the number of animals drawing them, even up to 12s. when a wagon was pulled by six beasts; and droves of animals were charged per score, anything from 2½d. to 10d.

However beneficial turnpike roads turned out to be — and they were beneficial – because they required the payment of tolls they were described as 'unpopular to a considerable degree in every county on their first erection and in many counties the opposition of the people to them hath been so strong as greatly to retard and, in some cases, totally to prevent their being carried into effect'.[20] Statute labour had benefited landowners and their larger tenants by improving access to markets, and turnpikes increased these advantages but neither statute labour nor turnpikes helped those who lived at more or less subsistence level on very small holdings. They had no need of access to markets any more than did townspeople who grew a few crops on little plots of land outside their burghs.[21]. *Statistical Accounts* from all around the country described antagonism to turnpikes: ' . . . the opinion of the country in general seems to be against them';[22] or 'many people think it will be too expensive',[23] while that for Dallas, Morayshire, was delightfully parochial and stated that 'turnpikes would be altogether inefficient in Dallas'.[24] When the first Turnpike Act in Scotland was proposed for East Lothian in 1750, the inhabitants of Haddington complained loudly of the oppression that was to be laid on them by making them pay toll for every bit of coal they burned. Near neighbours of turnpikes complained that it was putting a heavy tax on them, in addition to what they already paid for statute labour.[25] Everyone's opinion was summed up by a statement which said that turnpike roads would be very acceptable 'if the ceremony of collecting money at the toll-bars should be dispensed with . . .'[26]

The *Statistical Account for Kilspindie, Perth*, said ' . . . of late there has been in this, as in some other counties, a sort of outcry against turnpikes'.[27] One of the counties where there was the most violent opposition was Berwickshire, although initially it began in a very democratic way with meetings of 'heritors, farmers and others' in and around the county town of Duns when they heard that a Turnpike Bill was being laid before Parliament by some of the landed gentry in 1791-2. Minutes of these meetings are now held in Duns Library and from them there appears to be a little doubt about just how many heritors opposed the Bill. William Hall of Whitehall, near Chirnside, is the only one styled 'Esq' in the minutes, a style which at that time indicated a heritor; but even if few heritors attended these meetings, some certainly gave financial support later on when in February 1792 this group sent subscription papers round the county to raise money to enable them to petition Parliament. They engaged a solicitor and decided to pay the expenses of one of their number, Robert Chirnside, to go to London should someone be required to attend a House of Commons committee. But their efforts were to no avail and the Bill became law that summer although they considered that they had had a minor victory because their opposition had resulted in lime being charged at half-rates. All this effort cost £116. 15s. 6d., raised by a levy on the number of their supporters' horses — 6s. for a horse, 3s. for a mare. William Hall must have felt very strongly about turnpikes and tolls because he was prepared to put his money where his mouth was and at his own expense accompanied Robert Chirnside to London, stayed there for four months 'attending on Parliament' and in addition paid for the transcribing of papers and printing. Surprisingly, the lawyer who advised on the propriety of sending a deputation to the House of Lords refused their offer of 5 guineas as a fee and would only accept one, although his clerk readily took

9   Dryburgh Toll-house from the South. Courtesy of Miss Robb, St Boswells.

10   Old Toll-house near east end at Dundee turnpike, built c.1790. Source:
Scottish Ethnological Archive, Royal Museum of Scotland.

10s. 6d. Robert Chirnside's expenses seem incredibly little compared to today's prices — 'travelling in haste to London' cost just £5 and his expenses there and his return journey came to a mere £9.

Once the Act was passed at least seven toll-bars were erected, two of which were at the east and west ends of the town of Duns, and the levying of tolls was fixed to start on 4 July 1792. To this there was strong opposition and on the night of 3 July a considerable number of people in Duns decided to destroy these bars, and did so, burning the wood at the town cross. The authorities appeared, but only in a small way: a sheriff officer tried unsuccessfully to arrest one woman, women taking an active part in the proceedings, but it was the following afternoon, the 4 July, when she was finally apprehended, only to be rescued by a large crowd. On Friday 6 July, two of the men implicated in the trouble were arrested and as this became known people began to gather in the streets. There was considerable unrest, with some of the younger men wanting to rescue those arrested but yielding in the end to the advice of wiser men who did not advise this course. The following day the Sheriff managed to persuade the people to go home and order prevailed once more. That same week the toll-bars at Paxton and Newwater were wrecked by a mob armed with hatchets, pick-axes and other weapons. It must have been an unnerving experience for the toll-keeper at Paxton who was a woman. Like all other toll-keepers she had had to pay rent for the privilege of collecting tolls and yet there she was, on only the second day in this new role, with the toll-house partly demolished, her furniture burnt outside and what remained of the toll-house then set on fire. It seems obvious that there was an organizing hand behind these various riots, which are described in a letter written by Ninian Home of Paxton House to his uncle Col David Milne Home of Wedderburn Castle, a letter now in the Scottish Record Office:

> Paxton House,
> July 13 1792.
>
> Dear Sir,
> I have been expecting you every day for a good while past and therefore have not written to you, but a letter I received yesterday from Campbell says you are not to leave town for a week; so this letter may reach you. In truth you have been as well out of the way. We have had more disturbance and riot in the county about establishing the toll-gates than I could have believed possible and I fear they are far from being at an end. Seven gates that were erected have been pulled down and burned or thrown into the Tweed; the toll-house at Paxton Gate burned and a great part of the wall thrown down; a temporary house put up at Idington Muir is also burned. There has been no open violence since the 5th but you see insolence and ill-humour in the faces of almost everyone you meet on the road; and they threaten, if the toll-gates are put up again that they will burn and destroy the houses and property of every gentleman in this part of the county who has been concerned in putting up the gates; and if we are not protected by a sufficient military force, I dare say it will be the case. Three troops of dragoons have been

in Dunse since last Saturday which has kept everything quiet, but they speak of moving some of the dragoons. I was in Dunse yesterday and we wrote to Lord Adam Gordon pointing out our situation and telling him that unless we had a sufficient force not only to enable us to erect the gates, but that force to be continued with us until the country was quiet, we could not attempt to do anything. His answer will arrive tomorrow or Sunday and the Trustees will meet again on Monday. The whole of the farmers to a man almost are at the bottom of the business or they could easily have restrained their servants; but they do not act themselves, and it will be difficult, I am afraid, to fix it on any of them. The whole town of Chirnside, man, woman and child, I believe were concerned in the riots. The Sheriff went from Dunse last Sunday night with a party of dragoons, but they had scouts out everywhere to give them intelligence, and not one was taken. Three of them, however, were taken the night before last with one or two others. They will be examined on Saturday (tomorrow) when the Sheriff, who was obliged to attend the trial (as a witness) of Taylor, one of the Edinburgh rioters, is expected to be at Dunse again. Two of the Dunse rioters are carried to Edinburgh by a Justiciary Warrant. We shall not have peace until some examples are made: and I think you had as well pass a few weeks at Buxton or Harrowgate until things are settled. The Col. is at Caldra. I passed a day with him last week. Mrs. Home, Miss Mary and Miss Grahame were here alone the night the gates were burned. I was at Caldra. You may believe they were very much frightened, and are not a little so yet.

I ever am, Dear Uncle, Affectionately Yours,

Ninian Home.

There is a strong indication in this letter that William Hall's group, largely based as they were on Chirnside, while initially organizing opposition in a democratic and orderly manner, were perhaps not averse to giving it a helping hand at a lower level – but that may be unfair. For their rioting, two women were sent to the Tolbooth for four months, then bound over to keep the peace for life under caution of 1,000 merks; and three men were also sent to the Tolbooth for four months, then banished from Scotland for seven years and bound over as the women were. On charges of fire-raising, two cases were found not proven, one man did not appear and was outlawed while another was sent to prison for four months and banished from Scotland for life. These sentences may seem harsh but in the case of fire-raising they were mild as at that time it could carry the death penalty. In December of that year of 1792, Gallatown, near Kirkcaldy in Fife, was the scene of more turnpike rioting. The villagers had pulled down parts of the toll-house so often that the trustees had to bring in constables to guard it. This achieved its object for a couple of nights but on the third night a crowd started throwing things at the constables and broke the toll-house windows. The following night the constables were attacked and driven back and this time the toll-house was completely destroyed. When the toll-bar was re-erected, the Sheriff Depute arranged with a Kirkcaldy mill-owner to provide six 'stout hands' to be a guard and with a large number of the manufacturers of the district promising support if needed, there was no further trouble.[28] There was opposition elsewhere, as has been said, and this was in the forefront of the trustees' minds all the time, so much so that in 1811 when there was £3,500 owing on the Lauder–Kelso road, the trustees were anxious not to have to erect a new toll-house, 'a measure they are conscious would create much public dissatisfaction'.[29] At no time did trustees realize that a great deal of the opposition to turnpikes could have been avoided by allowing special rates to people living so close to toll-bars that they inevitably had to pass them several times a day.[30]

Certain bridges also came within the remit of the turnpike system, under bridge trustees, and Kelso Bridge over the River Tweed was the setting in 1854 of what the local paper, the Kelso Mail, called 'disgraceful scenes'. The Bridge Acts provided that once money borrowed against tolls or pontage dues had been paid up, along with interest, then tolls or pontage should cease. For this reason the Kelso Bridge trustees considered giving up pontage on the bridge and the public got it into their heads that this was indeed going to happen. However, if money was required for upkeep — something which was surely inevitable — then the Act allowed a proportion of toll or pontage to continue to be levied, and the trustees decided in this case to let the tolls for at least six months more, to the fury of the townspeople. In March that year a meeting of the Convenery of Kelso discussed the report of a committee appointed to inquire into the Kelso Bridge Trust. Among other conclusions, they decided that the Trust, before extracting any more money from the public 'though not legally bound, are in honour and in justice bound to show the public in unmistakable figures, why this is necessary. And that the Convenery, as part of that public, can have no confidence in an vidimus which the Trustees are either ashamed or unwilling to publish'. These strong words appeared prominently on the front page of the Kelso Mail on 6 March that year.

New Burgh Acts had brought the village of Maxwellheugh and several farms, all on the south side of the river, within the burgh of Kelso and people naturally felt aggrieved at having to pay pontage to cross the bridge to go from one part of the town to another. Feelings came to such a pitch that a mob, apparently organised, took advantage of the Queen's birthday which was celebrated at the end of May and 'after committing many wrong acts' set off from the Market Place for the bridge, carrying a pole topped with a sack full of shavings and other fire-lighting material. They did not succeed in firing the toll-gate because, in their enthusiasm, they inadvertently threw their incendiary device over the rails but they tore the large gate from its hinges and threw it over the bridge, only to find that it had not landed in the river, so they rushed down to where it lay and pushed it right into the water. It floated off to the cauld below Maxwellheugh and at that point word came that the police were coming and the mob fled. The next day what began as a more constitutional demonstration took place, although it did not end that way. At midday, Mr Patterson, the Covener, and two others formally entered a specially hired carriage at the Town Hall, drove once round the Market Place where an immense number of onlookers had gathered and then headed for the bridge, with cheering all the way. Their intention was to cross the bridge without paying or to do so only under protest. To the accompaniment of a great deal of noise from the crowds, the toll-keeper seized their horse's head and demanded payment. Mr Patterson and his companions said they would only pay if they got a ticket but the toll-keeper knew nothing about tickets and had to go and ask the Clerk to the trustees, only to return to say that there was no need for them. Loudly declaring, 'I will not pay you', the Convener drove on but on his return, so as to behave in a legal way, he paid toll and this time did receive a ticket. During all this, half the people were inside the toll-gate, which must have been rescued from its watery resting place, and several horses and vehicles were pulled over the bridge by the crowd amidst cries of 'No toll'. In spite of the odds against him, the toll-keeper seized the head of every horse he could reach and asked for payment but received none. Throughout the rest of the day, the bridge crossing was for all practical purposes free and people passed and re-passed at will, in spite of the demands of the unfortunate toll-keeper who, after all, had agreed to pay £715 for the privilege of receiving the half-year's tolls.[31]. The press reports of this incident end somewhat surprisingly by saying that it was expected that the Convener and others would bring a prosecution against the Bridge Trustees for repetition of the toll duty as a Summary Debt summons.[32]

Naturally enough, people tried to avoid payment of tolls whenever possible. Carriers set out on cart journeys just after midnight so as to complete journeys in one day and so avoid the payment of double toll,[33] cheerfully disregarding the risk of falling asleep at the reins and ending up where the horse took them rather than where they wanted to go.[34] Others jumped toll-bars on their horses and one gypsy is reputed to have carried his donkey through the gate so as to avoid paying for it. Some people in Inverness hit on a good way of getting rid of bridge toll — one Sunday as people left church, they and the minister were shocked to see others playing shinty on the green at Muirtown. They explained that they could not pay the toll and so could not get to church and had nothing else to do but amuse themselves. The minister applied to the Magistrates and as a result no toll was thereafter charged on Sundays.[35] Sometimes people broke through enclosure fences so as to slip around toll-bars and the farmer at Clackmae, Roxburghshire, always maintained his own private diversion round a nearby checkbar. It was at that particular checkbar that an incident occurred which was reported in the local press in 1847 under the heading, 'Toll Case. Important to Toll Gatherers'. A farmer was charged with refusing to pay toll and won his case with expenses on the grounds that the name of the toll-keeper was not displayed on the toll-house as it should have been and that the list of dues was out of date.[36]

In spite of the toll-keeper at Kelso Bridge not knowing about tickets, possibly because being the end of May he had just taken over as toll-keeper, these were meant to be issued and some of the conditions under which this was done are implicit in a case reported in the press in 1855 under the heading of 'Illegal Issuing of toll-tickets'. Donald Macdonald, a toll-keeper near Kelso, was charged with refusing to accept a toll ticket granted at another toll-bar although it was on the same line of road and within the statutory distance which entitled a person paying at one to exemption at the other; and this in spite of the fact that the toll-keeper's rental conditions had clearly stated that pass tickets should be given and received. He was fined £5 plus expenses. At the same time another toll-keeper, John Turnbull, was fined £1 plus expenses for issuing a ticket which did not specify the toll-bars to which it gave exemption.[37] One can well understand how annoying it must have been to toll-keepers when their toll-gate was the one passed freely while another man received payment. Having undertaken to pay rent, they had to make as much out of their toll-gathering as they could and sometimes they were none too scrupulous about how they did it and press reports often show how disputes, particularly to do with bridge pontage, had to be settled at a higher level. In 1836 the people in Inverness were said to be 'turning sulky' and refusing to pay the pontage on peat carts and this was only settled when the Burgh Council allowed the toll-keeper £2 in lieu.[38] An argument there in 1838 over pontage charged on grain went to the Sheriff[39] while much earlier, in 1817, one of the townspeople wrote to the press about a charge of 2s. 6d. for a wedding party at one of the bridges, which was considered exorbitant and presumably was a try-on by the toll-keeper.[40] Toll-keepers were therefore obviously not the most popular of people and there are various reports of attacks on them but perhaps John Turnbull, who did not specify exemptions on his tickets, was a particularly difficult man because, whatever the reason, in 1855 a woman called Ann Cunningham or Dixon was charged with wickedly and feloniously attacking him by 'striking him upon the face or head with a sharp stone or other missile, and biting his hand with her teeth, to the injury of his person and effusion of his blood', for which she was fined 10s. with the alternative of ten days hard labour.[41]

Just as people tried to avoid paying tolls, so trustees tried to prevent this happening. In the case of bridges, they had the authority to close both fords and ferries which provided alternative crossings; and all these powers were ones which they used. For instance, when it was proposed in 1793 to apply to Parliament for a Turnpike Act for several roads near a Border town, one of the first things considered by the trustees was choosing a spot for a bridge so that 'little danger of evading the pontage could arise'.[42] In 1803 the trustees of Kelso Bridge persuaded a landowner who had always allowed the public to use a footpath to a ferry, to close the path and themselves closed the fords on a stretch of the river and declared that 'all persons using the said fords or footpath after the 22nd November will be punished in terms of law'.[43] This was very harsh and nowadays would be regarded as a gross infringement of civil liberties but it does not seem to have provoked the outcry one might have expected; and such rulings were common all round the country. A Dumfries writer felt very strongly about the powers of the trustees in this respect, saying,

> They should never wantonly shut up other roads which are of importance to the country, nor use any oppressive methods to compel persons to travel on the turnpike road only. They should ever remember that turnpike roads are made for the country and not the country for them; and that no man in a free country will easily submit to illegal or unequitable compulsion.[44]

The Kelso Bridge trustees went even further however in their desire for exclusive rights. When a railway bridge was proposed over the Tweed in 1847, close to their bridge, the trustees petitioned Parliament, not to prevent the bridge being built but for compensation on the grounds that it would materially diminish pontage dues, which must have been over £1,000 a year, by diverting traffic from it. The trustees incurred heavy expenses for this claim in the House of Commons and won their case but it was a hollow victory as it caused the railway company to abandon their plans for the branch line for which the bridge was intended.[45]

The higher the rent that could be obtained for toll-bars, the more money was available for road-making and, as up to 10 per cent more was offered where the toll-house was licensed[46] so it was that the selling of alcohol by toll-keepers became common, in spite of the fact that it was forbidden by Act of Parliament. The old toll-house at Ashkirk, near Selkirk, still has no less than three large cellars below it, running the whole length of the house, a very clear indication of the amount of alcohol consumed there. Allowing alcohol to be sold at toll-houses was easy to justify. 'This is an evil which it must be difficult to remedy so long as the trustees of the roads have the power of granting licences because each is anxious to secure to his own particular toll-house that by which the rent is augmented,' said the writer of the *New Statistical Account for Carnwath, Lanarkshire*, adding that all six toll-houses in the parish were licensed, even though some of them were within a very short distance of a licensed inn.[47] Another opinion was '. . . the more it is vindicated by the increase in toll-revenue, the more it ought to be reprobated for the demoralisation it creates'.[48] Such ready availability of alcohol along the roads was found to be a great source of trouble although for many travellers it must have been welcome and perhaps sweetened the pill of toll-paying. Certainly the men who carted wool over the ridge separating Liddesdale and Rulewater in the Borders thought it a splendid idea to have some refreshment on the way. This was at a time when Liddesdale had thirty to forty sheep farms, the wool of which, packed in bales, came to eight or ten cart loads per farm.

Moving this was such a task that it was usual for farms to help each other out, with several co-operating to take all the wool of one farm one day and another's the next and so on. The wool was taken to an agreed spot, half way between seller and buyer and either the bales handed over or the carts temporarily exchanged. A favourite place to do this was at the isolated toll-bar at the Note-o'-the-Gate. The carters loved these trips and the ongoings are said to have kept the gossips busy for the proverbial nine days.[49]

Naturally enough, the social effects of toll-house drinking were not good. It was considered 'very prejudicial' to allow spirits to be sold at toll-houses[50] and the consumption of spirits could be enormous.[51] Half the evil might have been removed if toll-houses had been restricted to the selling of ale[52] but they weren't and the position was summed up by one minister thus, ' ... our country roads are to a considerable extent maintained by the gains of intemperance'.[53] In spite of its being illegal, licensing of toll-houses was 'stubbornly maintained by the road trustees'.[54] In those days, candidates for normal ale and spirits licences were generally required to produce a certificate of good character from the minister of their parish, but while JPs paid lip-service to this principle, they did not adhere to it in regard to toll-houses and licensing of them was in fact achieved through Acts of JPs themselves, many of them being road trustees.[55] Anyone applying to quarter sessions with a certificate from a JP received a licence, in certain areas anyway, without production of the ministerial certificate of moral character usually demanded and in Biggar one toll-keeper had no difficulty in getting a licence even though a certificate of character had actually been refused on the grounds that he was a man of bad character. Because toll-keepers only had annual leases, they were a shifting population and were therefore less concerned to keep up standards than were normal inn-keepers and in order to make as much as possible out of their high rents, they were often tempted to encourage excess; but because of the extra rent offered it was very difficult to abolish the practice.[56]

Some toll-keepers, however, did not bother to obtain a licence but cheerfully sold alcohol without one which, of course, was not popular with the authorities. In 1847, three toll-keepers in the vicinity of St Boswells, Roxburghshire, were charged with selling excisable liquor in this way. In 1855, four more in much the same area were all found guilty of the same offence and were each fined £1. 15s. with 10s. expenses. While selling alcohol at a toll-house could cause trouble, so could refusal to do so, presumably from a not unnatural expectation that it would be available there. An instance of this occurred at Sprouston, Roxburghshire, when two men, thought to be navvies working on the railway being built at that time, began smashing the toll-house windows when they were refused admission and drink and it took the efforts of the villagers to stop them doing even more damage.[57] With all this liquid provision for humans, it is nice to know that a horse trough was usually available at toll-houses for horses to slake their thirsts too.

But selling alcohol was not the only way in which toll-keepers could make some extra money. At the time of fairs, Highland games and similar occasions they were allowed to provide and charge for special access to these events. Writing of St James's Fair in Kelso in 1842 the *Kelso Mail* said,

> A wooden bridge was, as usual, erected across the Tweed a little above the Anna, for the convenience of foot-passengers frequenting the fair. This erection is made by the tacksmen of Kelso and Teviot bridges who enter into it as a profitable speculation, pontage at the wooden bridge being exactly double the sum charged at the other bridges. We mention this for the purpose of complaining of the very incommodious and unsafe temporary bridge which was erected on Friday. Immense crowds passed and repassed at this bridge, which was so carelessly and imperfectly constructed that scores of persons were immersed in the river in the course of the day and particularly towards evening, and had it not been for the shallow state of the river, very serious consequences might have followed. If the tacksmen find such an erection a profitable speculation, they are surely bound to make sufficient provision for ensuring the safety of passengers and it is certainly the duty of the authorities to ascertain that such provision has been made, before the bridge is allowed to be opened. It will be too late to make a fuss about the matter after some fatal accident shall have happened, and we trust, therefore, that this will be attended to in future years, or that otherwise a temporary bridge will not be permitted. The lives of such immense crowds, a great many of whom are females and children, ought not to be allowed to be trifled with in such a manner, merely to gratify the avarice of the parties concerned.[58]

The problem did not arise the following year as the river was too high to allow for a temporary bridge to be put up but the paper's broadside must have done some good as in 1844 it was able to report that a wooden bridge of very superior construction to those of former years had been erected, with the result that great numbers went by it to the fair.

Yet another way for those toll-keepers who were near the border with England to make extra money was to go into the marriage business. In Scotland two unmarried people of the opposite sex were considered legally married if they declared themselves to be man and wife in the presence of at least two witnesses. When an English Act of 1754 stopped Fleet marriages — those performed without a licence by debtor–clergymen in the Fleet prison — young couples fled to Scotland to take advantage of her more lenient laws. Gretna Green was one of the most popular places for this and several men — not toll-keepers — set up as 'priests' there. Some six or seven years after the opening in 1830 of the Carlisle–Glasgow road via Gretna, Simon Beattie became tenant of the toll-bar about half a mile south of Gretna and began performing marriages in the little circular white-washed toll-house and, being fractionally nearer the Border than 'priests' in the village of Gretna, he did well at it. He also did well during the Carlisle Hiring fair when young couples 'made it up'. He had several strapping daughters and it is said that if he was away from home for any reason, one of them would not hesitate to dress up like him and perform the ceremony in his place. The income from marriages increased the yearly rent of this toll-bar considerably and in 1843 another man, John Murray, took over, presumably having outbid Simon Beattie. The toll-house at Coldstream bridge was another where marriages were performed, as was Lamberton Toll in Berwickshire. At all these places, of course, Scottish couples also were married, taking advantage of marriage without the formalities demanded by the church and one can only assume that the trustees either approved or turned a blind eye, so long as the rent was increased.[59]

From the time of Alexander II (1214–49) and perhaps earlier, travellers were entitled to spend a night on the highway, such as it was, and to graze their beasts there so long as they did not allow them on to what was obviously cultivated land or meadow.[60] But as new roads were built and the land on either side was enclosed it became impractical to allow wayside grazing of animals and road trustees did not want to have their new roads spoilt, any more than landowners and farmers wished to have enclosures broken, and so it was that in 1832 the *Kelso Mail* carried a notice saying that pasturing on road sides was forbidden, except over common or unenclosed land, under a penalty of 5s. per beast. Any animal found grazing would be seized by the trustees or their surveyor and held for three days to allow the penalty and any expenses to be paid. If these were not forthcoming within three days of the notice of detention being given on the two nearest toll-bars on the road where the beast was found, it could be sold with the authority of the Sheriff or any JP of the county and the owner would receive whatever remained after penalty and expenses were deducted. Gypsies were obvious victims of this new enactment. In their wanderings it was essential to camp and to graze their horses and donkeys by the wayside and press reports often show that they were fined for doing so, and for camping on Roman roads which gypsies regarded as ancient highways to which they had every right of access. In general they were less likely to be molested on Roman roads than elsewhere and large numbers of them camped for days together on these old routes.[61] But when part of a Roman road was incorporated into a new road, things changed and there was an interesting case about this in 1848 when a gypsy, Alexander Young, was fined for camping and pasturing on a stretch of Dere Street, a Roman road which runs partly through Roxburghshire, a section of which had been made into a highway in March that year. Young's summons was put into the keyhole of the house he used in Jedburgh during the winter months, a stupid thing to do as he had by then set off on his summer travels and did not find it in time. He later appealed against the charge on the grounds that the road or land, being a Roman road and the property of the Crown, could not be taken possession of by the trustees and, that in attempting to make it a highway, they had not obeyed the provisions of the Act.[62]

Unfortunately there is no further report of this case with its interesting legal implications. The prevention of grazing and camping, along with the imposition of tolls, were among the things that ended the wandering ways of gypsies although many of them became carriers or carters which allowed them to travel and to keep horses as they had always done. Grazing prohibitions and tolls also affected pedlars whose income was small but to whom travelling was essential, as was a bite for their beasts along the way.

It is understandable that payment of tolls, closing of certain roads and compulsory use of certain bridges was unpopular but over and above these grievances, there were some surprising complaints about improving road conditions. Cattle drovers bewailed road damage to their animals' hooves, unconcerned with the damage that these hooves might do to roads; and human beings in some areas lamented the wear and tear that gravelled roads caused to their feet. So against innovation were the people in parts of Skye that for a number of years after roads were built, they would not on any account walk on them. They said the stones and gravel both bruised their feet and wore their shoes down and they preferred to stick to the old paths, uneven and boggy as they were, although they did in time become reconciled to good, level, firm, dry roads.[63] Although not applicable to turnpikes, the same sort of mentality was found by a Shetland minister who made a road of sorts through the glebe to the church only to find that the people did not like it because it damaged their footwear.[64]

Great though the benefits of good communications were, they could encourage the entry of the undesirable as well as the desirable. 'Improvements have taken place in the modes of communication with other parts of the kingdom,' said the New Statistical Account for Strath, in the island of Skye,

> ... but although the benefits ... are great yet some of them are attended with disadvantages, as they are the means of introducing into the country a variety of vagrants such as gypsies, rag-men, vendors of crockery, tinsmiths, egg-dealers and old-clothes men. By characters of this description, manners and habits which were formerly unknown to the lower orders, are gradually introduced, such as tea-drinking, tobacco chewing and smoking.[65]

In the parish of Pettie, in Inverness-shire, there was the same kind of problem:

> This district, from its being traversed by the public road to Aberdeen, is peculiarly infested by imposters pretending to be shipwrecked sailors, clerks and schoolmasters whose health has failed and vagrants with forged or out-dated passes or begging certificates furnished with too much facility. We expect a remedy to this evil from the adoption of the Constabulary Act by the county and the rural police now in course of formation.[66]

Fife with a thoroughfare from east to west though the county suffered in this way too and the people were 'much oppressed with beggars and vagrants'[67] while in the town of Cupar the inhabitants were 'daily subjected to their importunities and extortions'.[68] In the south-west it was the same story and Symington, Ayrshire, on the route between Portpatrick and Glasgow, was infested with Irish vagrants and beggars from elsewhere[69] while in Sanquhar, Dumfries-shire, 'the almost continual flux and reflux of vagrants through the town, which is a thoroughfare for both ends of the kingdom, is also a strong corrosive on the morals of the people'.[70] It was also felt that many of these beggars, half-starved and ill-clad, coming from the filthy lanes and closes of over-crowded towns, were naturally prone to disease and carried infection of all kinds with them in their wanderings. In parts of Argyllshire it was felt that typhus fever and other epidemics were being brought there by Irish vagrants[71] and in Moulin, Perthshire, where they were 'perfectly ate up with beggars', outbreaks of scarlet fever, whooping cough and smallpox were generally traced to them;[72] and their movement through the country during the cholera outbreak of 1832 was thought to have done much to help its spread too. But there are two sides to everything and in the county of Kincardine people were said to derive 'no small advantage from the number of travellers who are perpetually passing' thanks to the great north road which ran through it,[73] while the parish of Dunlop, Ayrshire, found that thanks to the roads running through it there was easy access to every part of the parish, and also to the country and town. 'In consequence of this, the people have frequent and friendly intercourse with one another, know the value of everything they have to sell and can bring it to the best market. To the same cause, perhaps, may be ascribed that polish and urbanity which they have in common with their neighbours, and that fondness for dress which is so observable on public occasions.'[74]

So although turnpike roads were initially received with doubt, hostility and even rioting, and although this chapter has to some extent concentrated on faults rather than virtues, the fact is that they were found to work well. The techniques of MacAdam and Telford were a great contribution to standards of road-building and, in addition, roads were better maintained. Statute labour money was freed for use entirely on lesser feeder roads, something which was of great benefit to people living off the beaten track. Better roads meant that far heavier loads could be pulled and wheeled traffic could move freely and fast, the very things that were necessary for the coaching age which flourished between 1780 and 1830.[75]

Tolls continued to be charged until the passing of the Roads and Bridges (Scotland) Act of 1878 when they were abolished and in some areas anyway, exactly at midday on 15th May 1879, intimation of their final demise was made by a shot fired from the windows of the various toll-houses.[76]

Appendix

Entries from the diary of Mrs Elizabeth Stenhouse, wife of Robert Hislop, farm steward at East Morriston, Berwickshire, show how she noted the condition of roads because they were so important in everyday life:

17 Feb. 1863, 'Nice dry roads'.
12 July 1863, 'Very dusty roads'.
2 Aug. 1863, 'Dusty roads'.
26 Jan. 1864, 'Dirty roads'.
28 Feb. 1864, 'Very dirty roads'.
27 Mar. 1864, 'Hard frost, dry roads'.
1 Feb. 1865, 'Sluchie (sic) roads'.
26 May 1866, 'A good dry day for flitters'.

A summary of Dorothy Wordsworth's comments on various Scottish roads in 1803:

Tolerable: Leadhills, Hamilton, Glasgow, Dalmally, Portnacroish, Killin, Loch Earn Head, Clovenford, Melrose.
Pretty good: Brownhill (near Dumfries).
Good: Annan, Dumfries, Arrochar, Tyndrum, Edinburgh, Roslin, Peebles, Dryburgh, Hawick, Longtown, Ambletree.
Excellent: Suie (near Tyndrum).
Most excellent: Callendar and part of the Ballachulish road.
Not bad, bad, baddish: Lanark, Tarbert, King's House, Kenmore, Dunkeld, Callendar to Falkirk.
Roughish: Jedburgh.
Very bad, wretchedly bad: Douglass Mill (near Lanark), Faskally.[77]

Into the late 1970s, old people in the villages of Hilton, Balintore and Shandwick, Ross-shire, remembered road-making there early this century, with stones carted from the shore or from nearby quarries, laid on the road, spread with clay, sprinkled with water and the clay worked in and flattened by a wide brush pulled by a horse. After this, from time to time, road metal was used to cover the clay and even up the surface.

5 TRAVEL ON TWO FEET

Although a diary kept by Mrs Elizabeth Stenhouse, wife of the farm steward at East Morriston in Berwickshire in the 1860s,[1] shows a surprising amount of social and business moving-about in a small area, that was at a time when road-building, coaching and, in southern Scotland, railways had all helped to make people aware of a wider world about them and how to get to it. But before there were proper roads, and even afterwards, the bulk of the population did not 'travel'. In the early seventeenth century it was hardly safe to do so anyway as all sorts of dangerous characters looked on country people as easy game and unless they were handy with a cudgel they stood to lose whatever they were carrying.[2]

In addition, working hours were long and occupied six days of the week and the only regular 'travelling' was to church on Sundays although the seating accommodation and size of churches makes it plain that by no means everyone who should have gone went, and going to the markets and fairs which occurred at regular intervals was to many the outside limit of any other travelling they ever expected to do. There was a general lack of movement and a significant number of inscriptions on rural gravestones show that a wife might be up to ten years older than her husband from which one can only assume that if one wanted a spouse one had to take what was available within a limited travelling area.

However, people who did all their work on foot thought nothing of walking miles, should that be necessary. Students for instance, walked from their homes to university, carrying with them the bag of oatmeal which they hoped would see them through till they next went home. Forty miles a day was considered a reasonable day's walk for younger people and even elderly gentlemen who might have been expected to ride a horse would sometimes go a considerable way on foot. In February 1834 an Elgin newspaper, under the heading of 'Unexampled economy worthy of imitation', told how two senior bailies of the burgh went on an official visit to Lossiemouth to see about the land necessary for a new harbour and in spite of its being a bad time of year, these worthy men walked 5 miles there and 5 miles back and spent only 1s. 6d. for whisky and 6d. for the waiter.[3]

According to Thomas Morer who travelled in Scotland in 1689, no boys were allowed to wear shoes till they were fourteen years old so that their feet might become hardened for war service should this be needed.[4] Where he got this story is a mystery but what is certain is that men went shod; women and children below a certain social standard went barefoot especially in summer and in fact some children might still be barefoot in the snows of winter as school log books show. That can have been no fun but going barefoot was no hardship to them in good weather and those who wore boots in winter longed for the spring when they could put them off until the autumn came and potato-lifting provided the money to buy the following winter's pair. This was still happening into the 1930s. The buying of these boots was an expensive business and the father of the family usually did what cobbling was necessary to maintain them. This included putting on 'protectors' when required. These were like tacks but, unlike them, were of various shapes — a selection could be got from the shoemaker — and a suitably shaped one was put on to the sole wherever it was getting a bit worn and protection was needed. Some older people still have 'protectors' among their bits and pieces.

Public worship demanded footwear and those who went to church did don boots and shoes, even if it meant squashing their feet into what no longer fitted. There are many references to women and girls in the eighteenth and nineteenth centuries walking to church with shoes and stockings slung round their necks[5] or more decorously in napkins[6] or just in their hands. When they got to some suitable spot near the church, they sat down and put them on, clean and unmuddied, and also donned their hand-borne bonnets and were able to go in to church looking their best. This was known as 'busking', one of 'busk's' meanings being to dress or prepare, and the custom gave its name to the Buskin' Brae in the parish of Coldingham, Berwickshire. But before any busking was done, those who had walked a long way to church sat down for a bite to eat — the kirk-bannock, as it was called, very necessary before a long morning service and possibly an afternoon one too. There is a reminder of this pre-worship picnic in the name of an old path, the Kirk Bannie, which runs between Ayton and Foulden via the Nunlands in Berwickshire.[7] Carrying footwear to church seems to have died out about the latter part of the nineteenth century.[8]

Relics of the days when people walked to church are the stiles made of through-stones in many churchyard walls and in farm dykes close to churches. Having walked a long way, no one wanted to go a step further than necessary and rather than go round to a gate, over the wall they went. The only entry to a walled graveyard at Dirlot, Caithness, is by a wide stile of this sort, with a ledge on top, of a suitable size to take a coffin being manhandled over the wall. A short cut to any destination was useful. In towns and villages, vennels between every four or five houses allowed people to cut through without going to the end of the street and, in the country, it was a wise landowner who put up a stile here and there rather than see his fences or walls damaged.

Such journeys as did have to be made were via the shortest practical routes, allowing for water crossings, and therefore paths beaten out by the feet of people and of animals became of enormous importance to local communities. Paths linked public places one with another and led to farms, mills, kilns, to peat mosses and to wells, and particularly valued were those to wells of health which had curative minerals in their water. Some paths were designed for specific purposes. There were routes used by fisherfolk going to places where bait could be found and running the gauntlet the while of country folks' sneering because, for some strange reason, they looked down on them. There were also 'ware roads' — cliff paths for carrying seaweed home from the shore to use as manure; other cliff or shore paths were used by those bringing salmon in by creel from outlying fishing stations to a central point. In a 6-mile stretch of cliffs in Nigg, Ross-shire, there were eleven paths to the shore, all of them of sufficient importance to be named.[9] In the Highlands there were funeral routes, with resting cairns along the way where the coffin was laid to give the bearers a break. These particular paths resulted from the Highlander's desire, no matter where he died, to be if at all possible buried with his forefathers. In the Northern Isles, long funeral routes were often avoided by taking the coffin over voes by boat. There were various paths used for bringing supplies inland from the coast, including salt roads and the herring roads in the Lammermuirs, such as one from Dunbar to Lauder, along which were carried herring which, salted, saw the people through the winter.[10] But valuable though paths were there were some who thought it confining to follow them. The Shetland minister who made a path through the glebe to the church, only to find that people complained that it damaged their footwear, said that there was also a decided disinclination to walk on it because it 'would imply a restriction to a particular path whereas the Shetlander's delight is to roam uncontrolled and "to wander free as the wind on his mountains".'[11]

Paths were treated as rights of way but without thought of any legal implications. It was only when they were closed for any reason, such as enclosures, sporting activities on moorlands or because new roads provided adequate alternatives, that the cry of paths having been used from time immemorial was raised, and usually silenced as well. But improved roads in the late eighteenth and in the nineteenth centuries did help the foot traveller very much. Surfaces were better, there were milestones to show how far he or she had gone and what distance lay ahead, and there were sign-posts too, particularly useful for visitors to Gaelic-speaking areas where inquiries about the way could not be understood let alone answered.

But people could only walk where water permitted. A short boggy patch could be overcome by laying planks across it but if it was large, the only alternative was to go round it. A peaceful burn in summer could easily be jumped but when it became a raging torrent in winter rains it became impassable. Many tales are told of important travellers, such as judges and advocates, being held up for hours or even days because of this[12] and so fords and safe crossing places were vital. Words indicating old crossing places are still commonly found although a knowledge of place name meanings may be necessary to spot them.

Some fords were natural, others man-made by laying a bed of large stones on the floor of the river at suitable places. They were only practical where the river banks were fairly flat or at any rate where they levelled out towards the river mouth and so they are more commonly found in gentle rivers than in

11   Lilliesleaf ford, Roxburghshire. Source: Scottish Ethnological Archive, Royal Museum of Scotland.

steep-sided ones. Even so, fords were often very dangerous, such as one in the parish of Roberton, Lanarkshire, which was of considerable importance to travellers and was also used by pack horses but, because of a fierce current, 'the crossing ... was often attended with loss of life'.[13] The nature of fords could change due to floods and, in the case of those near river mouths, due to high tides as well. In the parish of Urquhart and Wester Loggie, Ross-shire, several fords went in a zig-zag direction and this, with variations from natural causes and the swiftness of the River Conon made them a 'hazardous passage which proves fatal to many' and the minister who came in 1774 said that hardly a year had passed in the following twenty years without at least one person and sometimes two, three or more being drowned, while about 1786 seven people were lost crossing the river at various points in the parish.[14] The River Loth in Sutherland had no ferry boats on it and there was no alternative but 'to enter the stream' which resulted in several drownings too.[15] Until the eighteenth century's bridge-building got under way, there was a 60-mile gap between Peebles and Berwick with no bridges over the Tweed and people were often drowned at fords between these two points;[16] and these are only a few instances of what one writer called many similar 'heart-rending visitations'.[17]

The suitability of fords for either foot or for horse travellers was sometimes indicated as, for example, at Couttie in the parish of Bendochy, Perthshire, where a 'riding stone' and a 'wading stone' marked the right places for a rider or a walker to ford the River Isla;[18] and wading was often necessary, for instance, at a ford at Bonar Bridge over the Kyle of Sutherland, said by Thomas Telford in 1811 to be 3 feet deep at low tide.[19] Even where there were bridges, a pedestrian often preferred to use a ford if it would shorten his journey. People were used to getting wet and, within limits, preferred that to additional mileage. An instance of this was in Crailing, Roxburghshire, where 'There was, indeed, an old bridge but being above the direct line and inconvenient of access to it, it was little used unless the ford was greatly swollen'.[20]

But fords did not just cross rivers; they also crossed estuaries, bays and

12   Signpost pointing to ford over Nigg Bay sands, Ross-shire. Photograph, A P P Ricketts, 1967.

arms of the sea where there was sufficient tidal fall to expose the sands and where these were firm enough to be safe. Sometimes tree trunks or wooden stakes were used to show the way[21] but many fords were unmarked and required common sense and care in crossing. Some tidal fords were less precise than those on rivers; it was sufficient to know that it was safe to cross at certain states of the tide within the area of certain landmarks, although there were always hazards. A ford across Nigg Bay, Ross-shire, is a case in point: the sands were an excellent source of shells for lime but digging for them resulted in the formation of pits which made the sands dangerous, especially to strangers 'some of whom, falling into these pits before the tide is thoroughly gone, unhappily lose their lives'. Several travellers drowned in this way in the earlier part of the nineteenth century and one particular pool, Poll nan Ron, the Seal's Pool, was 'fatal to every one that touched its waters' but there was 'no danger to the traveller who keeps to the eastward of a line drawn betwixt Tarbat House and the Church of Nigg'.[22] This is an instance of the common use of the words east and west in direction-giving when north and south would be more accurate.

This particular ford was of great use to the people of Nigg. There was no peat in the parish and it was only thanks to the ford that they could get to a neighbouring parish for supplies and when there was a secession from the parish church in 1756, almost all the congregation who left it, crossed the ford for years to worship elsewhere. The Nigg minister's wife is said to have complained to her husband that on Sundays the sands were black with people heading for another church via the ford but he was totally untroubled saying, with truth, that they were not taking the stipend with them.[23] On the subject of fords, there is a memory of the minister of Creich, Sutherland, who when he went to dine at a house on the other side of the Kyle of Sutherland, waded the Kyle at low tide with his evening clothes in his arms, changed into them when he got to his destination, stayed the night and returned home, as he had come, at the next low tide.[24]

The drove trade used several estuarial and river-mouth fords and many fords over both rivers and tidal stretches were shown on maps as main roads. The Nigg Bay ford is an example of this: an atlas of 1893 showed the road from Nigg Ferry going across the ford and thence to the town of Tain, with nothing to indicate that there was a bay to cross at low tide which could cause a delay of hours.[25] There was also a sign post pointing over the ford, indicating a main route which, though by then illegible, was still standing in 1975. It must have been frustrating in the extreme for travellers to think there was a road all the way to their destination, only to find a temporarily impassable ford in the way. The old military surveys were clearer about this and showed land roads with double lines which broke off if they came to a ford and only re-started on the other side. Well after roads were built, fords were still used, and the Nigg Bay one was being used by cars into the 1920s, by farm carts going to a mill on the other side till 1947 and by riders till the 1960s.

A very good way of hopping over a river was by stepping stones which were in fact most basic form of bridge, whether natural or placed in the water by man. They were often referred to simply as 'steps' — the *New Statistical Account for Dunipace, Stirlingshire*, speaks of pedestrians crossing the River Carron by steps (carriages went by a ford prior to the building of a bridge in 1824).[26] They were useful too in cases where, for instance, the village was separated from the 'big house' by a river. This was the case at Ancrum, Roxburghshire, where, although there was a bridge, it was by rather nearer stepping stones that people in the village crossed to work on the estate of Ancrum House, where at one time forty people were employed.[27]

Crossing a ford could mean getting wet, as could a careless slip on a stepping stone, but one way to cross an unbridged river, given the will and the skill, was by using stilts, although successful stilting can only have been managed where the river bed was suitable. Uneven, slimy stones such as are found in many rivers would have made it impossible. About the 1760s to 1770s the people of Dollar, Clackmannanshire, were very expert at crossing the river in this way. Each stilt was made of a suitable branch of a tree, with a cleft or small protruding branch of a size to take a human foot, about 18–20 inches from the base. 'Upon these, the person being mounted, with a foot on each cleft or projecting branch, and the top or small end of the stilt in each hand, they walked through the river at the fords. This they call stilting. There are still some who cross in this way but since the bridge was built, the practice has been generally laid aside.' This was written in the 1790s and although stilting may have been 'laid aside' in Dollar at that date[28] there are still old people in the Border valleys who remember stilting and there is certainly at least still one pair of stilts in existence in private hands in that area. Not only could people cross rivers themselves on stilts, they could carry children over too, always taking care to move slightly upstream, not the other way, and the delightful book, *Aunt Janet's Legacy*, by Janet Bathgate describes how a shepherd not only carried a child over the river, but did so with her bundle of clothes held between his teeth.[29] At some fords stilts could be hired for a penny or two and then left on the other side to be collected later; this happened just below the present chain bridge near Melrose, Roxburghshire. A conveniently situated branch of a tree by the side of a stream, from which a rope could be hung to swing oneself over the water, was a very good alternative to steps and stilts.

A sidelight on walking days is the 'Kelso Convoy'. Old Kelso people did not say goodbye to a guest on the doorstep but saw him all the way home, in return for which kindness the guest saw his host back home too. An 'Aberdeen Convoy' is said to have been taking a guest half way home, whereas a Scots one was merely seeing him 'over the doorstance'.[30]

13 Stepping stones across a river. What man could use, so could beasts.
Source: Scottish Ethnological Archive, Royal Museum of Scotland.

14 Crossing a ford on stilts. Drawing by Anne Carrick.

As horse transport developed, people walked less and less and Rev Thomas Rain of Hutton, Dumfries-shire, describing a century's changes in 1898, posed the question, 'Will human legs be as serviceable at the end of next century as they are at the end of this one?'[31] Foot travel was often arduous but it could have compensations, even when these were combined with bad conditions. In a description of the town of Helensburgh, the Old Luss Road was said to be very rough, with pools, boggy sections and stepping stones which provided such uncertain footing that young girls in their best bonnets and boots had to be helped and tended with dextrous care over them. 'There was, therefore, a fearful joy in the evening stroll which no smooth highway could ever impart . . . it was an encouragement to fond declarations . . . it was a highway to matrimony.'[32]

6 FERRIES

Before bridges were built, where there were neither stepping stones nor fords and where the river conditions made stilting impossible, the only way to cross water, short of swimming, was by ferry and so ferries became an integral part of land routes. Some were over rivers, some over arms of the sea and others on tidal waters which though fordable at low water needed a boat to cross at high tide. Records of early royal progresses often mention use of ferries, as do the accounts of other early travellers. A few of these ferries still exist, many are well remembered, others are still spoken of and some places retain the word 'ferry' in their names although the ferry itself has long since gone, while other ferries are implied in names like Boat of Garten on the River Spey and Coble of Dalreoch on the River Earn.[1] Church records are sometimes a clue to the site of a long-forgotten ferry, with baptismal rolls and delinquents' lists giving the names and locations of boatmen whose children or behaviour caused them to be named in these documents.

Ferries belonged to the landed proprietors on either side of the crossing or to Burgh Councils if they fell within a burgh and, in pre-Reformation days, sometimes to Church foundations. These various individuals or bodies let the right to operate the ferry to a ferryman who thus had a monopoly and a jealously guarded one at that, as James Hogg, the Ettrick Shepherd, found on one of his Highland tours in the early years of the nineteenth century. He tried to get a lift in a boat across Loch Carron and even offered three times the fare but the men in it refused to take him, saying that it would deprive the ferryman of his right.[2] Being a monopoly, abuses crept in. Some of them are obvious from various Acts of the Scottish Parliament passed between 1470 and 1490 which ordered that the rates on the Forth and Tay ferries should be no higher than allowed by statute and use and wont, and that people must not be kept waiting.[3] One Act decreed that any ferryman at the ferry of Port-on-Craig, Fife, who charged more than a penny for each man and horse would be fined 40s. Scots, payable to the king, James III (1460–88), and imprisoned at the king's will,[4] and in 1551 a further Act decreed that ferrymen who overcharged would lose both life and goods.[5]

The best known ferry in Scotland must surely be Queensferry, called after the pious Queen Margaret, wife of Malcolm III (1057–93), who arranged that the ferry should be free for those going on pilgrimage to St Andrews.[6] Because of its long history and importance, this ferry is well documented and some of the regulations for its running show the problems that affected would-be passengers. Until 1784 the ferrymen owned the boats but that year the owners of the ferry refused to renew their leases, bought up the boats and let them yearly by roup. The *Statistical Account for South Queensferry*, written shortly after this happened, said that it was a help but admitted that the landing places required improvement as it was 'painful to see the difficulties which passengers have, the dangers to which they are exposed as they have to scramble a considerable way among rocks and large stones made slippery by being covered with wet seaweed'.[7] At Tulliallan, Fife, things were as unpleasant and people often had to wade through mud for forty yards in the days before a pier was built.[8] The improvement made at Queensferry, and criticised at the time, meant that fifty or so years later, there were still 'inconvenient features' which included no suitable piers, no superintendents, boats kept only on the north side where the boatmen lived and the arrangements at such landings as there were, were so bad that crossings could only be made during $4\frac{1}{2}$ hours of each tide. Following an application to Parliament in 1809, trustees were appointed with the power to build landing places, to buy land for boatmen's houses and so on. As so often in Scotland, when any change was proposed, there was great opposition but improvements were made although it was 1820 or slightly later before things were put on a really good footing. (See Appendix.) Regulations made then required several boats to be kept on the south side and at least eight boatmen to live there too. Crew numbers for each type of boat were specified, although in stormy weather the superintendent was allowed to increase this number. Boatmen were forbidden to take any money over and above the official charges and all signals for boats had to be attended to punctually by having a lookout on duty night and day at the signal house on the north side.[9] At Queensferry the signal asking for a boat to come over to the south side was usually given by lighting a 'blaze';[10] elsewhere it might be by something like hauling a black board up against the wall of a white building and it was up to the ferryman to keep an eye open so long as visibility permitted the signal to be seen.

Although important ferries such as Queensferry were hedged about with regulations, those in outlying areas came under no such compulsion and thus it was that the minister for the Orkney parish of Stronsay and Eday said,

> The ferries in this district and throughout all Orkney, except on the post road from Caithness to Kirkwall, are not under proper regulations. There are no stated ferrymen, the freights are accordingly imposed at the pleasure of the boatmen who cross over with passengers, which renders the expense and trouble of travelling through these islands very great, and difficult to be ascertained.[11]

The habit of overcharging was only too frequent but a subtle way in which a ferryman could get a little extra was by asking for the price of a dram of whisky over and above the fare, even if the request was charmingly put. When Mrs Murray, who travelled in Scotland at the beginning of the nineteenth century, was crossing from the island of Kerrera to Mull the fare was 6s. 'and you may if you please add a shilling to the boatman to drink your health'.[12] James Hogg met with the same thing when the ferryman finally took him over Loch Carron on the trip already mentioned. Many ferry-houses sold whisky which must have often been badly needed by wet and chilled passengers; and some of them provided accommodation for travellers,[13] all of which added to the ferryman's income.

Initially ferries were served by rowing or sailing boats and a decree of the Scottish Parliament in 1639, referring to the Forth–Tay area, ordered good boats to be provided.[14] Under the 1669 Act for repairing Highways and Bridges, the one that introduced statute labour, those implementing it were also required to visit ferries 'and appoint fit and sufficient boats', but this was something more easily said than done. Ferries could be very dangerous and boats cost money but their importance to communities was such that even Kirk Sessions contributed to them, usually after some disaster had befallen an original boat. The Kirk Session of Fettercairn, Kincardine, for instance, gave £3 in 1730 towards replacing a boat on the Northwater and Coldingham Kirk Session, Berwickshire, contributed something towards the 'making of a new boat on the New Water' because the old one had been 'broken' the previous winter. Disasters or near-disasters could result from using unsafe boats and one can imagine the consternation in Dumbarton when the Provost and the minister nearly lost their lives because of this in 1634. The Burgh records describe the event quaintly but graphically: 'The ferriaris at the west braid ferrie of Clyd having ferryit wt ae unsufficient boit, and this day thairby put the provost and minister of this burgh in hazard of thair lyff, giff God had not brot them to schore, Cautioned and actit thaim nevir to repeat the lyk.'[15]

Even when there were good piers, nasty accidents could happen at ferries. At Queensferry it ultimately became the practice to drive coaches on to the piers to meet passengers off the boats but in 1838 the custom was stopped when a coach went over the edge and two women in it were drowned.[16] There were other problems also with ferries. Stormy conditions or a swollen river could easily cause a boat to be swamped or overturned and in addition several fatal accidents resulted from ferry boats being grossly overloaded. In 1809 the boat at Beauly, Inverness-shire, was crossing the river of that name with such an 'immense number' of people who had been to Communion on the other side, that it simply sank. Although the water was deep, it was fortunately not a very wide crossing and everyone got safely to land although many were hurt.[17] All was well in that case but there was dreadful loss of life when a ferry

15   Dornie Ferry, Loch Long. Source: Scottish Ethnological Archive, Royal Museum of Scotland.

boat sank about the mid 1700s on the occasion of a Selkirk fair,[18] and in 1809 there occurred the Meikle Ferry disaster on the crossing between Sutherland and Ross-shire. On an August day, some one hundred and twenty people boarded the boat to cross the Dornoch Firth to attend the market in Tain. This was far in excess of what the boat could safely carry and half way across it sank and ninety-nine were drowned. Many of them were fathers of families and because of the market a good number of them were carrying money to pay bills, or to buy raw materials such as leather for their work; some were tenants on the move who had converted stock into cash and were taking it to the bank in Tain; and some were described as 'recruiting parties with their all, except wives and children'. So not only were many families bereaved but the family savings went to the bottom of the firth too, a terrible thing to happen when there was no social security as a safety net.[19]

The fact that ferry boats carried travellers' horses and other animals too did nothing to promote safety. Anyone putting a recalcitrant horse into a horse-box may think it a difficult task, yet horses were frequently loaded on to small boats by means of boards used as gangways or 'bridges', as they were called. The Scottish Parliament in 1425 ordered that these 'bridges' should be provided at all ferries taking horses,[20] this decree being repeated in 1467, 1469

16   Dornie Ferry. Source: Scottish Ethnological Archive, Royal Museum of Scotland.

and 1474 for the boats on the Forth and Tay,[21] the crossings with which Parliament was always the most concerned. The need for these 'bridges' was described thus,

> It was often so dangerous to boat horses from a ragged craig [rough rock] that the Legislature in 1474 interposed their authority, ordering the ferriers to make briggs to their boats [a kind of timber platform to be laid from the most proper part of the craig to the gunwale of the boat] for shipping horses more safely and easily.[22]

Providing these bridges was again referred to officially in 1655 in Instructions given to Scottish Justices of the Peace[23] and even in the 1790s when piers had been built at many places, the bridges at Port-on-Craig, Fife, were still kept in case high winds or tides made it necessary to load horses from the rocks.[24] Sir William Brereton who visited Scotland in 1636 described a 10-ton ferry boat at Portpatrick as '. . . very dangerous for horses to go in and out; a horse may easily be lamed, spoiled, and thrust into the sea; and when any horses land here, they are thrown into the sea and swim out'.[25] Unfortunately horses often did not wait to be thrown into the water on the other side but jumped out of the boat en route and many accidents and drownings of both men and horses were the result. Horses, in fact, could cause accidents or save life. Where a ferry-boat capsised for any reason, a horse could swim ashore with someone clinging to it, whereas human beings in those days could hardly ever swim. However, a horse could only swim if it was allowed to and in an accident at the Kessock Ferry near Inverness, on a boisterous day in 1846, when a horse leapt from the boat when about half way across, taking with it the ferryman who had been sitting on the edge of the boat holding it by the head, both man and beast were drowned because its head was so firmly held down by a martingale that it could not swim and so could save neither itself nor him.[26]

Cobles and yawls could take a couple of horses at a time and a rowing boat might take four or five horses or ten cattle or twenty sheep. The Western Isles and part of the indented coastline of Argyllshire were served by ferries which by the end of the nineteenth century 'wafted over' nearly 2,000 cattle a year, as well as a considerable number of horses.[27] Drovers' beasts which moved in large numbers were made to swim through rivers, sometimes several in one day, and getting frightened and unwilling cattle to swim needed great skill and was a difficult and tiring business, always with the risk of them drowning or getting chilled if a cold night followed river crossings.[28] It was just as difficult for farmers taking beasts through a river to get to market, especially if they were unsold and had to be taken home and it is probable that many an animal was sold below its value rather than have to take it back again through the river. It was of tremendous help to have ferry boats on such routes even though loading and unloading was far from easy. When it came to taking vehicles on ferry boats, there was the sheer effort of lugging loaded carts or carriages on board, and unloading them on the other side, and then going back for the horses. Often there was fear when there was no danger and sometimes there was complete unawareness of risk when there was real peril.[29] Naturally, no one ever wanted to have to pay much for a crossing and in 1827 a complaint was made to the JPs of Stirlingshire that the rates for ferrying cattle by sailing boat over the Forth were so high that drovers avoided the ferry altogether. As a result, charges were fixed at 4d. for each animal up to six in number, reducing to 3d. each after that up to a score which cost 5s. In 1828 a steam boat was put on the river at this ferry, charging 6s. 8d. a score and, even at this higher rate, it was sufficiently popular with drovers for their beasts and ordinary passengers to have to take turn and turn about with the boat.[30]

As time went on, various clever forms of ferry boats were devised. In 1849 the *Inverness Courier* reported that the ferry over the River Ness had been 'rendered convenient by an ingenious contrivance. Large posts have been fixed on the bank on each side and landing quays constructed. From two of the posts a stout rope spans the river. A block travels across this rope and the boat is attached to it by a short line. The boat is thus held to the rope and the strength of the stream acting on the keel and the helm is sufficient to carry boat and passengers from the one side to the other in less than a minute'.[31] A variation of this was the type of chain boat provided about the 1830s over the River Clyde in the parish of Carnwath. This was a float which ran on a chain and was worked by machinery so easy to operate that a boy could do it. Moreover the charge was modest[32] and it could take two or three loaded carts. Another version of the chain boat was called a fly-bridge, described in the *New Statistical Accounts for Caputh* and for *Logierait*, both in Perthshire.[33] It consisted of a large platform, moveable on pivots, placed on two long narrow boats, parallel to each other but several feet apart. By a simple mechanism the boats were so angled that the action of the water propelled them to the other side and a chain stretched across the river and passing over a fly-wheel on the boat kept it on a straight course. To re-cross, the relative positions of boats and platform were easily altered and the crossing made in reverse. Such a boat could take four loaded carts without unyoking the horses. The introduction of steam brought steam boats like the one on the Forth in 1828, on to major ferries but their charges were generally considered high; in time, motor boats were started on many ferries and gave excellent service.

As with roads and bridges, ferries were an asset to landed estates and those who owned them did much to improve them through the years, increasing the value and rents of their properties as they did so. The chain boat at Carnwath was provided by the proprietors at a cost of £500 and was exceedingly useful as parts of the Clyde nearby were impassable at fords for nine months of the year.[34] John Erskine of Mar, writer of the *General View of the Agriculture of Clackmannanshire* in 1795 and advocate of improved methods of road

building, built piers at a ferry in the parish of Airth, Stirlingshire, to make it
'commodious for passengers and all kinds of carriages, with or without
horses, either at high or low water',[35] and very many others did the same sort
of thing and contributed greatly thereby to the needs of ordinary people who
had to travel.

For many years ferries did not operate on Sundays but gradually the
prohibition came to be only on ferries running during the time of public
worship and by the 1790s, 'modern times allowing a slacker rein',[36] many a
ferry was busier on Sundays than on any other day of the week, which is not
really surprising as it was the only non-working day for the bulk of the
population. On the subject of Sabbath observance in transport, though not
strictly applicable to ferries, the New Statistical Account for Falkirk,
Stirlingshire, said that because no vessels were allowed to pass through the
Forth–Clyde Canal on Sundays, the town of Grangemouth generally
contained a larger number of idle sailors that day than any other and it
suggested that there, as in other seaports, a part of the church should be
allocated to these men as a 'means of preserving them from spending the day
in idleness and drunkenness'.[37]

As harvest time came on each year, large numbers of Highland shearers –
harvest workers – moved south to cut the lowland grain crops. They must
have been quite a sight, described as 'bootless and bonnetless, the women
with their petticoats gathered up, their sickle on their arm and with a snow
white mob cap on their heads'. For these workers, there were greatly reduced
charges at all principal ferries, for instance 6d. as against the usual 9d. at
Dundee and at Queensferry 1d. instead of 6d.,[38] but these reductions may have
contributed to some pretty cavalier treatment for these people. During the
first fortnight of August 1824, well over 2,000 shearers from Mull, Skye and
elsewhere in the west, passed through the Crinan Canal in three steam boats,
one of which was allowed to become so over-crowded that a number of the
shearers were put off at Crinan and made to walk down the canal bank, a very
good 6 miles or more, to Lochgilphead.[39]

Well managed or not, with or without reduced fares, ferries could not be
avoided if one had to cross certain waters at certain points. It was only
something exceptional, like an Act of God, that altered this, for example the
intensely cold winter of 1813–14 when, in many parts of the country, the
rivers froze over making the ferries inoperable. In the town of Kirkcudbright,
people could walk and even ride over the frozen river[40] and on the opposite
side of the country and much further north, the Kyle of Sutherland
was frozen so hard that 'men, cattle and wagons might cross the arm of the sea
above the bridge and it was passable also below it as far as Creich'.[41]

Some crossings were particularly tricky and required boatmen who knew
them inside out. About the beginning of the nineteenth century an attempt
was made to replace the old boatmen of the ferry at Inverkeithing but it was

found that no one, unless brought up on that crossing, could manage it without danger and delay.[42] A similar intimate knowledge of the ways of the sea was shown by Geordie Gibson, the Cromarty–Nigg ferryman in the early years of this century, who sometimes drank too much but at his most inebriated would declare that he could safely make the trip because 'every wave in the ferry knows Geordie'.

The building of bridges for roads and railways did away with the need for many ferries, as did the introduction of steam ships on coastal routes. Short-haul steam ships were also of great value; when a sloop of 40 tons with a 'neat cabin' and a hold for animals and carriages was put on the Burghead–Golspie run across the Moray Firth, it took a mere 6–8 hours instead of the time needed to travel 100 miles overland, making use of the ferries of either Ardersier or Kessock and of Cromarty in what had been described earlier in 1813 as 'open, crazy, ill-rigged boats'.[43]

However, for many years ferries had an important role to play in conjunction with other forms of transport. A case in point is Meikle Ferry which links Ross-shire and Sutherland and which was the scene of the great disaster of 1809. In 1864 the railway had reached as far as the southern side of that ferry and there were good roads on the north side and the link between the two, avoiding a much longer land route via Bonar Bridge, was the ferry. The *Inverness Courier* in June that year carried an 'Important Notice to the Inhabitants of the Northern Counties and all Travellers', to the effect that the Inverness firm of Croall & Ellison had agreed to operate the Meikle ferry for a period of years and intended 'at the term of Whitsunday first to place a steamer of considerable size and power on the ferry'. It was to start at fixed hours and they felt confident that 'the passage will always be made with certainty, safety and comfort'. They went on to say that their 'coaches will run in connection with almost every train and the hours of crossing the Firth will be made to suit them as well as the requirements of travellers on foot'. (These coaches took passengers the short distance from railway to pier.) 'The rates will be regulated by a due regard for economy so as to establish the Meikle Ferry route between south and north as at once the cheapest, the most direct and the most pleasant that can be adopted by travellers, whether on business or pleasure'.[44] This ferry, which at the time tied in so well with the railway, has long since ceased to operate but at the time of writing it is being strongly promoted as the site for a road and rail bridge. Many other ferries have been bridged since the Second World War, not least of them Queensferry, but a few are still in use and industrial developments have brought at least one back into use, the Cromarty–Nigg ferry which was resuscitated in the 1970s after a gap of some fifteen years, to bring oil-rig workers from the Black Isle side of the Cromarty Firth over to Highland Fabricators' yard at Nigg.

Appendix

Regulations for Queensferry, c.1822

These included, 'Complaints against boatmen or those to do with the ferry ...
may be left ... in writing ... with Mr Mitchell at the Inn' or with a named
person in Dunfermline or a W.S. in Edinburgh, and the complainers would
have no need to appear further.[45] The average number of crossings per annum
at Queensferry c.1822:

40 hearses and mourning coaches.
145 coaches.
665 chaises.
16 curricles.
770 gigs.
1,530 carriage horses.
4,110 carts.
4,310 cart horses.
5,860 saddle horses and market horses.
31 mules and asses.
4,500 barrel bulk of goods and luggage.
16,000 black cattle.
30 calves and hogs.
23,300 sheep.
3,600 lambs.
2,340 dogs.
77,500 foot passengers.
3,500 Highland shearers.

Mails, guards, military baggage, carts and troops and Government stores all
had free passage.[46]

Charges at Queensferry, 1820[47]

	s.	d.
Coach, barouche, landau	7	6
Hearse, mourning coach	10	
4-wheeled chaise	6	6
Curricle	5	
2-wheeled chaise and taxed cart	3	6
Horses used in drawing any such carriage	1	
Wagons, carts etc. not over 10 cwt	2	
20 cwt	2	2
22 cwt	2	4
25 cwt	2	6

For every cwt more, not exceeding 30 cwt, 1d. for each.
For every cwt not exceeding 40 cwt, 2d.
   for each and for every cwt more, 1s. each

Horses used in drawing wagons and carts		8

	s.	d.
Saddle horse	1	
Mule or ass		6
Lowland ox, bull, cow or heifer		6
Highland ditto		5
Calf, sow, boar or hog		3
Sheep or goat		$1\frac{1}{2}$
Lamb or kid		1
Dog or puppy		1
Grain or merchandise per barrel-bulk		6
Passenger in pinnace or yawl		6
Ditto in large boat		3
Highland shearer		1
Hire of boat in daylight	2	6
Hire of boat in darkness	5	
Hire of large boat in daylight	5	
Hire of large boat in darkness	6	

Charges at Meikle Ferry, Ross-shire, 1919[48]

	s.	d.
Hearse with 2 horses and driver	15	
4-wheeled coach or chaise, 2 horses and driver	8	
Ditto, with 1 horse	5	
2-wheeled gig, 1 horse and driver	4	
Each additional horse	2	
2-wheeled loaded cart, not over 25 cwts, horse and driver	4	
Small country cart, 1 horse and driver	3	
Empty cart	2	6
Each additional horse	1	
Travelling caravan drawn by 1 horse	8	
Each additional horse	1	
Saddle or led horse	2	
Stallion	4	
Bull	3	
Ox, cow, heifer	1	
Calf, sow, boar, hog		6
Sheep, up to 12, 2d. each, each additional sheep 1d.		
Passenger with stock		9
Merchandise per barrel-bulk		$4\frac{1}{2}$
Barrel of herrings		6
Hogshead of wine, spirits, porter, ale	2	
Half ditto	1	3
1 anker ditto		9
Quarter of grain, up to 10 qrs, per qr		3
Each additional quarter		$1\frac{1}{2}$
Sack of meal or flour		3
Sack of potatoes		$1\frac{1}{2}$

	s.	d.
Bag of wool		3
Plough, pair of harrows		6
Iron and general goods not specified, per cwt		4$\frac{1}{2}$
Hire of boat by one passenger	1	
Ditto for 2 passengers, each		9
Ditto for 3 passengers, each		6
Ditto for 4 passengers, each		4$\frac{1}{2}$
each additional passenger		4$\frac{1}{2}$
Cycles		6

Exempted from above rates:
1. Passengers in charge of stock where the ferriage is 1s. or over.
2. Passengers' luggage not exceding 5 cubic feet.
3. Dogs used by servants in charge of livestock.

Ferry runs between 6.00a.m. and 10.00p.m. daily
In cases of emergency the ferryman will cross the ferry at all times, weather permitting.
When ferry is not normally open, the charge is 1$\frac{1}{2}$ times the said rates.

7 BRIDGES

Although a few *Statistical Accounts* and *New Statistical Accounts* liked to attribute certain bridges in their parishes to the Romans, the likelihood of this seems doubtful although bridges, like churches, tend to be built on previously used sites and it takes experienced eyes to detect the various stages of use and construction. There must certainly have been a few bridges built in connection with early routeways but, as they would have been made of timber, nothing of them has survived and for very many years the restraints caused by rivers were very great. 'One can get along a bad road more safely than over a swollen river,'[1] is a very true statement and lack of bridges produced 'serious and distressing effects, particularly in the case of the post, surgeons called to the sick, the minister and the people in getting to and from church, and in travelling about their affairs, marriages, christenings, burials, markets, to go to mills, smithies etc.'[2]

It seems slightly surprising to realise that good bridge-building preceded good road-building but this was because a bridge is a one-off construction, of use as it stands, whereas a road is of little use unless linked to others and constantly maintained. Early Scottish bridge-building owes much to the church, both pre- and post-Reformation. Bishops of the Roman Catholic Church were responsible for the erection of several important bridges at strategic points although most of them have not survived in their original form. One of these is the Brig o' Balgownie over the River Don in Aberdeen, said to have been built by Bishop Cheyne under the direction of King Robert Bruce. It partly fell in 1587[3] but was largely rebuilt and Sir William Brereton who saw it in 1636 described it as one of the fairest bridges in Scotland.[4] Glasgow Bridge, built in 1345 to replace an earlier wooden structure, is attributed to the efforts of the Bishops of the cathedral there[5] and it too Sir William Brereton found 'very fair'[6] but it fell in 1675 and again in 1761 and was finally demolished in 1856.[7] Another churchman, Bishop Wardlaw, was responsible for building the Gair or Guardbridge in the west of the parish of St Andrews on the road to Dundee in 1420[8] although the present structure is said to have been erected in the 1530s.[9] The Bishop appointed a family named Wan to be hereditary keeper of this bridge with a 'perpetual fee' of about 10

17   Brig o' Balgownie, Old Aberdeen. Photograph George Washington
      Wilson. Source: GWW Special Collections, University of Aberdeen.

acres of land adjoining it. When wheeled vehicles came into use, post chaises
were allowed to cross the bridge but presumably to save it from too much
wear and tear, carts were prevented from doing so by a chain stretched across
it and they had to use a tidal ford below which caused them a lot of delay, but
ultimately the chain was removed and carts allowed to cross it too.[10]
Dunblane Bridge, built in the early years of the fifteenth century, is also said
to have been the result of the efforts of the Bishops of the nearby cathedral[11]
but according to Dr Pococke, an Irish Bishop who visited Scotland in 1760,
it was demolished and rebuilt.[12] Bishop Elphinstone planned to build a bridge
over the River Dee in Aberdeenshire but died in 1514 without doing so.
However, he left a legacy for its construction and his successor, Gavin
Dunbar, added to the fund himself and had the bridge built in 1527.[13]

   Another early bridge was a three-arched one over the harbour at North
Leith, near the church, built originally by the Abbots of Holyroodhouse and
apparently rebuilt in 1602, only to be removed later to enlarge the harbour.[14]

In the parish of Cambuslang, Lanarkshire, an old bridge over the River Calder was known as the Prior Bridge, because it was built either at the expense of or for the convenience of the priory in Blantyre.[15] At Dunkeld, Perthshire, there was a plan in 1469 to throw a bridge, partly of wood and partly of stone, across the Tay but there is no evidence that this was done. The foundations of another bridge were laid in 1513 by Bishop Brown at a point close to his palace, and completed by Bishop Gavin Douglas. This bridge was later either washed away or demolished. The *Statistical Account for Dunkeld* said in the 1790s that a bridge at that spot would be particularly useful as the river had been known to rise by as much as 17 feet at the ferry, making it 'highly perilous' so that people who would have preferred to go to market in Dunkeld had to go further away to Perth instead.[16] Yet another bridge connected with the Roman Catholic Church crossed the Spey near to where the Burn of Mulben joins it. It was mainly made of timber and meant only for pedestrians and horses and was reputed to have been built on the site of a Roman bridge but whether this was so or not, it certainly existed in the thirteenth century[17] and connected with it, on the Boharm side of the river, was a religious establishment called the 'Hospital of St Nicholas at the Bridge of Spey'. It is thought that when the Reformation closed this Church foundation it deprived the bridge of its means of repair and so it decayed and was finally swept away in a flood. A ferry boat was put in its place and the crossing came to be known by the name of 'Boat of Bridge'.[18] About two hundred and fifty years later the ferry boat gave way to a suspension bridge erected by that noted builder of such bridges. Captain Brown RN.

A pre-Reformation bridge built in the parish of Hamilton, Lanarkshire, was traditionally attributed to yet another clergyman, although his reasons for constructing it were not the most worthy. A matter about which there was considerable dissension was to be decided at a meeting of churchmen in Hamilton on a certain day and a priest living south of the town had been particularly anxious that his view should prevail, to which end he had persuaded a large number of the brethren in his own neighbourhood to support him. But when the day came, the river was so swollen that they could not cross and his opponents won the day. He was so angry about this that he used some of his considerable wealth to build a bridge in order that such a thing might never happen again.[19]

The 1560s saw the Reformation and the end of the great Roman Catholic establishments with their rich clerics and from then on that church could do no more for bridge-building in Scotland although in time the reformed church, as will be seen, was to play an even more important part in this work, providing bridges not just at strategic places but where they were also of benefit to local communities. There was a reduction, but not a total halt, in the building of stone bridges between 1540 and 1570[20], presumably due to the run-up to the Reformation and its aftermath. Church lands fell into private

hands and many landowners prospered very much as a result and for some
years thereafter it appears that it could only have been them who built
important bridges which are known to have been erected. Had they been built
other than privately, it would be on record but as it is not, many early private
efforts are unknown. Fortunately there are at least some accounts or
traditions of what individuals achieved, sometimes in fact even before the
Reformation. One such was a bridge, the only one at the time in Hawick,
Roxburghshire, built over the River Slitrig in the reign of Alexander II
(1214–49) by a pious woman to give worshippers a safe crossing to the church
of St Mary. Stones for this bridge were brought by pack horse along an old
Roman road and it was so well built that it stood for six hundred years
although it needed repairs after floods in 1767. It was demolished in 1851 and
replaced by a wider bridge, suitable for carts.[21]

As with roads and ferry-boats, it made sense for landowners also to build

18   Stow bridge leading to the old church of St Mary of Wedale, not to the
newer church in the background.

bridges, big or small. It made their own lives easier and it gave their tenants access to markets and thereby increased the rents they would pay. Throughout the years up to the introduction of statute labour, landowners built bridges; and afterwards they were involved in road- and bridge-building as trustees, a situation which continued right through turnpike days until these matters fell to the local authorities in 1878. Sometimes landowners paid the whole cost of a bridge themselves, sometimes they organized subscriptions from neighbours, and under this heading one may perhaps include groups like the Corporation of Bakers of Dundee who built a bridge over the Dighty Water in the late eighteenth century.[22] In the parish of Duthil, Inverness-shire, all the bridges were originally built at the expense of the proprietor;[23] in the parish of Kilmacolm, Renfrewshire, at the end of the eighteenth century, all thirteen bridges there had been built and were maintained by 'the family of Porterfield';[24] and in the parish of Edinkillie, Morayshire, Miss Brodie of Lethen organized subscriptions from round about and some help from county funds too and had a most elegant 72 foot bridge thrown over the River Findhorn. Sadly, this splendid structure was badly designed and within a month of completion it gave way one night and fell into the river, which must have been most distressing to those who had had such high hopes for it.[25] Many other bridges were built by landowners, usually erected primarily to benefit an estate or a house but available to local people and of inestimable value to them. Even very small bridges could benefit communities enormously. An example of this was at Ormiston, East Lothian, where the Earl of Hopetoun organised a subscription, which he himself supplemented, to build three small bridges on the public road in the immediate vicinity of the village. One was over the little Puddle-burn where floods and melting ice could affect it badly; the other two were built only 20 yards apart immediately below the mill, and the road between them was raised to their level. Although these were only very minor improvements, they seemed major ones to the people living there as that small section of the road was constantly covered with water coming from the mill trough and in winter was barely passable even by horses and carriages. The word 'subscription' in connection with these bridges may not be strictly accurate because it implies voluntary giving when this, for some people, may have been compulsory, as happened in 1799 when tenants were charged between 1s. and 6s. according to rent for building Thurso Bridge — although nominally subscription, this was in fact assessment.[26]

Not all private bridge-building went smoothly. About 1727 the stone bridge over the Dullan Water in Banffshire was destroyed in a flood and it took until 1752 for the people to manage to collect sufficient money to replace it with a wooden one. This new bridge was swept away in 1768 and replaced with yet another wooden one which was also lost. Arguments then began about a new site and a Mr Macgregor declared that no bridge would be of real use until there was a road to it and as each landowner wanted the road to be on his land, there was great rivalry about this. While this was being discussed, a tree trunk was thrown over the river as a temporary measure. There must have been various machinations going on in the background all this time and one Sunday, as two people were negotiating the tree trunk, one of Mr Macgregor's workmen jerked it so that they both fell into the water. This did nothing to help matters and in the end those opposed to him managed to build the new bridge where they thought most suitable, even although it was thought necessary to arm some of the workmen with guns as well as tools.[27]

Some bridges were built as a consequence of personal grief and suffering. At Anstruther in Fife, the Cunzie burn was very dangerous in winter floods and one Sunday as Bailie John Loch was returning from church he heard a cry go up that a child had been drowned in the burn. It turned out to be his own beloved little girl. When his wife had recovered from her immediate sorrow, she persuaded him to do something practical to prevent such a tragedy recurring and the following entry appears in the Burgh records: '28 Oct. 1719. John Low represented that John Loch, merchant in this burgh, is content to lay out as much money of his own as will sufficiently pend the Cunzie Burn and make the same passable either by carts or wains, and that without taking any interest from the Town.' The result was a contract with a firm of Pittenweem masons to arch the burn and lay down a causeway 10 foot wide in the summer of 1721.[28] The *Book of the Chronicles of Keith* by J F S Gordon gives two traditions regarding the building of a bridge there, one being that it was erected by the parents of a boy who was drowned in the hope that such a thing would never happen again,[29] showing the same concern for others that Bailie and Mrs Loch had exhibited. A spirit not of grief but certainly of caring for others is described in the *Statistical Account for Kells, Kirkcudbright*: 'A bridge of two arches over the large burn of Paharrow is the private donation of one Quintin MacLurg, a tailor, who lived in the neighbourhood some sixty years ago. Being often in fear and danger of his life in passing and repassing this burn to serve his customers, he resolved that no one after him should be in such jeopardy again and erected this bridge out of the earnings of his trade, which was never more than 4d. per day. His name still remains engraven on a large stone on the top of the bridge.'[30] Another tailor, but one with a less kindly spirit, erected a bridge over the River Teith near Doune in Perthshire. Robert Spittel was tailor at the court of James V. Tradition says that about 1535 he wished to cross this river but found that he had left his money behind and so, naturally, the ferryman refused to take him over. Spittel was so enraged at this that he built a bridge in order to get his own back by ruining the boatman's business. In spite of this bridge's tradition of having been built out of vindictiveness, the *New Statistical Account* gives a quotation referring to it as a 'godly edifice which was a work of charity'. However, the people, always mistrustful of anything new, initially viewed it with suspicion and dislike.[31] It is tradition, yet again, which says that the North Water or Old Bridge in the parish of Logie and Pert, Angus, was built in the sixteenth century by John Erskine of Dun, Superintendent of Angus and the Mearns as a result of dreaming that unless he built a bridge at a place called Stormy Grain, of which he had not then heard, where three waters met, he would be miserable after death. Shortly after this, he was walking along the banks of the river when he met an old woman who happened to tell him that the spot was called Stormy Grain. Immediately he set about building a bridge but, even as the work was going on, it was swept away. When the same thing happened a second time he fell into a deep depression but fortunately, like King Robert Bruce, he was encouraged by seeing a spider repeatedly trying to spin its web and so he began again, this time with success.[32]

Some time after the Reformation, when the Protestant Church had found its feet, it became involved with water crossings but on a much wider scale than the Roman Catholic Church had done. For some reason, many parish churches are sited near rivers or sizeable streams and water being a great restraint, how to get people over it to attend worship became of great concern to the Church. Until the late eighteenth century, ferries did not normally operate on Sundays although, as has already been said, the church often gave financial assistance towards the repair or replacement of boats. One example of this was on the River Tyne in East Lothian where the ferry boat largely depended for its maintenance on the Kirk Session of Tyninghame before whom Magnus Clark, the ferryman, frequently appeared asking for help. But the Church disapproved of all inessential work on the Sabbath (although Tyninghame Kirk Session paid Magnus Clark £3 to ferry strangers and the poor over the river to church)[33] and it may have been an acceptance that they could not have it both ways — forbid Sunday ferries and still expect people to get to church from the other side of rivers — that caused the Church in Scotland to become involved in the seventeenth and eighteenth centuries with the provision of bridges. The Church of Scotland was a very strict disciplinarian of its people and many parishioners were required to appear before congregations to confess their sins, sometimes as often as twenty-six Sundays before absolution was granted. An entry in 1703 in the Kirk Session records of Hawick, Roxburghshire, tells how the elders excused the absence of a man and a woman 'because the water was not passable', and while this sort of excuse was genuine it must have been an added incentive to provide crossings so that no delinquents should have an opportunity to avoid church censure. Almost worse, of course, than no bridge was a dangerous one such as that at Ayton, Berwickshire, over the River Eye, where the parishioners were said to have risked their lives every Sunday until it solved the problem by falling of its own accord, fortunately without hurting anyone.[34]

At its simplest, a water crossing to church might be provision of stepping stones through a river. In 1704, the Kirk Session of Ashkirk, near Selkirk, considered 'that the want of a bridge over the water proved a great hindrance to frequenting the church' and instructed two of the elders 'to cause stones to be layed in the water and them that layed them to be payed out of the box', which came to 18s. Scots. Two years later, they paid 5s. Scots for 'stops' through the water, again to enable people to get to worship. The Kirk Session records of Greenlaw, Berwickshire, prior to 1766, have frequent entries 'for laying steps [through the River Blackadder] in front of the manse', thereby giving access to the church as well, and similar steps were laid elsewhere in the river too.[35]

Provision of bridges was a logical step for churches to take and explains why often a bridge is to be found near to an old parish church. What the Church provided by way of bridges to start with might be very basic but nevertheless practical. Kirk Session records in some cases show the purchase of tree trunks to be used as ad hoc bridges; those of Alyth, Perthshire, show that in 1641 43s. Scots was given 'for tua trees to big the brig of Eronanchie',[36] while in the parish of Edinkillie, Morayshire, a plank between two rocks 7 feet apart, over the River Findhorn, gave access to church to a considerable number of parishioners from the west side of the river.[37]

Be it stepping-stones, tree trunks, planks or more conventional bridges, the Church did its best to provide crossings of some sort and to see that they were maintained. Some examples from a Selkirkshire parish give a good idea of this work:

> 1697, 7th November, Report that bridges over the burns in the parish was decayed ... which was a great hindrance to people in repairing to the Kirk, and that it was the custom for the Session to uphold them, therefore appointed two ruling elders to agree with a workman for mending them.
>
> 1698, This day payed to Patrick Lockie, wright, for making a new bridge on Langhope burn with mending the blindhaugh brig (sic) and for repairing that on the other Headshawburn £6. 18s. Scots.
>
> 1701. Jan. Reported that the bridge over Headshaw Miln Burne was now quite useless, ordered arrangements for a workman to repair it again.
>
> 1704, Nov. Report that the bridge over Langhopeburn was greatly wasted and was a great hindrance to coming to church so ordered two elders to agree with a workman to by timber for repairing it, £7 16s. Scots.[38]

When it came to building bridges to give access to churches, a few parishes were lucky enough to have ministers able to provide them. Although clergymen are not nowadays regarded as being highly paid, they were people of reasonable substance in the eighteenth century. The fact that some manses have butlers' pantries[39] is a comment on the financial position of certain ministers and Rev David Hume, incumbent of Greenlaw, Berwickshire, from 1603 to 1637, was one of those able and prepared to dip into his own pocket which he showed when he built a wooden bridge over the Blackadder. Greenlaw seems to have been particularly fortunate in respect of bridge-builders as, although Mr Hume's bridge does not seem to have lasted very well, Thomas Broumfield, farmer at Greenlawdean, who died in 1667, left money not only for a church bell and for the relief of the schoolmaster, but also included the following in his will: 'I leave for the pritt building of ane stane bridge over the water of Blaccader above the Wester rawe at Grinlaw qr Mr David Hume, some tyme minister, built ane timber bridge, the sum of 4,000 merks.' This was £222. 4s. 6d. Scots and the bridge built with it served the community well although it is interesting that the Kirk Session was also laying stepping stones in the eighteenth century in much the same area of that river.[40] Another ministerial bridge-builder was Rev Dr George Morison of the parish of Banchory-Devenick, Kincardine, who erected a suspension foot-bridge in 1837 over the River Dee which cost £1,400 not including the price of the embankment on the south side to make an approach to the bridge. This gave access to church and school for seven hundred people on the Aberdeenshire side of the parish. He also left money for its maintenance[41] but he was not a man who concealed his charity and mentioned this good work when he wrote his parish's entry for the *New Statistical Account*.[42]

Kirk Sessions might find themselves involved in the care of a bridge even though it was not built by or for them. In 1732, James Black, a tenant farmer in the parish of Edzell, Angus, decided to build the Gannachie bridge over the North Esk on the west side of the parish of Fettercairn. He provided the materials, arranged with a mason to do the work for 300 merks and, being a very handy man, built the parapets himself. All this was a lot for someone in his circumstances to do but he also left 50 merks for its upkeep, this money to be managed by the Kirk Session.[43] Unless there were such benefactors, money for building and repairing bridges to churches came from kirk funds but these had many prior claims upon them, such as the primary one of paying the Session Clerk's and Kirk Officer's salaries and using what was over for caring for the poor, apart from what had to be spent on other expenses. And so it was that Kirk Sessions frequently resorted to holding special collections on Sundays for particular purposes, of which bridges were one. An example of this is reported from Howman, Roxburghshire: 'May 20, 1738. Considering the ruinous condition of the bridge above the kirk, which is now rendered very unfit for passengers, especially for such as attend the ordinances, therefore to remove the said Inconveniency the Session thinks it proper that people according to their severall Abilities may give in their collections against next Lord's Day which shall be gathered at the church doors for repairing the said bridge that those that attend the said ordinances may both come to and go from the same with all possible Conveniency.'[44] Money did not grow on trees and one feels that whatever was raised was made to do; at Fettercairn, Kincardine, a special collection for a bridge in 1722 raised £6 and £6 was the cost of the bridge.[45] Very often the cost of building a bridge could be beyond the resources of one Kirk Session on its own and it was necessary to apply to nearby parishes for assistance. About 1729 the minister of a neighbouring parish wrote to the minister of Fettercairn 'craveing some supply' towards the construction of a bridge, obviously one which gave access to the church. Fettercairn Kirk Session 'taking the same into consideration and understanding the necessity thereof, and that it was already built, and being so pious a work' decided to contribute £4 Scots to it. Where a bridge would be of general help to the public, even if not leading to a church, a Session might look on it with sympathy. In 1733 James Guthrie who lived in the parish of Fettercairn petitioned the Session for help in building a bridge 'anent the saw mill' and was given £1 Scots towards it because it was regarded as something necessary. Only two years later, in 1735, this same Kirk Session was asked by the minister of Strathcathro and by a man called John Preschok of the market ford for a contribution towards a wooden bridge at that ford because it was 'on the public road between Fettercairn and Brechin, very useful for such as travel on foot that way'. At the same time that this appeal came in, there was a petition for help for a family in desperate straits and the Session, finding both requests just and reasonable, resolved to support both of them so far as they could 'without wronging the ordinary poor of the parish'. The Session was already short of funds because of a very large number of poor on the roll at that time and because there was so much bad coin in their ordinary collections, a common occurrence with only about a third of it being good. The solution in this case was the usual one, a special collection on a Sunday for both causes. It was not uncommon for a joint appeal to be made in this way and this was an example of this being done. Over £12 was raised and the Kirk Session allocated about a fifth to the bridge and the rest to the needy family.

It was not just neighbouring parishes which sought financial help to build bridges to churches. Instructions often came from the General Assembly for special collections, frequently nationwide ones, to assist with this cause. One of these collections is referred to in the records of the parish of Auchterhouse, Angus, in 1723, when by Act of the General Assembly a collection was intimated for 'building a brig for making a convenient passage to and from the churches of Lethnot and Navar'.[46] There was great necessity for such bridges because people in their anxiety to attend church would cross rivers even when it was very dangerous to do so. The Scottish desire for education cannot be underestimated and for many people the only opportunity they had of receiving any instruction at all was at church because although parish schools developed in the seventeenth and early eighteenth centuries, they were not free and provided learning for only a very limited number of the population. Going to church had other attractions too: it was an opportunity to meet people, to exchange news and catch up on all the gossip, to hear any public announcements made there and, best of all, to see delinquents punished.

H R G Inglis, in an article in the *Proceedings of the Society of Antiquaries of*

Scotland, 1911–12, refers to the bridge-building period of 1600–80 as the 'collection bridge' period. Practically every bridge close to a church was built during those years.[47] These bridges were designed for people and horses, not vehicles, and were narrow and steep and seldom over 9 foot wide and any bridge fulfilling these conditions almost certainly dates from this period.[48] An outstanding example is at Stow, Midlothian, clearly visible from the A7 road, 6½ feet wide with one main arch and two lesser ones. It was built from collections made between 1654 and 1655 in order that parishioners on the west side of the Gala Water could attend church.[49] A lesser known but delightful bridge at Ancrum, Roxburghshire, which appears to have been widened now to 10 feet, with one arch, would appear to be of the same vintage.

Between the dates of 1600 and 1680, which Inglis gives for 'collection bridges', and even later, the Church was the only national organisation which could be used for fund raising and so found itself in the position of having to do this for the general interests of the country. Where bridges — or indeed other public works — were considered of more than local importance, churches were ordered by Parliament with the encouragement of the General Assembly, to arrange Sunday collections, usually on a national scale but occasionally confined to a specific area such as 'south of the Forth'.[50] Parishes were expected to comply even though the object of the collection had nothing to do with church life and the bridge or public work might be at a great distance from them and of no interest either. It was thus that a bridge was built at Inverness in the 1680s and one over the River Clyde at Lanark in the 1690s, 'so good a work and Christian a purpose', as it had been described earlier.[51] Many other bridges had the Church to thank for their funding, such as those of Linton and Leith (1668), Coldstream (1671), Dumbarton (1683), Bridge of Dye (1688) and the Teviot Bridge at Ancrum (1798). These were at least on the mainland but one wonders what parishes made of a General Assembly edict for a national collection for the Bridge of Strong in Shetland in 1715.[52] Parliament sometimes authorised private individuals to raise large-scale collections as in 1661 when William Baillie of Littlegill was empowered to have a voluntary contribution in the parishes south of the Forth in order to build two bridges in his part of the country.[53]

It was normal practice for Kirk Sessions when their funds were fairly healthy, as they could be if the number of the poor was not too high, to lend the poors' funds out at interest to individuals or to public bodies, and here also bridges might benefit — the trustees of Kelso Bridge were one of the organisations making use of such funds, when they borrowed from the Kirk Session of Bowden, Roxburghshire, in 1756, repayment to be made thirteen years later.[54] There was a further way in which the Church might contribute to bridge-building, but this was indirectly. When a church was vacant — without a minister — the stipend which was provided by the heritors was unused and it became quite common for the Scottish Parliament to order that this money or part of it should be applied for the building of bridges or highways nearby. In 1685 Parliament regulated the position by passing the Act concerning Vacant Stipend, ordering that this money should be used by the patron of any vacant church 'for pious uses and in building and repairing bridges, repairing churches and maintaining the poor', failing which these patrons would lose their right of presenting a minister to the parish. 'Pious uses' included training men for the ministry, helping ministers' widows and children, contributing to universities and so on.[55] There were many bridges built with vacant stipend such as the Old Bridge (Cuddy Bridge) at Innerleithen, Peebles-shire, built in 1695–7,[56] and, like the Bridge at Stow, Midlothian, only 6½ feet wide on the crown of the arch.

Because burghs almost always lie on or close to rivers, their Councils could not avoid being concerned with water crossings either, even if it was only in providing a ferry boat and letting it out to a ferryman as part of the burgh revenues.[57] They might even subsidise a ferryman as the Burgh of Lanark did in 1662 when they gave 10 merks to some boatmen to help them build a boat[58] and in 1671 when they gave £10 Scots to other boatmen to help to provide a new boat.[59] Obviously bridges came within their scope as well. After the Reformation, those bridges which had been built and maintained by Roman Catholic foundations frequently fell to the care of the relevant Burgh Council. The bridge at North Leith, the one originally built by the Abbots of Holyroodhouse, became the property of the Town Council as the result of an Act of Charles I[60] and although this was the general pattern, such acquisitions could be potentially expensive if large repairs were necessary and the bridge over the River Dee, planned by Bishop Elphinstone and finished by Bishop Dunbar, was only taken over by the Council of Aberdeen after lengthy negotiations and with great caution in spite of the fact that its position must have made it one they wished to control.[61] Similarly any important bridges which appear to have been built by private effort at strategic spots also appear to have been taken over by the appropriate burghs. While there is nothing to show who built the bridge over the Tweed at Peebles or when — although this is thought to have been in the fifteenth century — the Burgh Council of that town was certainly involved with its maintenance and was using compulsory labour on this bridge well before it was introduced for roads. In 1468 the Council decided that anyone failing to turn up for work on it, having been ordered to do so, would be fined 4d. forthwith 'and this not to be forgiven'.[62] Compulsory work or payment in lieu for this sort of thing was normal and was obviously unpopular so that in 1571 the Council had to threaten that anyone not paying for or carrying out their day's work on the bridge would have their goods poinded,[63] the same sort of thing that happened two hundred years later under statute labour regulations for roads. Another instance of maintenance of bridges by burghs appears in the records of Stirling where in the summer of 1699 the Treasurer was ordered to 'help' the bridge and to see that the 'fallen doune and louse stones' were built up again.[64] People seemed to enjoy throwing down bridge parapets, described in another area as 'a practice disgraceful though not peculiar to this parish'.[65] Lack of parapets was obviously dangerous and in 1711 when the Council of Stirling passed an Act for repairing a bridge it especially mentioned the necessity of 'ledges' — parapets — on the north side so 'that the damnage which ordinarilie has fallen out to goods passing that way in droves may be prevented in the future', an indication of the difficulties which the droving trade had in crossing bridges.[66] In the early eighteenth century in Dumfries-shire, cattle crossing the bridge over the Eden near Carlisle panicked when they met a coach approaching them on the bridge and in the ensuing melee the parapets broke and both cattle and men were thrown into the river beneath.[67]

Because stone bridges were expensive to build and required skilled masons, many burghs tried to make do where they could with lesser structures, and so it was that in 1628 the Burgh of Dumbarton was involved with providing some very basic 'bridges', (as Kirk Sessions found they had to do too). In April of that year, they laid some 'tries' — tree trunks — over Gruggie's Burn only to find that this was not satisfactory for in September they decided 'to caus mak a brig over Gruggie's Burn'. That year too they arranged to 'caus calsey and help to repair the tua staine brigs, and big and repaire the same'. The bridging of Gruggie's Burn must have been a constant source of trouble for the next thirty-five years as in 1663 the Burgh records have an entry which says, 'In respect of the manifold charges in upholding the timber briggs on Gruggie's Burn these past years, which might have by now built a stane brig, order a stane brig to be built; appointed the Master of Works and ... to be overseers, and for the better care of the work, a member of Council to go out each day that they shall be warned'.[68] They had realised that to be of real use bridges had to be of stone and many other burghs found this too, such as at Elgin where about 1630 the Magistrates built the first bridge over the River Lossie, the steeply arched Old Bow Brig, so steep in fact that it had to be lowered in 1789.[69] Any bridge with a high arch made it cruel work for a horse to drag a heavy load up the incline and over it; and where the roadway narrowed on the arch itself there was only room for one cart at a time and sometimes traffic in both directions was completely halted when two stubborn drivers, going in opposite directions, met on a bridge and a third person often had to be called in to sort things out, as the long-established rule of the road did not operate in such a case. This rule, which appears in the earliest volume of the Acts of the Scottish Parliament, said that on a bridge or other narrow way, when anyone alone or with a single beast met with a number, then the single one must turn back and let the number pass.[70] On market and fair days a narrow bridge could become densely packed with people crossing back and forth but to one man at least this was an advantage.

It is said that at the beginning of the nineteenth century a local exquisite in Hawick, Roxburghshire, liked to mount the parapet of the bridge on the excuse that he could find no other way through and strode back and forth on it to give everyone ample opportunity to admire his elegant form and fashionable dress, thus gratifying his own vanity while livening up the scene.[71]

It was mainly between 1680 and 1710 that Burgh Councils, JPs or Commissioners of Supply built what Inglis termed 'local bridges', raising money by public subscriptions and also by using what was called 'bridge money'. A Road Act of 1686 allowed the Commissioners of Supply to assess landowners at not more than 10s. Scots for every £100 of valued rent, as had been provided for in the 1669 Act, but what this could bring in was so little that it was in practice only for bridges, hence the name,[72] and because no road works of any consequence were going on then in any case.

A fault of public subscriptions (as opposed to those that were really assessments) and individual philanthropy was that money came from the well-to-do who always had vested interests and could more or less dictate which bridge was to be repaired or where one was to be built. Landowners could apply for bridge money to repair any bridge that suited them and these petitions were almost always granted, without any surveys being done to see where the first calls on bridge money should be. It was only when turnpike trusts began, with trustees and proper surveyors, that this problem was gradually overcome.[73]

Within Inglis's 'local bridge' period from 1680 to 1710 there was a partial halt to bridge building between 1688 and 1696 due, one assumes, to the Revolution of 1688/9 and the destitution of the Seven Years Famine of 1694–1701. It is a little surprising that this halt should have finished before the end of that famine. There was another break in bridge construction between 1706 and 1720, presumably due to difficulties with the Union of the Parliaments in 1707 and then the Jacobite rising of 1715.[74]

Burghs were among those who applied to the Privy Council for permission to launch national church door collections for building bridges and the Burgh of Dumbarton was one of those which did this in order to bridge the River Leven. They were granted permission in 1680 to have such a collection[75] and, as already said, the bridge was built in 1683, but good though congregations were about donating money, it did not come in overnight and raising sufficient for a decent stone bridge could take several years. This obviously happened in the case of this appeal by Dumbarton because it was not until October 1685 that Provost Smollett reported to the Council on 'his diligence concerning the bridge'. He had put great effort into the enterprise and had gone far afield to negotiate with Burgh Councils and parish ministers and had visited 'mony touns' including Dalkeith, Dunbar, Duns, Dumfries and others besides.[76] The *Statistical Account for Inverurie, Aberdeenshire*, noted the exertions some hundred years later of the Provost there who, along with the

Earl of Kintore, raised subscriptions of £2,000 for a bridge over the River Don.[77] Provost Smollett's need to negotiate with other Burgh Councils may well have been because all burghs kept a close eye on what they gave to others, to ensure that the money was used for the intended purpose and nothing else. Sometimes they also laid down certain conditions in return for their donation. Glasgow, for instance, supported all appeals within a 50-mile radius on condition that her citizens should be exempt from toll and, wisely, in view of the time that could elapse between a bridge being planned and its completion, handed over no money until the parapets were begun.[78]

One burgh with an unorthodox attitude to bridges was Annan, whose Provost in the earliest years of the eighteenth century was the Earl, later Marquis, of Annandale. Such a person in such a role was a continuation of the days when the Church depended very much on the burghs' prosperity and the Provost was often chosen, not from the citizens, but from noblemen or landed gentlemen so that they could use their power and influence should that be necessary.[79] The church in Annan had been vacant from 1700 to 1702 and the Earl allotted the stipend for those years for a bridge which was completed in 1705. That autumn the Burgh Council passed an Act of its own to fix bridge dues, something which should only have been done by an Act of Privy Council, and in addition they decided to levy 12s. from all heritors and wadsetters in the parish of Annan and 6s. per annum from all tenants for the benefit of the bridge as well as 12s. for each wedding or burial. This was obviously decided in the absence of the noble Provost as it was minuted that it would only apply if he approved. It was an extraordinary thing to fix these dues without proper authority and then to suggest rating the whole parish for maintenance of the bridge. The Marquis, as he was by 1707, looked after his own tenants, and consequently his own interests, by securing in that year exemption for them from *burgh* dues, not just bridge dues, something granted for the 'great and good services' done by him. Burgesses usually paid no dues in their own town and it appears that Annan must also have had negotiations about the bridge with the Burgh of Dumfries as its citizens were allowed special rates of pontage while its Magistrates and Council, along with their horses, were exempt altogether.[80]

Although tolls on roads were strongly opposed, tolls themselves were nothing new as they had been imposed on many bridges for very many years, although not on all — a bridge at Rutherglen, for instance, built in 1775 by subscription, with the Burgh contributing nearly £1,000, was free.[81] Pedestrians not carrying loads were usually free too. Just as Act after Act had to be passed to permit the making of more and more toll-charging turnpike roads, so Acts or warrants had previously been passed by the Privy Council permitting the levy of tolls on bridges. Without such an Act it was illegal to charge, as Annan had proposed to do, and illegal too to increase tolls without further permission. Although the Scottish Parliament did not become directly involved in the building of bridges, it did all it could to encourage others to do so by authorising Burgh Councils, parishioners or private individuals to levy tolls if they built them themselves. Instances from just one year, 1661, give an idea of these: a warrant was granted to the Magistrates of Wigtown to impose a toll for the support of a bridge; another to the Magistrates of Musselburgh to raise the toll on Magdalen bridge from 1d. Scots to 2d. Scots per horse load; one to the parishioners of Liberton to charge toll for eleven years for the repair of bridges in the parish and yet another to William Baillie of Littlegill, who has already been mentioned in connection with a voluntary collection in the parishes south of the Forth, to levy custom on the Clyde bridge for twenty-seven years to enable him to build another bridge over the Clyde at Ramwell Craig and one over the Dunedin. There were also warrants to Ferguson of Craig-darroch to exact toll for building a bridge over the Cairn at Minniehive and to Murray of Bruchton to charge a toll for building and maintaining a bridge at Gatehouse of Fleet.[82]

An idea of the levies charged on bridges is given in the Records of the Burgh of Lanark in 1705. After intimation by 'tuck and drumb' that the customs of the bridge were to be let for the following year, the following rates were fixed:

> Burgesses and inhabitants to be free.
> Horse and merchant's pack, 12d. Scots.
> Horse and man, 6d.
> Horse and load 6d., except for loads of peat and coal which were 4d.
> Each draught of timber 4d.
> Cow 6d. Horse 8d. Sheep 2d. Lamb 1d.
> Footman (not free on this particular bridge) 1d.[83]

The charges for the bridge at Annan included 6d. for each foot merchant's pack and 1s. 6d. for a merchant's pack.[84] Not unnaturally, people tried to avoid payment of these bridge dues by using fords which were free, but on occasion these were denied to them, even before the turnpike days when fords were closed by road trustees. An instance of this appeared in the records of the Burgh of Stirling in 1710 when the Treasurer was instructed to pay £6 Scots to a man as part of his charges in 'pursuing the drovers for passing with their droves at the foords of Forth and not at the Bridge of Stirling, in prejudice of him as tacksman'.[85] When the Scottish Parliament passed an Act in 1663 to impose dues on certain commodities at two bridges over the North Esk and the South Esk at Dalkeith to help to pay for repairs, the people simply used fords instead but, not to be defeated, a petition was lodged with Parliament in 1670 for power to collect customs at the fords too and this was granted. The petition referred to the customs levied at the two bridges and then went on: ' ... but divers persons to frustrat and prejudge your petitioners of the said small custom at the saids tuo bridges, passes at the foord of Elginoch upon the North Esk and at the foord on South Esk that

leads towards the west end of the toun of Dalkeith whereby the collection at
the saids tuo bridges is so inconsiderable that it does not pay . . .'[86] These
Dalkeith bridges were important ones which had previously been repaired
thanks to Parliament in 1594 when a tax of 40d. Scots on each millstone and
8d. on each cart load of wine or timber crossing them, was imposed for three
years for their repair.[87] Certain commodities seem to have been regarded as
fair game for taxing for bridge maintenance. In 1695 an imposition of one
merk per boll of malt ground at the town's mills was granted to the Burgh of
Irvine, Ayrshire, for ten years for repair of the bridge there[88] while in 1700
there was an Overture for a nationwide Act to exact from brewers 2d. Scots
per pint of ale for repairing bridges,[89] and of course the 1669 Act which
introduced statute labour for roads, also allowed for the imposition of
modest tolls at bridges, as well as ferries and calsays, should the stent not be
sufficient to keep them up.[90] The fact that toll was paid at a bridge did not,
however, necessarily mean an easy passage across and in Stirling in 1736 the
bridge was found to be so 'much damnified' by the crossing of carts with
heavy loads that the Council ordered all loads to be taken off carts and
manhandled across, failing which the tacksman of the bridge had to prevent
them going over.[91]

Just as there were sometimes difficulties between individuals about
bridge-building, so this could happen within burghs too. Hawick Burgh
Council, in Roxburghshire, decided in 1738 to put a bridge over the Teviot
only to find that there was hot dispute about which of two sites should be
chosen and, afraid that this might turn into open rebellion, finally left the
decision to the local landed gentry. While the building work was in progress,
the Council decreed that the common haugh and another green should be
available only for the horses and other beasts of burden belonging to
tradesmen working on the bridge and no one else's animals were allowed to
graze there while the work was in progress. This must have been a very real
hardship to the many townspeople who kept animals and relied on these
grazings and one cannot help wondering how legal such a ban was.[92] A
bridge-building problem that affected the contractors was not just grazing for
their animals but finding sufficient of them in the first place to carry stone and
lime in the required amounts.

One way and another, many local bridges were built prior to, but largely
during, the early years of the eighteenth century and there was always one
important feature during what would nowadays be called 'site visits', an
example of which appeared in the burgh records of Cullen, Banffshire: '1730,
for ale drunk by the Council when they inspected the bridge at the Townhead,
£1 Scots.'[93]

As wheeled traffic became more common in the eighteenth century, roads
which had till then been just for local use were required for a much wider
traffic and it was essential that they should be bridged wherever necessary and

not just at churches, burghs and points chosen by landowners. The development of roads went hand in hand with an increased demand for bridges, each encouraging the other.[94] The 1720s saw the start of modern bridge-building on the network of Government-financed military roads from Carlisle to Portpatrick and from Stirling to the Highlands, when bridges about 12 foot wide, which allowed for two-way traffic, were built on these routes.[95] Statute labour was used to build small local bridges and when this was commuted into money, this helped still more — in the first forty years of the nineteenth century, no fewer than sixteen bridges were built in the one parish of Alvah in Banffshire, for instance.[96] As the total cost of these sixteen bridges was only £730 they cannot have been large but to the ordinary people going about their daily life they were tremendously useful, in addition to opening up general communications, and of course there were no tolls on these little bridges. But even with all this progress, the picture was different in more isolated areas and the parish of Edinkillie, Morayshire, was one where even in the 1790s no aid had ever been given for a bridge over the River Findhorn even though the great post road between Inverness and Nairn crossed the river and the mail was often delayed for many hours when it was swollen.[97] The writer of the *Statistical Account for Castletown, Roxburghshire*, gave a diatribe on roads there saying that although they had been built in other parts of the country, yet in that parish 'not a yard of road was attempted till within these last few years' and continued, 'As we have hitherto had no roads, it is not to be expected that we should have had bridges. The rivers Liddel and Hermitage divide the parish for twenty-six miles but there never was a bridge over either of them'. However, at the time of writing, he was able to report that vacant stipend, along with the ordinary road fund, had paid for the building of a bridge over the Hermitage and another over the Liddel which, along with the part of the road already made, were proving of great benefit to the community and to the many travellers who were beginning to use that route from Carlisle to markets in the north and Berwickshire, it being shorter than going by Langholm and Mosspaul.[98] In Dalry, Kirkcudbright, in the eighteenth century there was still no bridge over the River Ken although it was often impassable with boats;[99] and the further north one went, the worse things got. At the same time, the parish of Dornoch, Sutherland, was 'destitute of bridges'[100] while Rogart, in the same county, had no bridges except some wooden ones for foot passengers and everything had to be carried on horseback as a result.[101] Even further north, in Shetland, roads and bridges were said to be non-existent.[102] What can have happened to the church collection in 1715 for the bridge of Strong?

Under the turnpike system, bridges on turnpike roads were attached to them and have been mentioned in an earlier chapter. Inglis divided the building of turnpike bridges into three groups: early ones from 1754 to 1770; the later period from 1770 to 1800; and the heavy or mail road period from

1800 onwards when bridges were designed to carry fast, heavy mail coaches and were very fine indeed.[103]

The laying of foundation stones of important bridges, or the first crossings of them, were made with great celebrations, although occasionally these events were more dramatic than was intended. In August 1871, a suspension bridge at the old boat ford in Langholm, Dumfries-shire, was opened to save weavers having to go a long way round to cross the river by another bridge. It was to be a great occasion and a photographer was waiting to record the proceedings for posterity but he had barely put his head under the cloth when the bridge gave way — there were those who had all along doubted the soundness of its design — and slowly collapsed into the river which fortunately was not in flood. An enormous number of people had assembled on it, all of whom ended up in the water and there were stories of mothers dashing into the river to pick up a child and on finding that it was not theirs, dropping it back in again. Even so, surprisingly, no one drowned.[104]

Swollen rivers have been mentioned several times and throughout the years damage to bridges by flooding was a serious problem. Sometimes the floods which did damage were not really true ones but merely the normal state of a river in winter, which had not been appreciated when the bridge was built in the summer months. When bridges were of timber, things were that much

19   Schooner beached below the Bonar Bridge, built by Telford. Source: Tain Museum, Ross-shire.

20   Beauly Bridge, Inverness-shire, damaged by flood 1892. Source: Scottish Ethnological Archive, Royal Museum of Scotland.

worse as they were all too easily swept away.[105] There were also some spectacular floods which did great damage and must have caused bridge-builders much heartache. There were the great floods of 1659 which did such damage to the bridges of Dalkeith and in 1755 the Berwickshire area suffered very much, with the parish of Bonkle and Preston losing all its bridges except the one at Preston.[106] A flood in 1782 carried off nearly half of the bridge at Nairn which had been built about 1631 or 1632. All that the Burgh Council did was a temporary repair with timber — 1782 was after all the time of the famine known as the Black Year — but this was still the position ten years later and it was considered 'surprising that more has not been done as everyone knows a bridge over the Nairn is much more necessary than over the Spey and Findhorn which both have passage boats'.[107] On 25 October 1797 there occurred the flood which caused the collapse of the bridge over the Tweed at Kelso. When it looked likely that this would happen, a large number of people, including followers of the Caledonian Hunt, gathered at the east end to see the excitement and it was difficult to get some people to leave the bridge in spite of the danger. Fortunately, there was no loss of life although some people were marooned on the far side when the expected finally happened.[108] There were general floods in 1763 and in 1799, and 1829 was the year of disastrous flooding in the North of Scotland, particularly in Morayshire, where an enormous amount of damage was done to roads and bridges. The magnificent bridge across the Spey at Fochabers and the bridge over the Findhorn at Forres, both on the great coast road, were destroyed. The five-arched bridge over the Dee at Ballater, the three-arched one at Corrybrough over the Findhorn, the bridge of Carr over the Dulnan, the bridges of Kirkton, Alford, Craggan and Dava as well as many smaller ones, were all swept away and the beautiful 150-foot iron span at Craigellachie was in considerable danger. Temporary repairs were made but putting the damage right properly occupied Joseph Mitchell, then Chief Inspector and Superintendent of Highland Roads and Bridges, for the next three or four years.[109] Perhaps the most tragic bridge disaster was the collapse of the railway bridge over the Tay one stormy December night in 1879. The middle section of the bridge was swept away taking with it a passenger train from Edinburgh. Seventy-three passengers and four railwaymen lost their lives. There were many other floods, but a more recent one was in August 1948 which did great damage not only to bridges but also to stock and crops, especially in the Borders. In October 1977 a more local flood swept away the Selkirk bridge and British weather being what it is, there must always be some risk of bridges being damaged by flood water and what it carries along with it.

The floating of timber down rivers, especially the Dee and the Spey, did not do bridges any good either. When this method of moving timber began, in the eighteenth century, it was controlled by a man sitting in a currach — a type of boat in the shape and about the size of a small brewing kettle, made of hide and so light that it could be carried on a man's back. In it the man sat on a cross-stick and with the aid of a paddle moved ahead of a small raft of logs to which the currach was attached by a rope. The rope had a running knot tied around the man's knee so that he could quickly loosen it if the raft was brought to a sudden stop for any reason, as otherwise the currach would sink. He was then able to paddle round and free the raft and continue as before. The York Building Company, who bought large woodlands in north-east Scotland in 1730, soon devised a larger raft guided by two men, one at each end, with a seat and an oar but even with this, the occupation of wood-floater needed great skill to keep the raft in mid-river and it was difficult and dangerous work.[110] About the mid 1780s one company usually sent down the Spey once a year what was called a 'loose float' of some 12,000 pieces of timber which could do great damage to bridges if it struck them. After the very severe

21 The Tay Bridge, Fife, built by Thomas Bouch and opened to passenger traffic in June 1878, prior to the collapse of the middle section in December 1879 taking with it a passenger train from Edinburgh. Source: GWW Special Collection, University of Aberdeen.

winter of 1813–14 which froze many waters including the upper part of the
Kyle of Sutherland, the thaw brought down not only great blocks of broken
ice but also, jammed among them, nearly four hundred logs from the River
Carron which fortunately did not break Bonar Bridge.[111] Less fortunate was
the bridge at Potarch near Kincardine O'Neil, being built at that time. Timber
being floated from further up the River Dee destroyed much of the bridge
work but the consequence was not all bad as the accident resulted in the
passing of an Act that year to regulate timber floating and confine it to the
spring and summer months only.[112] After railways were built, the floating of
wood gradually fell off and in the Deeside area anyway had ceased altogether
by about 1875.[113]

Many old bridges have been lost for one reason or another but there are still
a number to be seen, some readily visible as in Musselburgh, some alongside
stretches of new road and some well away from modern routes, such as the
Maiden Bridge at the golf course at Newbattle, near Dalkeith. A very
attractive one is the tiny bridge over a mill lade in Kirk Yetholm,
Roxburghshire, which was specifically built for pack-horses, allowing room
for only one animal at a time and with parapets low enough for the pack to
clear them.

In some places, a form of cable-car was used in lieu of a bridge – a box large
enough to carry one person, which moved along ropes above the water, and in
other parts of Scotland, especially Berwickshire, there are Irish bridges, a
cross between a bridge and a ford.

8 THE RESPONSIBILITIES OF THE BURGHS

Burghs were not only concerned with their own water crossings and bridges; they were involved with many other aspects of transport also. Burgh charters conferred on them the right to impose customs or duties on all goods brought into the burgh for sale and on any wheeled vehicles, booths or stands used in such sales. This meant yet another tax for those transporting merchandise into towns and yet another tacksman of customs to tangle with, and there were many vociferous arguments between them and those being made to pay up. The scale of these charges in the Burgh of Kilmaurs, Ayrshire, in 1848 included:

> Packman's stand, not more than 1 yd long, 2d.
> Ditto, 4 yds long and over, 1s.
> Common stand, with apples or fruit, 1d.
> Each peep show, 2d.
> Each caravan or large show, 6d.
> Each cart with fruit or vegetables, 2d.
> Each cart, with parcels, selling on the street, 3d.

This particular burgh still had these powers in 1912 although such customs were in general given up well before that, being abandoned at different times by different burghs.[1]

Insufficiently controlled horses posed a considerable safety problem in towns and this came within the jurisdiction of Burgh Councils. In 1751 the Council of Stirling ordered everyone taking horses through the streets to lead them by the head 'and not allow the horses to go with the cart to the danger of children and others'. Anyone disobeying this injunction was liable to a fine of £5 Scots and the people who collected dues at entries to the town were enjoined to inform those coming in with horses and carts about the rule.[2] A related problem appeared in Fraserburgh, Aberdeenshire, where in 1793 there were complaints from the public that those in charge of horses and carts left them unattended in the streets, to the great danger of children, while they disappeared into various houses, presumably in search of alcohol. This was forbidden, as was the practice of allowing horses to wander on their own along the streets grazing beside the houses[3] — even when there were so-called streets, many houses in small towns and villages stood on rough grassy patches and it is easy to understand how carters must have been only too ready to make use of grazing that was freely available. There are many records from burghs all round Scotland of the problem of unattended animals and sometimes carters were required to give a pledge of perhaps 5s. against repeating the offence, and sometimes these pledges were forfeited.[4] And that was not all. Another implication of the hazards of uncontrolled horses appeared in the records of Lanark in 1660 to do with their grazing on the burgh moor. It was decreed that year that the owners of horses feeding there must bring them in at night or else pay a penalty of 40s. Scots plus the cost of any damage they might have done.[5] That year, too, a particular horse sickness prevailed and the Council ordered a fine of £20 Scots to be imposed on anyone who did not immediately bury properly any horse that had died of it.[6]

When horses, along with men, were pressed for army service this sometimes posed problems which Burgh Councils were prepared to try to alleviate. In October 1752, Stirling Burgh Council,

> being sensible of the great trouble and hardship that lies upon the carters in and near this burgh by being pressed from time to time, with their horses and carts for transporting the baggage belonging to the different troops that pass and re-pass through the burgh, and that frequently in seed and harvest time, and that the Government allowance is not equal to the common hire, they agreed to lay out £3 stg among the carters, as they deserve.

Being in sterling, this was more money than it may seem and moreover this donation was only one of several given for the same cause.[7] The pressing of horses by the Government was a serious matter for country folk, not just for carters, something which Burgh Councils realised — an example of this was in Fraserburgh in 1645 when the Council recommended that anyone with a horse should help a neighbour whose horse had been compulsorily taken.[8]

While burghs encouraged the development of horse transport, they ensured a fair deal for the citizens by fixing hiring charges themselves. In 1633 Dumbarton Burgh Council passed an Act anent Stablers decreeing that all stablers and others in the burgh who hired out horses should be paid 1s. 6d. Scots for each mile going and returning, plus any charges for a horse and boy should they have to stay all night; and if they stayed away longer than six days on a return trip to Edinburgh, they were to pay 6s. 8d. Scots for each additional day.[9] Cart hire did not escape the eye of Burgh Councils either and charges for this were also fixed, an example being those of Cullen, Banffshire, in 1765:

> Horse and cart with turf or peat from Aultmore to Cullen, 4s. Scots.
> Ditto from Cullen Moss to Cullen, 2s. 6d.

Ditto from another moss to Cullen, 1s. 6d.
Ditto from the shore with coal, stone, wood etc. 1s.
One yoking of dung in creels, 3s.
One yoking of a plough with 4 horses, 14s.
Horse and cart with a load to and from Portsoy, 6s.
Ditto, with a load to and from Fochabers or Banff, 16s.

So that no carter might exploit the public by using smaller-than-normal carts, the Magistrates of Cullen also decreed that any such carts would be burnt publicly at the Cross.[10] This desire to protect the public interest also appeared in Kirkcaldy where in 1731 the Council ordered carters to reduce their charges for carrying coal because the coal heugh was so near the town 'and the way so good and easy'.[11] In 1655 the Council of Glasgow summoned the carters who served the area of the River Clyde to remonstrate about their exorbitant charges for carrying goods from the river to various parts of the town. They laid down a scale of charges and intimated by 'touk of drume' through the streets that anyone infringing the new rules would never be allowed to operate as a carter in Glasgow again.[12] In Edinburgh in 1673 a special committee had to be appointed to consider what to do, not only about coachmen's prices, but about the furious driving done by them and the carters through the streets.[13]

Construction of streets and their maintenance was a duty of Burgh Councils and because a calsayed (causewayed) street — one paved with round boulders — was a great improvement to any town, this was something they liked to have done if possible. The compulsory labour demanded for burgh bridges also applied to laying and maintaining of calsays and everyone in a burgh was required to help with this. Thus in 1656 the Council of Lanark ordered 'the whole inhabitants to go to the Heiton port next Saturday with mattocks, shuiles [shovels] and clates [scraping tools], for helping the calsay and redding the burn', under pain of a fine of 6s. Scots for anyone who did not turn up. As this work was to be done in January it can hardly have been an attractive prospect for the unfortunate inhabitants.[14] When the calsays had needed work done on them at the end of 1563 the Council 'statut and ordanit that all the unlawis of the toun be tan up to the bigin of the cassay for ane quarter of ane yeir, and the counsall to cheis ane persoun to take up the said unlawis',[15] in other words, that all fines for three months should go to the building of causeways and that the Council should appoint someone to collect these fines. Building and maintaining of calsays were found to need more than that, however, and it became common to lay an imposition as it was usually called, on them, which was in fact a toll. This was sometimes called the 'calsay penny' as in the phrase 'to exact fra ilk persone strainger the sum of four pennies money as ane calsay pennie'.[16] It seems fair enough that strangers should contribute to these extra-good streets but it was just one of the many impositions which fell on the traveller. As tolls on bridges and on roads required Parliamentary authority, so did impositions on calsays, an instance of this being in 1661 when Aberdeen Burgh Council was granted the right to take a small sum to maintain a long calsay they had made in Cowiemouth,[17] a right which was continued in 1669 by a further Act which fixed the following rates:

> 2d. Scots for every footman
> 8d. Scots for every horseman
> 8d. Scots for every load
> 10d. Scots for every 10 sheep
> 4d Scots for each ox or cow
> 2s. Scots for every cart, whatever it contained.

The 1669 Act for Repairing Highways and Bridges[18] allowed for moderate charges at calsays should the stent — assessment — not be enough to maintain them and a further Act of 1686 provided that dues collected at calsays should be employed for their repair,[19] thereby implying that some at least of it was being diverted to other uses.

As carts were improved and their wheels came to be shod with iron, they were found to be very 'prejudicial to the calsays and streets', and although it was usual to let the right to collect duties yearly, in 1671 the Council of Edinburgh had a bright idea and let the duties of shod carts and coaches for life to a father and son who were calsay layers, in return for which they were to lay or have laid all the calsays in and about the town at a rate of £4. 6s. 8d. for 'ilk rud' of new work, and to mend and maintain all calsays at their own proper charges[20], an arrangement designed to avoid the haphazard work of compulsory labour. In Leith it was found in 1674 that the duty of shod carts did not bring in a sixth of the cost of the damage they did and that year the Treasurer and Bailies called together the drivers of these carts 'to see what length they can bring them to engage in to help the said calsays . . .'[21] and in 1676 the Council decided to levy a charge on each cart equal to the damage it did to the streets.[22] In 1695 Edinburgh's levies on shod carts were fixed for November 1696 as follows:

> Ilk draught of pension weight (a large cask), 6d.
> Ilk quarter of ane hundred daills in one draught, 6d.
> Ilk half draught of iron, 1s.
> Ilk pack lint, 1s.
> Ilk ball of mader or but of prunes, 1s.
> Ilk draught of three barrel weight, 1s.
> Each hired coach to pay yearly, £12.
> Draught of ilk brewers' cart made use of within the city, 6d.
> Ilk country cart coming to the city with coals, 2s.
> Ilk workman's cart made use of within the city, to pay for two draughts 6d.
> Ilk cart draught of stones (except cassay stones or stones for the good town's work) 6d.

All carts coming in to the city with plenishing, provisions, ale and coal belonging to noblemen, Lords of Session, Members of the College of Justice and burgesses were declared free of these duties, provided they were for their use alone.[23]

Like tacksmen of dues on bridges, roads or anything else, those in burghs had no scruples about trying to increase their income by over-charging and an instance of this appeared in Edinburgh in 1678 when there was a complaint by the brewers that the tacksmen of the shod carts exacted 2s. from them for every load of coals brought in for brewing, whereas the correct charge was 6d. a load, as the Council agreed. They also found that 'the present tacksman trubles the owners of muck carts for payment of duty, which they were never in use to pay nor the former tacksman in use to ask for it, nor were they included in the table', and so they forbade not only over-charging for coal but any charges at all for muck carts.[24]

With the road-building of statute labour and turnpike days, various villages found that these new gravelled but uncausewayed roads replaced the calsays which they had previously had through their streets. The village of Aberdour, in Fife, found that it suffered, like many others,

by its causeway being changed into a common road. Such a road in a narrow village continues long moist and is hurtful to the health of the inhabitants. They suffer great inconveniences too in winter from the depth of the road and in summer from the dust. Neither does a common road last in a village, being exhausted by attempts which are made to keep it clean. A paved causeway endures and no inconvenience which the travellers can find from it can balance the daily inconveniences to which the residenters are subjected by the other.[25]

Although calsayed streets, where they existed, were good according to the standards of the time, the footpaths alongside them were often shamefully bad in wet weather[26] so it was little wonder that the 'croon o' the cause'ay' was the safest place to walk. But in many burghs, improvements came surprisingly quickly once road-making got under way: by the end of the eighteenth century the town of Coupar in Angus had not only paved streets but also street lamps,[27] and it was only one of many. (Even so, there were still many little villages, even into the early days of the twentieth century, where the streets, if they could be called that, were rough and pot-holed and, being unlighted too, were very dangerous in the dark or in wet weather.)[28] An idea of just how quickly a burgh could get things moving if it was considered that something was desirable occurred in Inverness. On 3 July 1844, the Burgh Council appointed a committee to investigate the possibility of running a horse omnibus from the town to Kessock Ferry at a charge of 3d. per person, by offering a premium of £5 to a contractor. Three weeks later, their deliberations resulted in £10 being given to assist this project and the omnibus service began on 27 August 1844 just eight weeks after it was first proposed.[29] Even nowadays that would be good going.

9 TRAVEL ON FOUR FEET

Before the days of proper road- and bridge-building, the use of pack horses was essential. They could carry loads of up to $2-2\frac{1}{4}$ cwts in panniers or packs on their backs[1] of all sorts of goods — wool, grain, peat, coal, lime, ironstone, salt, lead or anything else that needed to be moved, including smuggled goods taken by devious routes during the night to their destinations, and they needed nothing more than paths — the so-called pack roads — and fords to do so, although they might have to go far out of their way to find paths firm enough to give a good footing.[2] They usually travelled in strings of thirty to forty, sometimes even as many as one hundred and fifty,[3] moving in Indian file, tied halter to tail. The first animal was led and the rest pulled forward by the tail of the one in front until they got to their destination, when they were

22   String of pack-horses. Drawing by Anne Carrick.

unloaded and the halter of the leading horse tied to the tail of the rear one, so that they were tied in a circle and could not run off.[4] Pack horses were much used in the days when tenants were required to give feudal services to their landlords. These services involved carriage and arriage — arriage was labour on the proprietor's land and carriage was transport of his goods — and were a great burden on tenants. To give an idea of just what carriage could mean, the monks of Kelso Abbey required some at least of their tenants, in addition to paying rent and giving five days work a year, to provide transport of peat from a peat moss at Gordon to Kelso, some nine miles each way, quite apart from the journey to and from the tenant's home; and to provide a horse once a year to go to Berwick, 24 miles each way from Kelso; and they could even be ordered to go to and from Lesmahagow in Lanarkshire, some 70 miles from Kelso.[5] Into the 1790s, long after church foundations had ceased to hold land, services were still demanded of tenants in some areas. At Kinnettles in Angus, at that time, those owning a horse had to provide two horseback carriages to Dundee — 12 miles — every year or else go another comparable distance. Larger tenants had to bring an amount of coal to the proprietor's house, possibly involving two or three days' work, as well as bringing in his harvest.[6] In Keith, Banffshire, at the same date, farmers were required to carry the landlord's grain to whatever port it was to be shipped from[7] and in the north and west, in the eighteenth century, tenants were sometimes required to ferry their laird's beasts from island to island. In the early days, these carriages were 'very unlimited and tyranically exacted'[8] and they gave additional offence when the order to perform them was intimated by the proprietor's officials at church doors on Sundays; but they were gradually reduced and clearly defined and by the very end of the eighteenth century were being incorporated into the rent. A form of carriage that might fall on country people was that of transporting and guarding prisoners en route for trial, as in the case of twenty-two men who were summoned in 1745 to 'carry and convey' Jean Miln, a prisoner in the Tolbooth of Elgin, on part of her way to Inverness to be tried for child murder.[9] Carrying for others by the farming community was not always a burden however; it could be profitable too if there was a seaport nearby to provide all the transport work they could want, at a good price, whenever they could spare their own time and that of their horses.[10] In general, the use of pack horses for long haulage ceased about the 1790s[11] as road-making made conditions better for wheeled vehicles. The last carrier in Kilmarnock to use pack horses was John Stirling, who had few animals but made up for lack of numbers by their appearance — all of them were white and, though very small, full of go. The leader had a bell hung round its neck, useful in the mists often met with on Mearns Muir. This attractive string of animals always brought shouts of joy from the Kilmarnock children, both on arrival and departure.[12] However, for many years after that, commodities of all sorts for local use were still carried on the backs of

23   Returning from market, knitting while they walk along. Source: Scottish
       Ethnological Archive, Royal Museum of Scotland.

animals, especially in the Highlands and Islands. Dung was taken to the fields
in semi-circular baskets or creels, hung on each side of the horse from hooks
on the saddle, which was put on over a straw saddle-cloth big enough to cover
both the back and the sides of the horse. The bottom of the basket was hinged
so that the load could be easily dropped to the ground,[13] while peats and
sheaves of grain were carried on 'crubans', shaped wooden panniers on which
they could be propped. A garron load of peats, as sold in Wick, Caithness, in
the 1790s for a penny, only consisted of ten to twelve peats which shows how
laborious a method of conveyance this was.[14] In Highland districts, meal was
carried in creels called cassies, made of long straw woven with ropes of twisted
rushes,[15] but elsewhere it, and items such as lime, were simply carried in sacks
tied over the animal's back.

      Initially, all that was asked of horses and ponies was back-carriage and being
used for riding; on farms, they also pulled the harrows but it was oxen that
were used for ploughing. It was only when roads permitted the use of carts for
horses to pull, that they were also yoked in the plough.[16]

      The quality of horses varied considerably. Town stables had a certain
standard to maintain if they wished to succeed in the horse-hiring business,
and people of means could afford to buy and keep good beasts and many
horses were prized by their owners and loved by those who worked them, but
taken all in all, in earlier years the care of working horses and ponies was very
poor. In Orkney they were described as 'subject to many diseases through bad
management for they are often given bad provender, both in stable and field;
they often lack food in sufficient quantity and are exposed to heavy rains

when warm from work or riding; their houses are often dirty and their skins not cleaned'.[17] Nor was that a state of affairs confined to Orkney. In addition, their harnesses were ill-fitting so that their skin became galled and with all this they had to struggle to drag heavy vehicles over difficult roads, their poor bodies being whipped or jabbed with goads the while. Press reports tell of horses falling in the streets and passers-by having to restrain their drivers from thrashing and kicking them to get them to their feet. Riding horses were better cared for but could have problems too. A very casual attitude lies behind an advertisement in the *Kelso Mail* in 1803,[18] headed 'Horse Left', and going on to say, 'There was left, on St James's Fair day, at the Cross Keys Inn, Kelso, a horse which has never since been called for or owned. Any person to whom this horse belongs, may have him by giving in the marks and paying expenses to Mr Yule'.

Putting animals to work before they were old enough was another problem for them. In Orkney, young horses were bought from Caithness at one year old, began working at two years and, if they survived, were sold back to Caithness when they were about eight years of age, at double their original price, although by then they were often past their best. At eight a horse or pony should be in its prime, not going downhill, and the cause was obvious. It was well described by Rev John Brand, writing about the northern isles in 1701. These animals, he said, would be more vigorous and live to twenty-six or thirty years if not worked till they were four years old. Little wonder that he thought that they should be allowed to develop properly before starting their working lives when some were so small that 'an able man' could lift them up in his arms, and yet these little creatures were expected to carry not only a man, but his wife behind him, for miles.[19] At the end of the eighteenth century there were some 2,400 horses in North and South Uist and the *Statistical Accounts* refer to the hardships they suffered. For most of the year they fed on sandy areas so that they were under-nourished and that very soil needed more manure than better land and so these animals had to carry even more dung and seaware than would have been the case elsewhere. This was very heavy work in spring and summer and, in summer also, they had to carry kelp ware up from the shore to the drying grounds and from there to the kilns. Getting fuel often meant another long haul as it frequently lay at a distance and such heavy work on inadequate feeding 'soon rendered them useless'. This description of the 'great fatigue and toil they undergo' was written at a time when people were by no means over-concerned with animal welfare so it is all the more telling.[20]

The number of horses required to do all this work did not allow for the keeping of breeding mares so that large numbers of new stock had to be imported to the islands yearly at about £5 each.[21] (A working horse suitable for the mainland cost £15–£25 at that time.)[22] This was a great drain on these areas and in the Orkneys, in particular, many farmers found oxen cheaper to buy, as cheap to feed, less liable to disease and, when no longer fit for work they could recoup their initial cost as meat.[23] All that could be done with an old horse was to shoot it or hit it on the head with the back of an axe and then bury it — unless one simply drove the poor beast over a cliff in the manner ordered by the Magistrates of Cullen, Banffshire, in 1635 during an outbreak of scab, a horse disease: 'if found in fields they salbe takkin and cassie ower ane craig till they be dead.'[24] The generally callous attitude to old horses was clearly shown at Peebles during the nineteenth century when a local carrier was in the habit of leaving his worn out horses to die on the green where the schoolboys amused themselves by stoning them to death — and no one cared.[25]

Where soil was very poor and feeding therefore scarce, only very small horses or ponies could be kept and this had a knock-on effect as more of them were required to do the work that could have been done by fewer larger animals. Throughout Scotland, far more horses were kept than was really necessary just because they were needed for back carriage and that was in itself a most inefficient mode of transport.[26] The *Statistical Account for North Uist* said, and this was something that could apply to the whole kingdom: 'If any method could be found that would enable the people to lessen their number of horses, nothing could turn out more to their advantage; using carts in place of creels, would help much to bring this desirable end. If the proprietor could supply a quantity of seasoned wood and some cart wrights to the country, so as to have carts made, adapted to the small size of their horses, which might be sold at prime cost, a great reduction of the number of horses might be the consequence. In that case, some of the corn now used to feed the horses might be saved; some of the money sent out of the parish then might be other-wise employed, and the people enabled to keep a greater number of black cattle.'[27]

Although wheeled transport was used in mediaeval times by armies, the Church and for royal progresses, carts were not generally used by other people until improved conditions made them practical. The first develop-ment of draught transport in rural areas was the car, sledge, slide or travois, as it was called. By whichever of these names, it was simply two parallel poles — possibly young birch trees — the front part of which acted as shafts for a single beast, while the rear part, suitably shaped, slid on the ground behind.[28] On the rear part were two cross-bars, forming a frame within which creels were placed to hold whatever was to be carried. To start with, the horse's collar was made of a thick withe of strong straw or rushes, twisted hard together; two bent pieces of stick, fastened at the ends with a leather thong or birch twig, were the haimes; and a hair or rush rope formed the halter.[29] As draught became more common, tradesmen began to make harness and implements and, in the fullness of time, carts also. Dung was carried on these slide-cars in wide-mouthed conical creels called keallochs, keallachies or

24 Slide-car. Drawing by Anne Carrick.

kellocks, made of woven broom or juniper twigs or whatever material the locality could provide; and the making of them gave work for some of the poor.[30] These keallachs were placed on the cross-bars of the slide-cars. One report says that they were placed base upwards which sounds as if the dung would be well spread before it ever got to its destination, although obviously all was well;[31] other accounts make it plain that the keallachs were placed on their sides on the cross-bars.

A development of the slide-car was the placing of small wheels at the ends of the poles on the ground so that they ran, rather than slid. The whole thing was very simple and not expensive: the slider and wheels cost some 4s. and the creel 1s. sterling.[32] They could carry goods which could not be easily put on a horse's back[33] and these slide-cars, or ordinary flat sledges, were also used in towns, as a reference in 1667 to the 'sledders of Leith' shows.[34] Sledges, drawn by a horse in traces, were still being used into the 1930s for certain tricky work, such as carrying cut bracken from steep slopes to be put into the foundations of grain stacks at harvest time.

The next stage of draught development was wooden carts called tumbrils which had wheels or rollers about 3 foot in diameter, into which a large wooden axle was inserted, on which the shafts of the vehicle rested. The axle turned with the wheels and it is not surprising that as a long string of these approached, the head of each horse tied to the rear of the tumbril in front, the noise was 'a musical concert, resembling the braying of asses, the screeching of night owls and the squealing of swine'. So much was this the case, that if the axle was not carefully and repeatedly greased, the tumbril and its load often caught fire and burned out completely, but even so, these tumbrils were a great improvement on slide-cars and sledges.[35] Farm carts of a more modern style gradually developed and this progress is clearly shown in the *Statistical Account for Campsie, Stirlingshire*. In 1744 there were just a few carts there, only used to take out dung in spring after which, as their wheels were not shod with iron, they were taken down until the following spring. By 1759 there were more carts and they were much improved with iron-shoeing. (In some places wheels were just lightly shod to start with, before it became the practice to ring them completely with iron.)[36] By 1794 Campsie had nearly two hundred carts 'equipped for any draught',[37] and a horse could, without distress, pull about a ton on a level road and between 11 or 12 cwts on an indifferent one,[38] a far cry from the pack horse's load of some $2\frac{1}{4}$ cwts. This was in keeping with the burst of agricultural improvement which went along with road-making in the late eighteenth century. So important were carts in a rural economy, providing among other things better transport from lime kilns and coal pits, that their numbers were given in *Statistical Accounts* in detail, although it was always made clear that the physical characteristics of a district played a considerable part in the degree to which carts were or were not used. In towns carts were used earlier than in the countryside, for obvious reasons, and by 1676, Edinburgh, for one, had discovered the damage which iron-shod wheels could do, which has already been mentioned. Although *Statistical Accounts* charted and welcomed the increased use of carts, no improvement comes without some resistance: apparently farmers in Glenae had conducted the carrying trade until about 1745 by pack horse to the south from Galloway and, fearing for their livelihood, smashed and burnt the first cart that appeared in that area.[39]

Morayshire had a special kind of cart known as the Moray Coach or more colloquially as the 'Morra' cairt', which was particularly good for carrying peats. It was made of rungs with gaps between, their flat side to the axle and the round side above, with pins up the side. About 1820 a man named George Kennedy, who lived in Cullen, was never known to say 'Whoa' to his horse; he simply put his legs, already dangling down through the rungs, firmly on to the ground and the horse knew it had to stop.[40]

Many country districts had to start by importing carts from areas more advanced than they were — for instance, the first carts used in Caithness came from Morayshire, although they were not 'Morra' cairts', and to start with their wheels were not shod as had been the case further south. Later, enterprising merchants bought second-hand carriage wheels from Edinburgh or Glasgow and sold them for about 15s. to £2. 2s. per pair to small farmers who then bought some birch wood for axle and shafts, fir wood for a box, and

25   Horse-drawn cart for pulling timber. Source: Miss Cranston, Earlston.

the local cartwright put the whole thing together.[41] Iron axles were introduced, wheels came to be made locally and carts proved of enormous help in country life. This was obvious in many ways but one small instance of it was on market days. When horses were loaded with creels it was difficult to display wares but when carts were used, they could be backed in to the sidewalks, articles could be easily shown and people could see what was for sale and compare one lot with another. Carts with shafts for horses could easily be adapted for a pair of oxen by fitting them with a pole and a yoke; if they were being kept for farm labour anyway, it was logical to use them for draught work too. In some cases, horse and ox joined forces and pulled side by side or in tandem, and of course donkeys did their bit too.

There were many nostalgic memories of these days. People still speak of the lifts they got, sitting proudly up in front with the driver or else comfortably tucked in the body of the cart. They remember getting a 'hurl' in the carts at

Not only were wheeled vehicles drawn by animals, they could be used to carry them too. A photograph of carts, each holding one cattle beast, was taken in the eastern part of Ross-shire about 1904, and into the 1930s four-horse bogies might be seen carrying a number of beasts to market or to the railway station. These were probably special animals, such as bulls. Otherwise until motor floats were introduced at the very end of the 1920s and early 1930s, animals were driven rather than carried and sometimes made life hazardous in market towns by running amok, even into shops and houses, with the occasional added excitement of an animal, maddened by all the excitement, having to be destroyed.[42]

26   Cattle bogies, c.1904, East Ross-shire.

27   Horse-drawn cart. Source: Scottish Ethnological Archive, Royal Museum
of Scotland.

harvest time as they went back and forth between field and stackyard and they also think of school and church picnics when farmers made carts available for the day — the excitement as they were heaved in, to tumble into a bed of straw with all the other children, the cheers when a cart got to the top of a hill, the wild thrill of crossing a ford, the fun of the picnic and then the whole journey again in reverse.[43] There are accounts of families going to church by cart[44] and then there were the flittings of farm workers at the May and November terms. In many parts these took place on the 28th of these months precisely — unless they fell on a Sunday — although people in the Borders also speak of 'flitting Friday'. At that time, there would be carts on every country road, piled high with furniture and bedding, hens and house-plants, the dog and the cat, and the family seated if they were lucky on straw-filled sacks. There is a tragic story told of one flitting in the Borders when a mother died in childbirth on the day of the flitting but the family had to make way for the incoming household and one cart carried in its load to their new home, the coffined mother and child, to rest there briefly before being buried in the churchyard.[45] Farm carts were still being used into the 1940s and 1950s and large stones at the corners of farm buildings are a relic of these days, placed there to fend them off and save damage to walls. Things became easier for the animals pulling carts as rubber tyres were introduced, but now tractors and trailers have overtaken them, although it is not unusual to see a little trailer which is just a converted cart — and just occasionally, one may be lucky enough to see a horse and cart still being used.

Throughout all these years horses and donkeys were also used for riding. In country districts there used to be nothing fanciful about this. Initially, the ability to stay on and get the animal to go in the right direction was about as far as it went. Aeneas Sylvius, travelling in Scotland in the reign of James I (1506–37), said that all horses were managed without a bit.[46] As late as 1720 in parts of the south-west, there were still neither bridles nor saddles, just halters made of hair, and people rode to market on breechams and pillions on the horse.[47] By then, in better circles, proper equipment had been introduced and men rode on well-turned-out horses and women learnt to ride side-saddle, but this required them to have a groom or attendant on another horse. However, in the eighteenth century 'riding double' — riding pillion, in fact — was quite usual among the upper classes. Almost all ladies going out on horseback, whether to church, to pay visits or anything else, rode on pads behind one of their menfolk or a man-servant, thus needing no skill in horsemanship, using only one horse and still having a male escort. As roads improved and carriages became common, this practice descended in the social scale and in *The Cottagers of Glenburnie*, a novel set in Scotland in 1788, there is a description of a visitor arriving on a 'double horse'. 'Riding double,' exclaimed the daughter of the house, 'I thought she was a lady!'[48] The loupin'-on stanes, either convenient boulders or specially made with nice steps, still to be found at country churchyard gates and at one time seen at nearly every house, are a reminder of riding double, to enable ladies to mount and dismount and to get in to carts too, but many a man made use of them as well, especially the stiff and the portly. Stabling at churches, for the horses of the gentry, can still be seen here and there, as can hitching rings in old villages where mounts could be tied up while their masters did their business or slaked their thirst before riding home; and the stable was always the focal point of any farm, where the gossip was exchanged as harness was cleaned, the Hallowe'en pranks planned and April Fool tricks thought up, in fact a social centre now sadly lost.

10 COACHING DAYS

It was only as roads improved that the luxury of coaching could develop. Scotland lagged behind England, where coaches are said to have been introduced either by the Duke of Rutland[1] who is thought to have had one in 1555 or else by the Earl of Arundel a little later; but however that may be, it seems certain that a coach was imported from Holland for Queen Elizabeth in 1564[2] although it could be that they were used in southern Britain before that.[3] The first glass windows in coaches appeared in one built for the Infanta of Spain in 1631[4] but it was some time before this refinement filtered through to coaches in general and until it did, they had windows of oiled linen or leather, making them both dark and draughty. Even so, Queen Elizabeth's coach so impressed the nobility and gentry living close to London that they copied her lead to the extent that an Act was proposed to 'restrayne the immoderate use of coaches' partly because riding in such comfort was thought to make men effeminate.[5] A writer in Queen Elizabeth's time said, 'The world goes on wheels with many whose parents were glad to go on foot' and in 1605 Old Parr said, 'Coaches have increased with a mischief ... and now multiply more than ever'.[6] By 1607 they had become so common in and around London that traffic in the streets was often interrupted and in 1619 a tax of £40 was imposed on all those below a certain rank who kept a coach.[7]

One writer gave his opinion of public coaches thus in 1662:

> These coaches make gentlemen to come to London upon very small occasion which otherwise they would not do but upon urgent necessity, nay, the conveniency of the passage makes their wives often come up who, rather than make such long journeys on horseback, would stay at home. Here, when they come to town, they must go to the Mode, get fine clothes, go to places and treats, and by these means get such a habit of idleness and love of pleasure that they are uneasy ever after.[8]

Another writer denounced coaches as the greatest evil of recent years, 'mischievous to the public, prejudicial to trade and destructive to lands. Those who travel in these coaches contract an idle habit of body, become weary and listless when they have rode a few miles and are then unable to ride on horseback, to endure frost, snow or hail, or to lodge in the fields'.[9] This attitude is very reminiscent of Highland chieftains who complained that the building of bridges made their people unmanly and less able to wade through rivers. In 1673 a writer who had obviously come to the conclusion that coaching could not be stopped, suggested that it might at least be controlled and its resultant evils reduced if only one vehicle were to be allowed in each county town and that it should make only one double journey a week, of not more than 30 miles in summer and 25 in winter, using the same horses all the time.[10] The fact that this would not have been a paying proposition does not seem to have struck him. But progress could not be halted, as he had realised and, in 1691, a mere eighteen years later, an Englishman reported glowingly on coaches in which one could travel considerable distances at a good speed in summer without suffering violent motion and sheltered from the weather.[11]

As to Scotland, an English ambassador managed to travel north to this country by coach in 1598,[12] a remarkable achievement considering what 'roads' were like at that time. Lord Seatone is said to have obtained a coach from France in 1560[13] — if so, he was even more advanced than Queen Elizabeth in London — while the Earl of Morton, Regent from 1572 to 1578, rode one day in what was reckoned to be only the second private carriage in Scotland.[14] By 1702, Thomas Morer was able to say that great men often travelled with coach and six, but added that they had to do so with such caution 'that, besides other attendance, they have a lusty running footman on each side the coach to manage and keep it in rough places'. He pointed out that in fact the roads would hardly take these conveyances and that the gentry, both men and women, preferred to ride.[15] It is said to have taken until 1715 before a coach was seen in the north of Scotland, but a public coach service of a sort had begun in the south of the country by the mid seventeenth century. In 1652 the Countess of Crawford was able to travel in what was called a 'journey coach' to visit her husband who was in the Tower of London and in 1657 such coaches were advertised as going from the George Inn at Aldersgate in London to 'sundry parts of England thrice a week; to Leeds, Wakefield and Halifax once a week, charge 40s.; to Durham and Newcastle once a week, charge £2; and to Edinburgh once in three weeks, charge £4. 10s.; in all cases with good coaches and fresh horses on the roads'. For the following fifty years, these long-journey coaches only travelled during the summer months, the roads being totally impossible in winter which meant that there could have been no more than eight or nine journeys a year between London and Edinburgh, even if the arrangement was kept up which seems doubtful as an advertisement from the same source the following year made no mention of Edinburgh, nor of anywhere north of York.[16] This probably explains why Thomas Morer also said that there were no stage coaches in Scotland in 1702, apart from a few hackneys in Edinburgh which could be hired to go into the country 'upon urgent occasions'.[17] (The term 'hackney carriage' also applied to sedan chairs.)

In spite of the tribute paid to English coaching in 1691, for some time thereafter a journey of a few hundred miles, or even less, was no light undertaking, especially in Scotland, and was the cause of much discussion and comment. 'The merits or otherwise of rival conveyances had to be studied and the intending traveller had to adjust his earthly affairs before starting, besides making his will if he had not already done so. A painful leave-taking took place between him and his nearest and dearest, but in addition, neighbours and acquaintances had to be visited and not unfrequently public prayer was offered for his safe return.'[18] Not infrequently, also, passengers went on such a journey armed in case of trouble on the way.[19]

The adventures of Lord Lovat and his two daughters on a journey from Inverness to London in 1740 illustrate some of the difficulties of coach travel at that time. Before setting out, two or three days were spent repairing the carriage but even so a wheelwright accompanied it as far as Aviemore and there declared it to be safe to continue without him. This assurance was not good as the back axle broke after a further 8 miles and his lordship and his daughters had to ride to Ruthven, the girls on barebacked horses behind footmen, and the carriage was dragged there by man-power. Two days were spent mending it but 4 miles on, it broke again and they were in a miserable state by the time they got to Dalnakeardach (sic). Once again the coach was mended and they got to Castle Drummond where they were storm-stayed for some days. Then off they set again and after 3 miles the axle of the front wheels broke and they had to wait on a cold hillside on a wild day until help could be got. Repairs took 5 or 6 hours and their journey that day was no more than 8 miles. Things seem to have gone reasonably smoothly after that but, all in all, they did well to get to Edinburgh in eleven days.[20]

Quite apart from breakdowns of this sort, one only has to read press reports of coaching days to realise that traffic accidents are by no means something that came in with the motor car. Coaching had its fill of them — horses fell and horses bolted, often dragging a groom with them to his injury or death; shafts and traces broke, wheels came off or people went under them, coaches got stuck in the mud, over-turned or went over embankments; outside passengers were thrown off and, in addition, there was the risk of footpads and highwaymen. Snowstorms were another dreaded hazard: James McGeorge and John Goodfellow, guard and driver of a mail coach lost in a snow storm north of the Devil's Beeftub near Moffat, Dumfries-shire in 1831, are commemorated in Moffat graveyard, a reminder of others who died in this way.

As coach transport developed for long journeys, so it became desirable for short ones too and attempts, albeit abortive, were made surprisingly early to introduce short-distance public coaches in large towns. In 1610 King James VI and I gave a Royal Patent to Henry Anderson from Stralsund in Pomerania (a country now divided between Poland and East Germany) to bring to Scotland coaches, wagons, horses and the necessary men to handle them, in order to run a public service 'transporting the lieges' between Edinburgh and Leith. Anderson received an exclusive privilege to do this for fifteen years on condition that he charged no more than 2s. Scots between the two towns. But nothing came of this. Fifty years on, in 1660, a man named William Woodcock tried to set up a hackney coach service on the same route. The hire between Edinburgh and Leith for each person up to three was to be 1s. Scots, should there be more than that, then there would be an increased charge but it was stipulated that on a very steep section, passengers must get out and walk.[21] But this project came to nothing either. However, in 1702 — in time for Thomas Morer to notice them — Robert Miller was granted the right to run coaches between Edinburgh and Leith for nine years and this time everything worked out and the route stayed open.[22]

Meanwhile, attempts had been made to establish a rather longer route between Glasgow and Edinburgh. In 1678, William Hoome, an Edinburgh merchant, was granted a warrant to run a coach between these two towns for seven years, having obtained from the Privy Council an exclusive privilege to do so, with an assurance that his horses would not be pressed for any kind of Government service. He had to provide 'a sufficient strong coach' drawn by six horses and able to carry six people 'and that every passenger shall have liberty to take a block bag or portmanteau for carrying of their cloaks, linnings or sicklyke'. The coach was to travel once a week 'whether there be persons to the number foresaid or none at all to pass therein'. Burgh Councils were always mindful of their own interests and in Glasgow's Burgh records it was stated that should there be more prospective passengers than seats, then 'the burgesses of this burgh shall be preferred to all others'. As William Hoome received an advance of 400 merks from the Burgh of Glasgow for this enterprise, this was fair enough; but the advance was given on the understanding that a proportion would be refunded should the coach be discontinued within the seven year period.[23] Presumably some money was returned, although there is nothing to say so in the records because, as had happened with the first proposals for an Edinburgh–Leith run, there seem to have been no practical results and it appears that it was not till some seventy years later, about 1749, that a coach was put successfully on that route.[24]

It was in 1753[25] that a successful attempt was made to run stage-coaches — regular passenger-carrying coaches which changed horses at stages — between Scotland and London, earlier attempts having fizzled out and, although the journey took ten days in summer and twelve in winter, coach travel caught on in no uncertain way. A London–Carlisle–Glasgow service became daily in 1779[26] while in 1767 coaches had started to run twice a week between Edinburgh and Stirling and three times a week between Edinburgh and Perth.[27] By 1825 over fifty stage-coaches left Edinburgh every day[28] and all this was due to statute labour and turnpike roads which between them made road travel positively easy and so coaching flourished for the next sixty to seventy years. Indeed, the *Inverness Journal* in the summer of 1809 reported the 'remarkable celerity' with which someone could by then travel in the Highlands, instancing the case of a man who had left Edinburgh on the Inverness coach and got to his home in Sutherland, a 215-mile journey, in $47\frac{1}{2}$ hours, a little over 4 mph on average.[29]

Stage-coaches were owned and run by individuals or groups, between whom there was great rivalry which did much to keep up and improve the standard of coaches, hence an advertisement in the *Edinburgh Evening Courant* in 1754 that 'for the better accommodation of passengers' the recently started Edinburgh to London stage-coach had been altered to a 'new genteel two end glass machine, hung on steel springs, exeedingly light and easy' which would be operated 'if God permits, by your dutiful servant, Hosea Eastgate'.[30] Although stage-coaches ran on regular routes at stated times, they could also be hired privately. An advertisement in Edinburgh stated, 'Whoever wants the stage coach for London may enquire at Mr Clark, vintner, over against the Earl of Murray's lodgings in Canongate, Edinburgh, where they may be furnished with good coaches and horses (beside the stage coach) for £30, from Edinburgh to London, on seven days advertisement, by the said Mr Clark. Likewise at the Black Swan Inn, in Holborn, London, at the same price to Edinburgh'. The reference to coaches other than stage-coaches was because up to this time, it was not unusual for someone intending going on a long journey such as from Edinburgh to London, to advertise for other people to join in the hire of a private coach or post chaise. Such a case is implicit in the following notice asking for passengers for a return journey: '1728, 13th August, set out from London to Edinburgh upon the 5th instant, a handsome and convenient coach and six, containing nine passengers, and being expected in Edinburgh on the 18th, will set out for London the 21st or 22nd, enquire at John Somerville's, gunsmith, Canongate.' A contract for such a journey in 1725 ran thus: 'London May 15th. Received from Col W Grant and Patrick Duff Esq, sex guinies of earnest for a good close bodyed coach and sex horses to sett out for Edinburgh from London on Monday 17th May, to travel sex dayes to York, to rest there two dayes and travel two dayes and a half to Newcastle, and three or four dayes from that to Edinburgh as the roads will allow, and to make for the said coach thretty pounds sterlinge. The half to hand, and the other in Edinburgh, and the earnest to be forfeited if the gentlemen do not keep punctuality. Sgd. Thos. Green.'[31]

Coach horses were changed every 10 or 12 miles, occasionally at toll bars, but generally it was at inns that these changes took place and keen competition could result where there was more than one inn in a town or village. The town of Kinross in the county of that name, found itself in this position and on one occasion it is said that the ostlers from the Kirklands Hotel linked arms across the road to prevent coaches going on to the Green Hotel. Inns quickly developed and improved to serve both coaches and travellers. Although some changes of horses were completed very swiftly, often a little time was allowed between arrival and departure for passengers to stretch their legs and have something to eat and drink. It was this that caused the Golspie Hotel, Sutherland, to advertise in 1864 saying that two coaches, one a mail coach, waited at the hotel for 35 minutes, going and returning, twice a day, 'and a liberal supply of every refreshment necessary will be

28   Coaching scene — unloading at a post-house. Drawing by Anne Carrick.

supplied to passengers at a moderate price'. Intending travellers were also informed that 'the wines and malt liquors are of the very best and most select description' and that the hotel had lately been 'improved, painted, papered, handsomely furnished and lighted with gas'.[32] What more could a cold, or hot, and weary traveller ask for? Coach passengers were often able to break their journeys for a night's rest at an inn when they were going a long way — as the quoted advertisement said — and this too was something for which inns began to cater.

To accommodate the many horses that came and went, inn-keepers provided stable blocks. At Mosspaul, for instance, on the Hawick–Carlisle road, there was provision for forty-two horses;[33] at Mount Pleasant in Berwickshire there was stabling for sixty;[34] and at Carfrae Mill Inn, at the southern end of Soutra Hill, eighty horses often spent the night.[35] At Border inns like these and in large towns it was easy to obtain fresh horses along the way but where a road was isolated, changing them could be a real problem.

Coaching speeds were initially 5–8 mph, rising as roads improved to 10 mph and on certain stretches even 12 mph.[36] Stage-coaches carried ten, fourteen and even sixteen passengers on top, as well as luggage, in addition to inside passengers[37] so it is little wonder that horses were lathered and sweating by the time they had completed their stage and the sight of these animals bringing a coach rumbling in to an inn yard was a thrilling sight to the local people who always waited eagerly to see the excitement, to see the ostlers run out to deal with the horses and the landlord welcoming travellers, to see what passengers wore and who they were — and this was something that could be a real problem for anyone travelling on private business and not wanting their every move to be a matter for local speculation and conjecture, and sometimes such people found it necessary to join or leave the coach somewhere along the route. Another attraction for spectators when a coach came in, was that when there was any special news to tell, be it to do with war, politics or just racing results, there was always someone among the passengers or in the crowd who was ready to read aloud from a newspaper, and so the arrival of a coach could be as informative as it was exciting.[38] Sometimes half-a-dozen or so of the more exclusive citizens clubbed together to have a newspaper sent weekly by stage-coach. Each kept it for a day but at the first house, the Reader of the parish usually came to read aloud from it to selected guests.[39]

The departure of a coach was just as stimulating. The horses were restless, the passengers could be seen scrambling aboard with the women, it is said, kilting their gowns over their heads if it was wet to save their bonnets; the driver had a last drink and finally the coach rattled away over the cobbles and the excitement died down, only to begin all over again with the arrival of the next one.[40]

Having provided stabling for the horses of others, it made good sense for inn-keepers to go into the transport business themselves and to provide coaches, post chaises, gigs or whatever else might suit their customers. As a result of this they were often known as 'stablers'. They made every effort to increase this side of their trade and lost no opportunity to do so. When a bridge was built over the River Tweed at Kelso in or about 1755, a local inn-keeper soon saw that this opened up possibilities for him and the *Newcastle Journal* of 25th September to 5th October 1762 carried the following advertisement: 'This is to give notice that John Waldie of the Cross Keys Inn, in Kelso, has now procured 4-wheeled post chaises and as the road between Newcastle and Edinburgh by Kelso is now good and free of any interruption by reason of the bridge over the River Tweed at Kelso, all persons travelling that road will be supplied with good chaises, able horses

29   Coach and four, on gable wall of Boar's Head Hotel, Laurencekirk.

and careful drivers at ninepence per mile, and travellers otherwise properly
accommodated by their most obedient, humble servant, John Waldie.'[41] A
later landlord of the same inn advertised in 1803, begging leave to inform the
public that his coach, drawn by three horses, would leave the inn for
Edinburgh at 7.00 a.m., three days a week, arriving at the White Horse Inn,
Canongate, there at 4.00 p.m. The advertisement included the statement that
he had 'engaged a skilful driver of known steadiness and sobriety. The coach
was purchased for the purpose and is completely fitted up'. Tickets cost 10s.
6d. inside, 6s. outside and 3d. per mile for passengers joining along the way.[42]
Something that says much for the coaching standards of inn-keepers is the fact
that when the Duchess of Buccleuch and her daughters, with their suite,
arrived in February 1854 at Galashiels on the way to their house at Bowhill,
the local press reported ' . . . the arrangements for the conveyances were under
the management of Mr Elliot, Bridge Inn, Galashiels'.[43] Not every inn-keeper
had a knowledge of this business, however, and it was a wise one who did not
do what he could not, hence this advertisement in a Highland newspaper in
1864, referring to the Caledonian Hotel, Nairn: 'The posting department
connected with this hotel is to be let, the landlord being unacquainted with
that part of the business.[44]

The posting business, as it was called, had faults. Travelling by post chaise was smart but in establishments where horses were always available for hire, they were required to do far too much. Instead of having a rest at the end of a stage, as others would have, they might be called out so often that they were going between 30 and 50 miles a day and during times of local excitement such as elections or race meetings, even more was demanded of them.[45]

Although there had been a mail service of sorts in Scotland from the early seventeenth century,[46] the use of mail coaches only began in Scotland in 1786 on the Great North road from London to Edinburgh,[47] and it was only in 1798 that the Edinburgh to Aberdeen mail coach began to operate[48] and from then on the service widened. The primary purpose of these coaches was to carry the mails as speedily as possible throughout the kingdom, but they also carried passengers and the mail coach came to be regarded as the best, the most comfortable and, because each coach carried a guard who was armed, the safest way to travel. It was also faster because there were no delays at toll-bars. The guard blew his horn 250 yards before any toll-gate and woe betide a dilatory toll-keeper who did not get the gate open in time for the coach to go dashing straight through.[49] The story is told of one guard who fired his blunderbuss through a tollhouse window, in exasperation at the keeper's habit of locking the gate at night to prevent cadgers and others from passing without paying, and then going to sleep so soundly that the guard's

30   The Aberdeen to Inverness Mail Coach 'Defiance', resurrected for a gala occasion. Source: Aberdeen Art Gallery and Museums.

horn fell on totally deaf ears.[50] For the privilege of not having to stop at toll-bars a yearly payment was made to the road trustees, and this cost was extracted from letter writers as an extra $\frac{1}{2}d.$ on every letter carried on toll-roads. In spite of this payment, the mail coach's right to go straight through at toll-gates was resented by people in general. 'Some proprietors complain, and with much reason,' said one writer, 'that the mail coach does much more injury to the road than any other vehicle which travels and yet it is wholly exempt from toll. The exemption from toll of the mail coach gives it an advantage over post chaises, which do much less injury to the road and yet pay better than most vehicles.'[51]

Although coaches were common by the early nineteenth century, there was something special about the mail coach. People loved to see it flying by and to hear the horn which had to be blown not only at the approach to toll-gates but also at the entrance to any town or village. A guard with musical ability might even play a tune on it and it all added to the enjoyment. Those who had the leisure to go walking made a point of being in the right place at the right time to see the mail coach pass; and cottagers ran to their doors for a glimpse of it. It is said that one old woman who lived near Langholm, Dumfries-shire, would always exclaim, whenever the coach was carrying anything like its full number of passengers, 'Dear me, where's a' the folk gaun the day?'[52] Surprisingly, some mail coaches ran on Sundays without causing offence. The *New Statistical Account for the parish of Kinross*, in the county of Kinross, tells how one passed on Sundays between 2.00 and 3.00 a.m. and between 7.00 and 8.00 p.m. and caused little annoyance; it was only when a second one was added that it was viewed in a different light and the Presbytery of Dunfermline, in which the parish lies, as well as that of Edinburgh and others too, tried to have this Sabbath desecration stopped but without success. To begin with, the coach usually carried no passengers on Sundays but within a few months the public desire for travel was such that there was little, if any, difference in the number of people using it on Sunday to any other day.[53] The writer of this *Account* perhaps forgot that when people worked six days a week, to be able to travel on the seventh was a real benefit to them.

It says much for the skill of mail coach drivers that they could more or less keep to time on night runs, with all the hazards of a road in darkness, and certainly some mail coaches did come to grief. Drivers had to be very competent and they and the guards were looked up to as special people. The guard had great responsibilities and wore the royal uniform of red and gold with a tall hat. He was in charge of the mails and to keep them safe was armed with a blunderbuss — which he might fire to celebrate anything like a great victory — and two pistols. Just how these were to be used was set out in a long list of regulations, which certainly did not permit firing weapons through tollhouse windows. He had to see that the coach kept time and was required to ensure that everything along the road was done properly and that the horses and their harness were in good condition, for without that good time-keeping was impossible. For this reason, a guard was usually required to have worked in a coach-building shop for some time before taking up his appointment, so as to be able to do running repairs on the road. Rather surprisingly, he was also required to help with changing the horses. For all that his job was so important, a mail guard was not highly paid — 10s. 6d. a week when working and 12s. 6d. when off duty, a most unusual arrangement. In the early 1840s this rose to £70 per annum but thanks to what were called 'fees' from passengers — tips in fact — both he and the driver had a good income. Fees varied but for long journeys 2s. 6d. from inside passengers and 2s. from outside ones seems to have been normal, although sometimes half sovereigns or even whole ones were given. There could be a nice little income too from carrying special messages, sums of money, legal documents and other items of this nature.[54] A mail guard would do almost anything to get the mail through. In February 1838, on a day of snow and intense frost, the guard on the Aberdeen to Inverness run had to take to horseback at Huntly and, even though he had to be rescued from a snowdrift near Keith, he still pushed on and got to Inverness in the end, taking just over 30 hours for what was normally a 12-hour journey.[55] A few years earlier, at the height of the great cholera epidemic of 1832, another Highland guard showed exceptional devotion to duty. He was on the Tain to Inverness trip when, a few miles from Inverness, he felt the onset of cholera, but managed to keep his seat till the coach arrived at its destination, delivered the mail bags and then managed to stagger home where he died some 4 hours later.[56]

Comfortable, swift and safe as the mail coach normally was, it was also rather expensive for travellers and as there was no monopoly on its routes services were started in specific competition with the mail coach, which did not harm mail deliveries and did nothing but good to the ordinary passenger. In Hawick, Roxburghshire, for instance, in 1822 seven men including the Town Clerk, began by obtaining a gig for public use and the following year started a coach to compete with the mail, and this sort of thing was common.[57] Competition also helped where mail services were not all they might be. Although one thinks of a mail coach as having four horses, in some places they had only two and about 1812 a mail coach with just a pair ran between Aberdeen and Inverness. Between Elgin and Forres it was drawn by two rather ancient animals known as the 'deaf and blind' horses. It was only in 1819 when a four-horse coach was set up in competition that the proprietors of this mail coach — the term proprietors perhaps indicating that this was a contract vehicle — took fright and put four horses into it and both coach services were able to prosper.[58] There was also great rivalry among the various opposition coaches and this did good but it also led to much dangerous driving. On one occasion a passenger complained about the speed at which they were going, asking the driver whether he had any regard for life and limb.

The answer was brusque: 'What's your life and limbs to me? I'm behind time.'
Passengers sometimes left the coach rather than travel at terrifying speeds as
coaches raced each other[59] but it was this very competition which made the
years between 1830 and 1850 the heydey of the coaching years of 1780–1850.
The roads bustled with horse-drawn vehicles of every kind — the travelling
coaches of noblemen, the phaetons and barouches of the gentry, post chaises
and gigs, stage and mail coaches, as well as the less spectacular traffic of carters
and pedlars. Wherever it was practicable and profitable, horse-drawn
transport was to be found and by linking up with the developing canal and
steamer sailings, the range of people's travel was tremendously extended.

There were, of course, places on the west coast and in the islands where sea
travel was always more important than land travel; and even on the mainland
there were places where the new, improved public facilities were not
available. Yet in the prosperous county of East Lothian, while most of the
parishes had coaches and public transport galore, that of Garvald and Bara
had no public transport through the parish apart from a carrier once a week[60]
— if one goes there it is possible to see why this was so — and the parish of
Morham had no public conveyance whatsoever.[61] This was considered a great
hardship. How surprising therefore to read in the *New Statistical Account for
Dollar, Clackmannanshire*, that a stage-coach which had recently begun to run
between Perth and Glasgow had been given up for lack of support; it may be
of course that this service was in some way unsatisfactory.[62]

By the middle of the nineteenth century, coaching began to be overtaken by
railways. During the 1840s to 1860s railway-building went on apace in
southern Scotland and by the 1860s had reached the Highlands. The
opposition that railways initially aroused disappeared and competition from
them began just as coaching reached its zenith and its limit. Even the few
coaches which had reached 12 mph could only manage that speed with the
greatest difficulty and it meant galloping practically the whole way. Horses
could go no faster, and so stage-coaches and mail coaches were taken off roads
where there was a railway alternative. This meant that drivers and guards,
from being people of importance, became unemployed overnight and many
of them seem to have made no provision for something they really should
have foreseen. Some found jobs as railway porters or guards and some drove
horse-omnibuses from stations. Some of the more provident became
landlords of inns on the routes they had known, although those inns must
have been very badly hit by the withdrawal of coaching traffic. All in all, there
was a terrible loss of jobs in the stables of coaching inns and in all the back-up
services that coaching had required.[63]

Although the social consequences of the closure of a coaching route were
serious, certain coach services decided to go out not with a whimper but with
a bang. An example of this was shown by the owners of the Engineer, a coach
which ran between Hawick and Carlisle. This service ended on 30 June 1862

31   Coach Party on the Pass of Melfort, Argyll. Source: GWW Special Collection, University of Aberdeen.

as the following day was to see the opening of the railway along the whole of that route. For the final run all the horses, both at the start and at the stages, were bedecked with silver-mounted and beribboned harness. The owners occupied the coach themselves, accompanied by a few special friends, and also a Mr Fenwick and Mr Gowanlock. Mr Fenwick had been an owner of the coach when he was landlord of the Tower Hotel in Hawick, and Mr Gowanlock's father had been mine host of Mosspaul Inn in the days when it could stable forty-two horses. Two of the members of the 5th Roxburgh Volunteers Band accompanied the party, playing their cornets all along the way. The driver was William Crozier of the Tower Hotel, Hawick, who had been a coach driver for many years but had presumably seen the way the wind was blowing and found a new occupation in time. A large crowd gathered to see the coach leave Hawick for the last time; schoolboys were allowed out of class to see it pass and everyone cheered it on its way. At Langholm, another large crowd was waiting and there the coach run ended, with the coach party sitting down in the Crown Hotel to an excellent dinner 'which was greatly relished', after which they spent the night there and returned home by train next day. The coach itself was sent to the Cross Keys Hotel, Canonbie, to be cared for by the landlord, Mr Elder, another former driver who had gone over to inn-keeping.[64]

Although railways — the very earliest of which were horse-drawn goods trains — killed the coaching trade on main routes, they made travel accessible to ordinary people at a reasonable cost and created a demand for feeder services to railway stations. There was also a continuing need for transport through town streets and for trips to the countryside and until the internal combustion engine was introduced, these wants could only be supplied by horse-drawn transport: coaches, cabs, wagonettes, omnibuses and a whole variety of vehicles. To a considerable extent, the opening up of railways brought tourists and travellers to many parts and gave an impetus to coaching in areas where it had not previously been of major importance. Hence the improvements done at the Golspie Hotel in Sutherland in 1864. The *Inverness Courier* of 21 July 1864 carried an advertisement saying that Croall & Bryson, a coaching firm, had made arrangements for an additional coach between Tain and Wick, in connection with the train from the south; and the same issue carried an advertisement for a posting establishment at Beauly, Inverness-shire: 'The subscriber is now prepared to turn out horses and carriages not to be surpassed in the north, for hire. Job horses carefully selected always on hand and given out at moderate terms with new conveyances and steady drivers.' The advertisement ended with, 'P.S. In connection with the above, a first class hearse and mourning carriages will be kept at the establishment after Whitsunday next,' because it had become fashionable as well as convenient, if money permitted, to convey the dead to their final resting place in elegant hearses. It was so that they could double up as hearse horses that carriage horses supplied by hotels and inns were very often black. Horse-drawn cabs survived along with motor transport for a surprisingly long time — there were three regularly drawn up in Bridge Street, Inverness, into the 1930s.

During all this time, there was always the alternative of travelling by the carrier's cart which went between large towns and villages but it was slow and uncomfortable and therefore only used by the poor. Part of its cheapness was because there was no tax on passengers when the speed was less than 4 mph, which these vehicles certainly did not exceed. Well after long-distance carriers give up in the face of railway competition, local carriers still operated and the carrier's cart fulfilled a real need. Elsewhere this need was filled by horse omnibuses, or horse brakes, the latter being just a long cart with seats which acted as a kind of rural bus. In the early years of this century one of these served the fishwives of the Seaboard Villages of east Ross-shire by taking them and their loaded creels to the railway station to join the train at the start of their day's round. A smarter version of this type of brake was the 'Burnfoot Tub' which plied around Langholm, Dumfries-shire. It was a cart, with seating round all four sides, and an enormous umbrella in the middle to cover everyone and keep off rain and snow.[65] For some time after coaching declined, carriage driving in its various forms continued as a pastime and it is interesting that this has been revived and is once more becoming an acknowledged sport.

Having said all that, one is left wondering what sort of vehicle it was that was referred to in an advertisement in the *Aberdeen Journal* of 30 September 1794 which went thus: 'To the curious in machinery. To be seen at Joseph Clark's shop, at the back of Mr M'Kenzie's house, on the Quay, at Aberdeen, his Four-Wheeled carriage that goes without horses, and goes so easy that a boy of 14 can drive it. Admittance, gentlemen 1s. working people 6d.'[66]

Appendix

Scottish Notes and Queries, vol. VI, pp 38, 39, has an article on Royal Mail Coach Tickets, by 'C'. 'C' had a collection of these, usually printed on thin paper, with blanks to be filled up in writing at the time of issue to show destination etc. The size of two specimens is $3\frac{1}{2}'' \times 4\frac{1}{2}''$.

Inverness cab fares, 1896 (Guide to Inverness and the Highlands, 1896, Alexander Mackenzie):

By distance, one mile or under 1s.
Every additional mile 6d.

Return, half-fare additional.

By time, making calls, shopping etc, 2s. for the first hour, 6d. for every additional ¼ hour.

For an outing in the country, 3s. for the first hour, 2s. 6d. for each succeeding hour.

From midnight to 5.00 a.m., double fare.

From 5.00 a.m. to 8.00 a.m., fare and a half.

Individual coaches had names, as railway engines do; the most common were Telegraph, Wonder, Comet, Despatch, Express and Rocket. In Scotland, they were also often named after the nobility, i.e. Duke of Gordon, or after well-known people such as Robert Burns, Sir Walter Scott, Wellington, Blucher.

Until about 1950, there was in Berwickshire, a building with two 'clocks', the hands of which were moved manually to show the time of the next coach in each direction.[67]

11 THE AGE OF THE TRAIN

As the Industrial Revolution progressed, so coal was needed for manufacturing purposes and it was to carry it and certain other heavy goods that the first railway lines were opened. These were really wagonways, built of wood with the trucks drawn by horses and, to start with, they were only short-haul lines, usually just from pit to seaport. Inverkeithing in Fife had a 5-mile railway of this sort, and so did Alloa, Clackmannanshire, where a line was built in 1766. Locomotive engines were introduced about the 1820s but, surprisingly, the Edinburgh–Dalkeith railway was still horse-drawn in 1844 because the Act of Parliament establishing that particular line had not permitted the use of engines.[1] Large amounts of coal were soon required inland too. Increasing industrial production meant that the existing supplies of water power were no longer adequate, so coal was needed instead and needed in such amounts that it could not be carried on the roads, and neither could the new machinery needed for modernisation, and so a proper railway system was the answer. The Highland Society of Scotland was so aware of this need that in 1822 it offered a piece of plate worth 50 guineas for the best essay on 'the construction of railroads for the conveyance of ordinary commodities', the essay to be accompanied by models or drawings to support its statements.

At the outset there was considerable aversion to railways because they were totally different to anything that people had seen or thought of before. Railway engines were large, clumsy and dirty; to some people they could be frightening because who could be sure that they really would stay on the lines and not run amok; when steam escaped at pressure the noise terrified men and beasts; engines huffed, puffed, jolted and clanked and at the end of it all, they sometimes broke down and horses had to be relied upon after all.[2] Whatever their faults, however, railways were much cheaper than any other form of land carriage. Goods could be carried on them at a third of the cost of going by road[3] and following the opening of the Glasgow and Greenock railway, there was a 50 per cent reduction in the fares of steam boats on the River Clyde, a clear example of the effectiveness of competition.[4] The railway companies soon found passenger traffic an excellent additional source of revenue and to the passengers this was good news. The Edinburgh–Dalkeith railway, originally intended for goods like coal, farm produce and manure, began to take people too — eight trips daily between the two places — and soon passengers were the chief source of profit. This was a fairly general picture around the country — little wonder that the *New Statistical Account for Neilston, Renfrewshire*, said, 'If the present mania for railways goes on, we shall probably have one ... running through the whole parish'.[5]

Railway lines were built with surprising speed but not without a lot of social upheaval locally. There was a vast amount of laborious work to do, with no heavy machinery to speak of — blasting, making cuttings and tunnelling, most of which was done by men who all the while risked being struck by wagons, earth slips or roof falls. Enormous numbers of navvies — what would be called travelling men nowadays — came to wherever railway works were going on, many of them from Ireland, but many too from other parts of Britain. The impact of such an influx was described thus:

> The scenes of drunkenness, Sabbath profanation, and horrid blasphemy, with which an unsophisticated country population has been familiarised by a residence among them of the very worst description of English, Irish and Highlanders, to the amount of 1500–2000 employed on the railways for the last two years ... [produced] ... most blighting and pernicious effects ... which it is to be feared, in many cases, will never be fully eradicated.[6]

These men were housed in camps set up by the railway companies, sometimes in outlying areas but sometimes on the outskirts of towns and villages. In much of southern Scotland this work was done during the Hungry Forties when there was already a lot of crime and lawlessness and the presence of navvies in a district did nothing to improve the situation. When pay day came around — and the men were paid for several weeks at a time — there was heavy drinking, wild rioting and fighting, which spilled over into the local communities with injuries to both navvies and inhabitants.

In September 1847 there were particularly serious disturbances in Galashiels, Selkirkshire, and some surrounding villages, not because the men got their pay but because they didn't. Due to some misunderstanding between the contractor and the railway directors, five weeks' pay which the men expected was not given to them. For the following two days, Saturday and Sunday, they were peaceful but when they gathered at the 'stores' which were camp shops, asking for bread, they were refused credit by the store-keeper. His reluctance to risk not being paid is understandable but many of the men had had no food since the Saturday and immediately there was trouble. Influential townspeople hurried to the worst spots and urged everyone to keep calm while an urgent message was sent to the directors in Edinburgh. The men were paid that evening but once unrest starts it is not so easily curbed and a number of special constables were sworn in and that night, when police arrested a very disorderly navvy, they were attacked by his comrades and there was a great deal of agitation. Similar things happened at two other camps in the area and a party of dragoons had to be sent from Edinburgh to Lauder in case of more disturbances.[7] Time and again the local press reported trouble in towns due to navvies' drinking and its consequences. In 1847 St James's Fair in Kelso was said to have been the scene of the worst drunkenness and disorderly conduct for years, both on the fair day and for two or three days afterwards,[8] and in 1849 St Boswells Fair, some 10 miles from Kelso, and also in Roxburghshire, saw what came to be known as the Great Riot. It was at 9.00 p.m. that the riot started with the arrest of a navvy, whereat his mates decided to rescue him and dashed to the adjoining stalls which they demolished to provide themselves with some sort of weapons and three hundred of them rushed the police. In the melee a young shepherd was killed trying to save his father. It was a very violent episode leaving, in addition to the dead man, sixteen hurt — four of them dangerously, several 'severely hurt' and two 'slightly' — while everyone who had gone to help the police was 'more or less' hurt. The incident produced a tremendous excitement in the whole district. The Sheriff and Procurator Fiscal came next day and gave orders for one of the ring leaders to be arrested so long as this could be done without putting the police in danger. On their arrival at the navvies' camp, the police found that the man they sought was immediately surrounded by a hundred protective navvies and so they withdrew and he wasted no time in decamping. The police were powerless and thirty dragoons were called in to arrest another navvy.[9] This was done simply because his clothing was blood-stained and he was hanged for the murder of the shepherd although this later came to be regarded as a miscarriage of justice.[10]

Public feeling about all this was expressed in a letter to the Editor of the *Edinburgh Courant* a fortnight later: 'For some years past, we have been in the habit of hearing of severe conflicts in different parts of Scotland with navvies and police; men have been killed and valuable property destroyed; and the majesty of the law for the time set at open defiance and invariably the ring leaders escaping.' Much of this was due, said the writer, to the defenceless state of the police 'and not being properly armed as in England and Ireland, many of these lawless navvies being natives of the sister isle, are more accustomed to steel and therefore have no dread of the baton'. He suggested that the police should be equipped with cutlasses in these cases as had been used in a recent outbreak of violence at Monkwearmouth Collieries when the Newcastle police drew their weapons and that was the end of the trouble. The Editor of the *Kelso Mail* which had copied this letter, was not sure that cutlasses were the right arms but certainly agreed that the police needed to be suitably equipped.[11]

To be fair to navvies in general, they did not have an easy life. The conditions in which they lived were appalling, especially when they had their families with them. In 1847 there were press reports of the 'railway disease' — scurvy — among the men working on railways in the Borders, with such bad attacks that medical advice recommended that all cases should be sent to Edinburgh Infirmary.[12] A correspondent of a local paper that year described walking through an area of navvies' huts near Galashiels, and finding that the occupants 'presented a melancholy appearance, their wasted forms, wan cheeks, and the difficulty with which they crawled along the street, showed plainly the ravages that the disease is making amongst them ... their houses are miserable in the extreme, there being from a dozen upwards of men, women and children huddled together in dark and loathsome apartments, where the tainted atmosphere generates disease; such a state of things is of itself sufficient to bring fever amongst us'.[13] When cholera broke out in Scotland in 1849, although it did not originate with navvies, their living conditions were an ideal breeding ground for it and a number of Border churchyards, in the vicinity of railway lines, have open grassy spaces which are 'cholera ground' where cholera victims of that time, very largely navvies, were buried with nothing to mark their graves.

Navvies were a tough lot — they had to be, and they are reputed to have murdered a bullying foreman by burying him under a load of earth on one line[14] — yet when they were needed for a work of mercy they were ready to help. In a terrible storm in 1847 which hit the Dunbar–Berwick coast particularly badly, a ship was driven ashore. Life-saving equipment was sent out from Dunbar and among those involved in the rescue of twelve men out of a crew of sixteen, were a number of navvies working on a nearby stretch of railway line.[15]

Railways came to be so useful that where more were to be built, with a possible choice of route, there was extraordinary competition among companies as to who should operate them and which line they should take. This happened in the case of the Hawick–Carlisle line, well described in *Waverley Route Reflections* by Bill Peacock. Naturally enough those on the Liddesdale route were wildly thrilled when it was the one chosen and when the news reached Newcastleton, Dr Murray, a native of the village and enthusiastic supporter of the poposed line, had his gig yoked and with flags flying from it, carried the news right to the head of Liddel Water.[16] One cannot help wondering whether some sort of inter-company rivalry lay behind a press report in 1847. Jenny Lind, the singer, was expected to perform in Edinburgh but her appearance had to be cancelled because, as one newspaper said, 'she caught a cold on the North British Railway'.[17]

People in those days were always ready for a celebration and railway construction gave them many opportunities to indulge in this kind of thing. Cutting the first sod for a line was one excuse for a special occasion. When this was done for the first railway in the north in September 1854, there was a holiday in the town of Inverness and the procession through the streets was 'one of the most brilliant ever seen on this side of the Grampians'. It was led by eight large navvies 'of Herculean proportions' clad in moleskins — a more practical garb than the 'spotless white' worn by railway stokers for the opening of the Inverness–Nairn line in 1855[18] — which were adorned with the conventional pearl buttons and each carrying over his shoulder a new shovel. Then came four pipers, three halberdiers, the Town Council, the Masons and the trades. Lady Seafield performed the ceremony by slipping a silver spade under a turf already cut and tossing it into a mahogany wheel barrow which the Chief of the Clan Macpherson, pretending to be a navvy, wheeled away 'amid the loud and long applause of the people'.[19] In Berwickshire, Lady Hume Campbell of Marchmont, wife of the chairman of a railway committee, cut the first sod for a line in 1862. The inevitable procession took place, in which the fairly recently formed Volunteer Company took a main part, firing a feu-de-joie from two cannons 'to add by their discharge to the expression of joy which noise is supposed to convey'. On these occasions, the dignitaries loved any opportunity to eat and drink and after the ceremony, luncheon was provided for them in the County Hall, Duns. There was a long list of toasts, 'almost everyone who had a remote connection with the county being toasted' and so not surprisingly the press report included the statement that proceedings lasted for several hours.[20] The opening of new lines or of extensions to existing ones provided further excuses for jollification. In 1849 the line connecting Duns to the main trunk of the North British Railway was opened — not the same line as the one just mentioned — amidst great celebrations. All the shops in the town shut at 1.30 p.m. and at 2.00 p.m. proceedings began with the start of the first train, with twenty carriages, filled with passengers admitted free by special ticket. At the station there were arches of flowers and evergreens over the line; a flag topped the hut which served as a station house; and there was constant music with the Duns Brass Band 'never ceasing the while'. As the train made its special half-hour trip, to be followed by two more train loads of special passengers, crowds of people, dressed in their best, waited to wave and cheer it on its way, and there was the usual dinner in the Town Hall about 4.00 p.m. for about one hundred and thirty people.[21] When a railway line was extended to the town of Fraserburgh, Aberdeenshire, in 1865, the town was en fete, with people from miles around coming to see the excitement, although many of them stood well back in case the train got up to high jinks. Everyone of any importance in the area was present, along with the chairman and directors of the company, and there was the almost obligatory procession through the town followed by dinner for two hundred. Two days later, a Monday, there was a public holiday so that people could take advantage of special cheap fares that day to Aberdeen. Everyone who could go did, but not everyone realised that it was easier to board a train at a station like Fraserburgh than at one like Aberdeen and many

of them caught the wrong train in the evening and widened their experience
of travel more than they had intended.[22]

It is nice to know that lesser mortals associated with the railways also on
occasion wined and dined. When Graham & Sandison, the contractors on
part of the North British Railway, had nearly completed their work, they held
a special sale of sixty horses which were no longer needed. The animals sold
quickly, following which their sellers entertained a large party to dinner. At
the New Year in 1854 the superintendent of the locomotive department on
part of the North British line entertained the foremen on a considerable part
of it to a 'sumptuous entertainment'. There were toasts to the chairman of the
company, the directors, the secretary and the managers, as well as success to
the railways, and more besides, 'all drunk with the greatest enthusiasm and
the evening spent in the happiest possible manner'.[23] In 1863 when Ridley &
Robinson, contractors, had completed their section of line near Newcastleton, Roxburghshire, so well and pleasantly had they done their work that
the two principals were given a dinner at the Commercial Inn there by a party
of local friends.[24]

Much of the early passenger traffic on the railway was for leisure,
particularly after the opening of branch lines, and weekends saw many a
family party setting off by rail for picnics and outings which, although only a
few miles distant, had previously been beyond their reach. The introduction
of the Mackintosh coat for rail travel in the first half of the nineteenth century
was a considerable benefit and contributed much to the comfort of
passengers. When the Highland railway opened about the 1860s a local
newspaper summed up the general attitude by saying, 'The excitement of
travelling when ever at all convenient, has now become a seeming necessity
with all classes'.[25] The railway also brought the opportunity of outings to a
variety of organisations who could never otherwise have travelled in such
large numbers. In 1842 about five hundred people were able to go from
Hawick to Edinburgh to see Queen Victoria thanks to the railway, although
the first part of the trip was by cart and on foot until they got to the
horse-drawn railway at Dalkeith which took them to the capital.[26] In 1849 the
Oddfellows and Foresters Societies of Kelso, Roxburghshire, went by train to
Tweedmouth and Berwick for the day and did so in style. Between 7.00 and
8.00 a.m., their members gathered in the market place and marched in
procession — always the passion for processions — to Sprouston, the nearest
station, which was some 3 miles distant. The Foresters went first, dressed in
their gay and conspicuous uniform; then came the Duke of Roxburghe's brass
band whose services had been kindly granted by the Duke, followed by a long
file of Oddfellows, whose only decoration was a ribbon and rosette. The
weather was perfect, refreshments were provided in a tent on the sands at
their destination and one can only imagine that it must have been very tired
Oddfellows and Foresters, along with friends who were allowed to go with

32   Oxton Railway Station, Berwickshire. Source: Scottish Ethnological
Archive, Royal Museum of Scotland.

them, who left for home about 7.00–8.00 p.m.[27] Of a similar trip, the press
report said, 'We hear of all the passengers being delighted with the scenery
and prospects to be obtained from all parts of the line and, as the crops and
foliage are at present in their most attractive state, the highly cultivated
country through which the line passes is seen to great advantage'.[28] Within
just a few weeks in 1849, a number of large parties from Edinburgh visited the
Borders, among them a band of teetotallers; schoolboys from George
Heriot's Hospital along with the Lord Provost and Magistrates; the girls of the
Merchants' Maiden Hospital and the High Constables; and on one day alone,
a train brought several hundreds of visitors from Falkirk, Stirlingshire. In one
of the towns visited, it was reported that the tradesmen were 'in very high
spirits about these trips — the inn-keepers have much reason to be so. We are
happy to be able to state that the pleasure seekers have almost without
exception conducted themselves with the greatest propriety'.[29] In 1855 what
was called a 'numerous pleasure party', no less than six hundred of them in
twenty-one carriages, came by rail from Newcastle to the Borders, arriving in
Kelso about midday. They walked through the town led by a band playing
merrily, then visited Floors Castle, and left about 6.00 p.m. 'apparently highly
delighted with the excursion'.[30] The impact of these trips on those who took
part in them and on the communities who received them, must have been
considerable. Not all these trips were rural outings for townspeople; the
country folk went to town too, in addition to special occasions like Hawick's

expedition to see the Queen. In 1849 over 1,500 people went from Duns to Edinburgh, the occasion being 'quite a holiday . . . as from the liberality of the merchants and farmers in the neighbourhood, all those in their employment anxious to take advantage of the trip were allowed to avail themselves of the opportunity'.[31] Many of these people would never have had a chance to go to the capital to see the sights were it not for railway excursions of this kind, and what was happening in south-east Scotland was happening all round the country where there were railway lines and a sufficient population to use them.

Not only did railway companies encourage outings but they went out of their way to offer special terms with suitable timings to encourage people to go to agricultural shows, parades and many other functions and school log books, by recording truancy, show how far afield people were prepared to go by railway to find a little amusement. Local entertainments were few and far between and the railway companies saw a market and catered for it. To take just one instance — the Easter and Wester Ross-shire Farmers' Clubs held a joint agricultural show at Invergordon in 1895. The show of stock was expected to be the largest and most important in the northern counties for many years and in addition there were to be a grand parade, horse trotting, driving and tandem driving, a pony race and jumping competitions. The *North Star and Farmers' Chronicle* of 15 August that year reported that the Highland Railway Company would issue cheap return fares from all their

33   Callander Railway Station. Callander was a major tourist centre for touring
     the Trossachs and Loch Katrine, and the coaches are out in force to meet
     the train from the South. Source: GWW Special Collection, University of
     Aberdeen.

stations, costing a single fare and a third, available for return that day or —
and this was particularly considerate — the following one. Special trains were
run for livestock and passengers, with stock being charged at the ordinary
rates and returned at half rate if unsold, provided that a certificate from the
show secretary was produced to that effect. No opportunity for business was
missed and in this same issue the railway company offered cheap fares home
from the east coast herring fishing between 1 August and 30 September — this
mainly affected the girls and women involved in gutting and packing — and
put notices in the press to tell the fisherfolk how to avoid delays by asking for
certain tickets rather than others. In addition to this, carriage of goods by rail
meant that shops throughout the country could carry stock equal to anything
found elsewhere in Scotland. This was so even in fairly remote villages and
thus domestic standards rose and even very humble homes began to contain
furnishings unthought of before. Railways also carried horses and carriages,
most convenient for those wanting a vehicle at the end of their journey — a
forerunner of Motorail. But when all was said and done, goods traffic apart,
those benefiting most of all from the railway were the working people who
could at last travel comfortably at a reasonable cost, so much so apparently
that the number of marriages at Gretna Green increased noticeably.[32]

Where railway lines superseded and by-passed coaching routes, inns along
the way suffered greatly, a classic example of this being the Castle Hotel at
Greenlaw, Berwickshire, which was such a busy coaching stage that the hotel
was built complete with extensive stabling to serve this traffic, only to have
railways open up almost immediately and destroy this trade entirely.[33]
Equally, hotels and inns near to railway lines enjoyed a boom.
Advertisements of the time show what improvements and extensions were
made to these establishments to catch the new trade and they always
particularly mentioned proximity to the railway station and whether or not
the boots met all trains and what local horse-drawn transport could be found
for guests to go on local outings.

So popular did rail travel become that there was a ready market for railway
handbooks, giving not just times and connections, but often describing what
could be seen along the route. One of these was advertised in the press in 1854
thus: 'Notice to the Railing Public ... where the "Rail" has laid its "iron
grasp" coaches are probably among the things that were. Persons can now
breakfast at home, travel hundreds of miles, transact business and be again
beside their "bleezing ingle" the same evening. This however requires method
— the time must be studied and the trains selected before this can be arranged.
But how is this to be accomplished? The course is plain.' The answer,
according to the advertisement, was to buy a copy of Brydon's *Railway, Coach
and Steamboat Directory* for all Scotland and the north of England, which was
stated to be under the patronage of the Royal Family and had already sold
over 10,000 copies.[34]

CALEDONIAN RAILWAY.

ROYAL MAIL ROUTE
BETWEEN
ENGLAND AND SCOTLAND.

DIRECT TRAINS run to and from LONDON (Euston), BIRMINGHAM, LIVERPOOL, MANCHESTER, LEEDS, BRADFORD, &c., with DUMFRIES, PEEBLES, EDINBURGH, GLASGOW, PAISLEY, GREENOCK, and the WEST; also, STIRLING, PERTH, DUNDEE, ABERDEEN, INVERNESS, and the NORTH.

A Sleeping Saloon is run Nightly between London and Glasgow.

To the Firth of Clyde and the West Highlands of Scotland.

The Company's Trains run Daily from Edinburgh, Glasgow, &c., to Greenock, in connection with the Steamer "Iona," for Dunoon, Innellan, Rothesay, Kyles of Bute, Tarbert, Oban, Iona, Staffa, Ballachulish, Glencoe, Fort-William, Caledonian Canal, Falls of Foyers, Inverness, Isle of Skye, &c.

Also, in connection with other Steamers on the Clyde, for Loch-Long, Loch-Goil, Inveraray, Kilmun, Blairmore, Arran, &c.

To Stirling, Perth, Aberdeen, Inverness, and the North Highlands of Scotland.

Trains run from Carlisle, Edinburgh, Glasgow, &c., to the North, in connection with Coaches from Callander for Trossachs, Loch-Katrine, and Loch-Lomond; from Crieff and Lochearnhead for Circular Tour via St. Fillans and Loch-Earn; from Killin and Aberfeldy for Circular Tour via Loch-Tay and Taymouth Castle; also, Tours via Dunkeld, Pitlochry, Pass of Killiecrankie, Blair-Athole, Inverness, Aberdeen, Isle of Skye, &c.; and from Tyndrum for Loch-Awe, Dalmally, Inveraray, Taynuilt, Oban, Iona, Staffa, Glenorchy, Blackmount Deer Forest, Glencoe, and Fort-William.

Tourists from England may break their journey at Beattock for Moffat, and at Lanark for Falls of Clyde, either in going or returning.

For particulars, see the Company's Time Table and Programme of Tours.

CALEDONIAN RAILWAY COMPANY'S OFFICES,   JAMES SMITHELLS,
GLASGOW, 1874.   *General Manager.*

34   Advertisement for the Caledonian Railway, 1874. From *George Washington Wilson Artist and Photographer (1823–93)*, Roger Taylor, 1981.

In spite of the enthusiasm for this new form of travel, people initially did not seem to grasp the fact that there might be any danger and one newspaper carried this fascinating warning in 1849: 'As accidents are continually occurring on railways from the sheer inattention or reckless temerity of passengers, it may not be out of place, at this time of jaunting and excursion parties, to call to mind the following simple maxims of the rail. . . .' The rules included:

> Never leap from a carriage.
> While in motion, do not move from one compartment to another. Accidents have occurred in this way.
> When near tunnels or buildings, do not put out your head at the windows. A fatal blow may be got by this indiscretion.
> Carefully eschew walking on the railway; many deaths have been caused by this stupid temerity.[35]

It seems incredible that such advice could be necessary, yet just three examples of how badly it was needed appeared in the space of a week in one Highland newspaper in 1864. When a passenger heard the station master call out the name of the coming station, he immediately opened the door and stepped out, even though the train had not stopped. Encumbered as he was with a plaid, he missed his footing, fell and was dragged under the train. Both his legs were broken and he later died. A woman in the same area also stepped out of a moving train, but it was not just passengers who did stupid things — railway employees could do so too. That same week the guard of a goods van climbed on to a truck to adjust a cover and whilst standing on it 'his head came in contact with one of the bridges'. Luckily for him, the train was going slowly and he managed somehow to get back to his van but the report of the incident said that his life was still in danger.[36]

The reaction of horses to trains was what might have been expected. In 1854 a correspondent of the *Kelso Mail* wrote that while driving along the turnpike road east of Melrose, Roxburghshire, he had been placed in great danger when his horse took fright at seeing the train on the line which ran very close to the road. The road was very narrow and several accidents had already taken place there, due to trains, in addition to 'innumerable escapes'. The writer strongly objected to passing railway engines being so openly exposed to the view of horses and suggested that the danger might be largely removed by erecting a screen to hide them.[37] In the summer of 1864, a blacksmith from Strathglass, Inverness-shire, and his wife were returning home from Inverness by cart when the horse took fright at the sight of a train and bolted. He was thrown out and badly injured and his wife broke her leg. The intriguing thing about this accident is that a passenger on the train saw what had happened, got off at the next station, returned to the scene, found the unfortunate couple and had them taken to the nearest doctor.[38]

There were many occasions when trains became stuck in snow-drifts but there cannot have been many like the New Year's Eve in 1874 when this happened near Galasheils, Selkirkshire, and the passengers were stuck for two days — two old lady farmers sent two cart loads of boiled potatoes to succour them, which must have been an unusual sight. Whether the potatoes got through the snow or not, is not known but certainly someone who was on the train said later that he had seen none of them.[39]

In spite of the Tay Bridge disaster in 1879, railways continued to be very popular although some people had reservations about certain aspects of them. Although the Leaderfoot viaduct over the River Tweed was considered a great engineering feat which even Queen Victoria came to see, Lady John Scott of 'Annie Laurie' fame had no faith in it and always arranged her journeys so that she never had to cross it.[40]

The operation of railways on Sundays caused problems. The *New Statistical Account for Erskine, Renfrewshire*, said how glad that parish was that the directors of the Glasgow, Greenock and Paisley Railway had decided not to allow Sunday travel because the parish 'from its beauty and its vicinity to Glasgow and Paisley would, but for that determination have been over run every Sabbath with visitors little likely to improve either the temporal or spiritual interests of the people'.[41] There was, however, such a popular movement for Sunday trains that a minister called Rev Andrew Thomson felt it necessary to write a tract on the subject which said among other things, 'We are unequivocally opposed to the running of communication trains on the Sabbath. The human profession made for travelling should just be for cases in which divine permission has been granted to travel. For a railway company, or any other company, to allow themselves to be carried beyond this mark,

35   'The High Flier', Caledonian Railway Company.

by popular clamour, is just to become partakers of other men's sins. It is replied that no company is able to distinguish such cases and that to provide trains for cases of necessity and mercy would, in fact, be to provide for all who might apply. Our answer is ready. The railway company has thus two alternatives to choose between — no trains at all, or common trains, and for our own part we believe the former of these alternatives to be infinitely preferable ... If two trains are granted to popular clamour, why not three; why not ten? Why not for goods as well as passengers? And if this is yielded on one railway, why not on all? Why not also in the case of steamboat and canal companies? As trains and traffic increase, more workmen are required — clerks in offices, porters, and cab-drivers at termini and steamboat piers — thousands are tempted to violate the Sabbath that they may retain their employment — the rural quiet of Scotland is broken, the Sabbath decorum of her cities disturbed, her Sabbath reduced to the character of a continental holiday...'. He finished by recommending that from the pulpit, the platform, the press and the Sabbath School as well as in the conversational circle, the law of Heaven in regard to Sunday railways should be urged.[42]

While people, especially in the south of Scotland, wanted to travel on Sundays, things were stricter in the north and in the summer of 1883 there was a remarkable instance of Sabbath observance in connection with the railway at Strome Ferry on the west coast of Ross-shire. It was planned to send a load of fish south on a Sunday but the villagers of Strome, armed with clubs and sticks, prevented the unloading of the boats or loading of the train. In addition, they prayed and sang in the railway station, not omitting to pray for the directors of the railway company. The police and rail officials tried to deal with this opposition but they were held off until midnight when the fish was finally sent off. Ten men were each sent to prison for four months for mobbing and rioting although the jury recommended clemency due to their ignorance of the law and their religious convictions and they only served fifty-six days before release, but not before questions had been asked in Parliament about the incident.[43] The rather odd thing about this is that unless the fish had been caught too late to catch the train on Saturday, they must have been caught on Sunday, something very much against the tradition of Scottish fishermen.

Much has been said of the benefits of railways, and there was also the spin-off benefit that railway-building led to a great demand for fir wood from northern Scotland, giving a lot of work in timber operations there,[44] but their introduction brought disadvantages to some areas. Railway lines did not always follow the line of roads and communities which formerly had coaches serving them sometimes found that these gave up and obtaining public transport was not so easy as it had been, and could mean a long walk to a railway station. One area which was badly hit by railways was the Black Isle in Ross-shire which for centuries had been a main route to the north by road

36 'The Jacobite', SRPS Special approaching Tulloch Station, Inverness-shire on route from Fort William to Edinburgh (the first time in over 20 years a steam engine has run on the main West Highland Railway). Photograph J Henderson, Banchory (c) 1987.

and ferry and suddenly found that this traffic, and the business it created, moved out of the district and on to the railway which ran via Inverness and Dingwall to the north, cutting off the Black Isle. In some areas there was an increase in the cost of living due to railways. This happened in the Elgin area of Morayshire, where it was said, 'The formation of railways has brought a great influx of strangers, particularly sportsmen, many of them with great wealth, into the district, who have raised the prices of provisions, of house rents, wages and of all commodities, so that Elgin is now almost as costly a place to live in as any part of the United Kingdom'.[45] On an even more local level, as people chose to travel by rail, social intercourse along the roads declined, something particularly felt in lonely areas. Where practical, farmers began to use the train to go to market, to do business or to visit other farms; no longer did they stop their gigs along the way for a chat with those they passed, nor could they drop in on friends as before, and those who had relied on such passers-by for news and company, missed this greatly.[46] In time, of course, as coaching suffered from railways, so railways were to suffer from motor cars and later still, from the axe of Dr Beeching who sought to make railways profitable by closing less-used lines.

12 REST FOR THE TRAVELLER

The necessity for inns to serve travellers and an equal need to regulate their practices was something which the Scottish Parliament recognised early on, as the following Acts show:

> 1336. 'All who sell bread and beer in burghs to receive travellers and supply their wants at the current prices, travellers who leave without paying to be arrested in the king's name.'[1]
> 1424. 'Hostelries with accommodation and food for men and horses to be provided in burghs and thoroughfares.'[2]
> 1427. 'Inns to be established in all burghs for the reception of travellers and their horses.'[3]
> 1496. 'Barons, magistrates and others having the direction and rule of thoroughfare and hostelries to set price of victuals, bread, ale and other necessaries.'[4]
> 1503. 'Deleted Act fixing payments for lodging at inns; the rate charged to be fixed by burgh officers and innkeepers at the sight of the lords justice and commissioners-at-aires.'[5]
> 1535. 'For eschewing exorbitant prices taken from travellers, the statutes of James I and other sovereigns to be enforced; burgh officers to cause hostelers to have sufficient accommodation and food at the usual rate in the neighbourhood; the rate of charges to be fixed yearly.'[6]
> 1551. 'The price of victual being doubled and trebled by hostelers, the provost and bailies to fix the price for dinner and supper at inns, so that the lieges be not grieved and hurt; a hosteler not obeying the law to be deprived.'[7]
> 1567. 'The old Acts anent hostelries to be put into action.'[8]

An element of monopoly appears in the following Act:

> 1425. 'Travellers to lodge in inns and not with their friends, unless they have many followers, who must lodge at the inn.'[9]

In this next Act, monopoly carried with it the burden for the inn-keeper of acting as customs officer:

> 1493. 'Masters of ships and merchants to lodge at the principal inn of the seaport, entering their goods as effeirs: the host of the inn to answer to the king for the

customs and duties of strangers passing away uncustomed and for money exported.'[10]

Late hours were also forbidden:

1436. 'Taverns to be shut at nine o'clock, persons drinking in them after that hour to be fined.'[11]

So was gambling:

1621. 'Keepers of inns and cook shops allowing cards or dice to be played in their houses to be fined £40 Scots.'[12]

In addition, fines could be imposed on inn-keepers by the baron court or JPs for receiving what were termed masterless men, rebels, vagabonds or criminals. A problem for the authorities was that it was largely women who kept taverns. Edinburgh taverns were so often hosted by women and were in reality brothels that in 1559 the Council forbade women to do so in future.[13] This obviously did not have much effect and in 1695 the Burgh records said that neglect of earlier Acts on the subject had caused much of the 'lewdness as is now found to abound within this City and suburbs thereof' and the employment of women servants in taverns, described as the reproach and

37   Crook Inn, Tweedsmuir. Oldest licensed premises in Scotland, founded 1604.

scandal of the nation and causing 'lousness' and debauchery, was forbidden under the penalty of £3 Scots.[14] Other burghs with similar problems passed their own Acts on this subject but in many places women continued to run inns — in the mid nineteenth century, eight out of thirteen inns in North Berwick were run by widows and the parish minister greatly doubted their authority over their customers.[15] Yet when one particular female inn-keeper *was* strict, what happened? In the Ayrshire parish of Kilmaurs, a decent woman was delated to appear before the Kirk Session for profane swearing when she refused admittance to several drunken men who came late at night to her ale house. Her profanity had consisted of nothing more than the words 'What the divill are you doing here?'[16]

When men were inn-keepers, there could be problems of a different sort. It was found in Glasgow in the seventeenth century that many of them were officials of the Council and there was such a problem with abuses in the election of Magistrates and Deacon Conveners who kept inns, that it had to be decreed that no inn- or tavern-keeper of any sort should be elected Provost, Bailie, Dean of Guild, Deacon Convener, Bailie of Gorbals or Water Bailie.[17]

Although the Scottish Parliament had encouraged the development of necessary inns, in 1656 it forbade the frequenting on Sundays of taverns, inns, ale houses, victualling houses, strong-water-houses, tobacco houses, cellars or shops but provided that the preparation and provision of food on Sundays in inns, victualling houses and cook shops was permissible for the use of those as could not otherwise be provided for — what was until fairly recently known as the bona-fide traveller.[18] Many laws of the Scottish Parliament had little effect and where this one was adhered to, it probably had more to do with the vigilance of the Kirk Session than the strictures of Parliament. Thus food could not, in some places, be obtained at inns for most of the Sabbath day. A traveller in the Hamilton area of Lanarkshire in 1723 said that travellers got nothing but bread and butter, with perhaps an egg, until evening sermon was over, when a hot supper was always provided.[19] Inns grew up where trade was to be found, be it the smithy, the ferry or the ford — but one of the best sites was close by or opposite to a church. In an account of the parish of Auchterhouse in Angus, the writer says quite frankly that as soon as church services were over 'there was a rush for the change house [ale house]'.[20] The close proximity of an inn to a church could mean that the former took its name from the latter — in Duncan's *Itinerary of Scotland* of 1823 there is a reference, in a description of Caithness, to the Reay Kirk Inn and at Canisbay, in the same county, there was an inn known as 'the house of the Kirk Style' which was obviously just over the churchyard wall where, according to the Kirk Session records people abused the Lord's Day by drinking and discussing worldly affairs after public worship. But whatever Kirk Sessions might say or do, at least one eighteenth-century minister, Rev Alexander

Thomson of Carnock in Fife, was more sympathetic when he wrote, 'It must be admitted that several houses of this kind are necessary for the ... accommodation of the people who come from a distance to attend public worship on Sundays'.[21]

Statistical and *New Statistical Accounts*, usually written by parish ministers, show some difference of clerical opinion about the presence of inns in general in their parishes. It was stated that the only way in which they were useful in the parish of Neilston, Renfrewshire, was for public meetings and to accommodate travellers and their horses overnight[22] while in Nigg, Ross-shire, it was admitted that while they were useful for travellers they were 'otherwise no blessing'.[23] In many cases it was the sheer number of inns in a parish that was condemned. In Ardersier, Inverness-shire, there were ten when three or four would have been ample[24] and the parish of Canisbay, Caithness, had far too many tippling houses — three in addition to ferry houses would be quite enough.[25] At Portpatrick, a busy harbour in the south-west, almost every house was an inn because sailors provided a ready trade, but the effects on them of so much drinking were not good.[26] Almost unbelievably, in North Berwick about the middle of the nineteenth century, there were thirteen public houses to a population of six hundred and fifty, one to every fifty people, men, women and children.[27] Rev Adam Forman, minister of Kirkintilloch, Dumbartonshire, regarded inns not as the cause of corruption but as its consequence,[28] while the minister of Liberton, Edinburgh, wrote sadly of the thirty-two ale-houses in his parish saying, 'One man is paid for teaching sobriety and thirty-two have an interest in defeating his efforts and human nature is on their side'.[29] Yet, other ministerial writers of these *Statistical Accounts* realised that inns had a valuable role to play, just as Mr Thomson of Carnock had appreciated that they were useful on Sundays. The pastor of Yarrow, Selkirkshire, considered the three ale houses there to be 'absolutely necessary for the accommodation of travellers' although he admitted that they could be 'somewhat demoralizing within a certain sphere',[30] and even the twenty-six inns of Auchtergaven, Perthshire, were not thought really harmful to the area as they were all on turnpike or other public roads, in other words, primarily serving travellers.[31] Some ministers actually expressed the need for a good inn. The writer of the *Statistical Account for Assynt, Sutherland*, a wild and remote area, said that good roads and decent inns would greatly improve the situation of the people[32] and in Clatt, Aberdeenshire, it was said that a proper inn in the village would make it 'a most convenient stage for travellers ... and the road being once frequented would contribute quickly to the improvement of the village'.[33] The same sentiments were expressed at Ormiston, East Lothian, where there was only inferior stabling at the inn: 'Were there one good inn, with accommodation for horses, it might be of great benefit to the place',[34] because stabling was very important, even before the days of wheeled traffic. In

38   Buccleuch Arms Hotel, St Boswells, c.1867. Source: Dr E Purdie.

Dingwall, Ross-shire, there were two inns 'kept by well behaving respectable people',[35] and at Closeburn, Dumfries-shire, there was a comfortable inn at Brownhill where travellers might expect to be treated with every civility.[36] It was plain common-sense that could see the benefit of a well-conducted inn but sometimes a bit of class-consciousness slipped into these *Accounts*: at Inverbervie, Kincardineshire, it was said, 'There are twelve ale houses, besides a tavern which is intended principally for the accommodation of travellers and the genteeler sort of company in the town and neighbourhood'.[37] In Moffat, Dumfries-shire, there were 'several excellent lodging houses where the best company may be accommodated'[38] and at Portpatrick, Wigtownshire, a large and commodious inn 'where nobility and travellers of rank frequently lodge in passing to and from Ireland'.[39] No ministers ever seemed to complain of the unofficial inns which opened in nearly every house in towns on market days, and often on the following day too, something that commonly happened at least until the 1830s.[40]

An unusual use of the inn—at least one hopes it was unusual—is said to have occurred in the village of Ferryden, Angus. There, if a man wanted to say anything of importance to his wife, he went to the inn, sent for her and then, in the hearing of all, said what he had to say. Possibly such a bombastic attitude to a spouse needed either masculine support or Dutch courage.[41]

By the late eighteenth century, however, there began to be changes, with the closing of many public houses ordered by JPs, under whose jurisdiction they came. It was reported from Cromdale, Moray and Inverness, that, 'Many public houses have . . . been suppressed of late. There are only four here now, two of them on the turnpike road for the accommodation of travellers'.[42] At Kirkhill, Inverness-shire, six inns were closed within two years, leaving only a couple, both on the public road.[43] Certainly there had been far too many public houses and certainly it made sense to have such as there were at places where travellers passed, but JPs were only too ready to licence toll-houses so that the problem of drunkenness does not seem to have been the reason for these closures. One cannot help but feel that drinking was being directed to where it could produce most financial benefit, either to proprietors through whose lands these roads ran and where inn-keepers would therefore pay a higher rent to them; or by increasing rents from toll-house licences which went to road-making. No one could call the twenty-six inns on the turnpike and public roads of the one parish of Auchtergaven, Perthshire, a small number.

While closing superfluous inns was sensible it could be very hard on the small man. In his *History of Kincardine O'Neil*, Robert Dinnie said that about 1825 there were eight licensed houses in the parish as well as several shops where alcohol could be bought for consumption off the premises, but these

39   Latheronwheel Hotel, from 'History of Latheron' (WRI, 1966). Source:
Scottish Ethnological Archive, Royal Museum of Scotland.

had been reduced to two. He pointed out that people of means could afford a conveyance for travelling but the poor had to go on foot, sometimes by night as well as by day, and when they called at one of the few remaining inns, they were often refused admittance because the landlords knew that they had little competition and knew they need not bother themselves for the small pittance of profit that would come from a poor traveller. And so these people had to trudge on, whatever the conditions.[44] An old Cromarty (Ross-shire) Estate rent book throws a sidelight on inn-keepers' attitudes to the social standing of guests, although admittedly the circumstances of this story are a little unusual. On the day after the Battle of Culloden in 1746, three tenant farmers from Cromarty decided to visit the battlefield. To do such a thing may sound very odd but many in the North of Scotland were anti-Jacobite and in fact the Presbytery of Tain, Ross-shire, met after the battle to give thanks for the seasonable deliverance it had given them from Roman Catholicism. The three farmers remained at Culloden for so long that they missed the last ferry boat home and went instead to Inverness which was full of English troops. The inn they went to was full up and they expected to have to sit up all night — until they had a brainwave. They would address each other with titles such as Provost, Bailie, Doctor, in the hearing of the servants and see what happened and, sure enough, in no time the landlord sought them out and gave them comfortable quarters for the night.[45]

Many people by-passed inns entirely because country people had a long tradition of hospitality, which was fortunate for travellers in areas where there were no inns. An early traveller, Taylor the Water-Poet, wrote in 1618 of a singularly generous home near Cockburnspath, Berwickshire, where a 'plaine home-spunne fellow' and his wife willingly fed and put up as many as came, and their horses too, and in the morning the reckoning was nothing.[46] Fynes Moryson, visiting Scotland some twenty years earlier, had found the same thing, that people in their own homes would 'entertain passengers upon acquaintance or entreaty'.[47] The more isolated the area, the longer this practice lasted. In very lonely districts, and in the Highlands, people did not travel much anyway but if they did, they found shelter with relations or friends; and for strangers too, the private house assumed the role of the inn but charged nothing. The Statistical Account for Reay, Caithness, put the position well: there were three inns where travellers could be put up but which were not very comfortable 'for the better sort' and 'the hospitality of the parish supplies the public instead of elegant inns'.[48] In Assynt, Sutherland, travellers simply went to tenants' houses where they could get a good, clean, woollen Highland plaid and a comfortable pallet or couch on which to sleep.[49] This welcoming attitude to travellers throughout the Highlands was such, in fact, that Thomas Pennant found in 1769 that in parts of Ross-shire it was virtually impossible to pass a farm without the mistress coming out and standing by the track, holding out a bowl of milk or whey for their refreshment.[50] Hospitality was given without questions being asked; in any case, a fresh face, some news and a good crack, made up for kindness shown. Asking no questions had hazards but apart from the obvious one of taking in bad characters, it could land the host in trouble with the Kirk Session. An instance of this occurred in the parish of Belhelvie, Aberdeenshire, where a man was convicted by the Kirk Session for taking in a stranger for three nights without any evidence of who or what he was; the well-meaning host had to make public repentance and also pay a penalty.[51] This incident arose because Kirk Sessions were always afraid that strangers might come into the parish but not leave it and end up as burdens on the poors' roll. To prevent this, they often demanded testimonials from them, without which no one was meant to shelter them— but Highland hospitality seems to have got round this prohibition quite easily. It takes exceptions to prove rules and this applies also to this rural tradition of welcome. The manse of Kildonan, Sutherland, was not a hospitable place, as the minister wrote in the *Statistical Account* under the heading of 'Disadvantages' that because there was no inn travellers above the common rank had to be put up at the manse. This, he said, was very inconvenient to travellers;[52] but as this was something they expected to do in such lonely areas, one feels that the inconvenience was to him and his household and, indeed, one can understand this even if it was not the Highland way. The story is told of a man named Kenneth Cameron who some time in the first half of the nineteenth century was driving sheep, along with a friend, from Ross-shire to Falkirk Tryst. In the Dalwhinnie area of Inverness-shire they asked for lodgings at a cottage but were told by the old woman who lived there that they could not come inside but could sleep in the pig-sty if they wished as the pig had recently died. Badly needing somewhere to sleep, this they did. On their return north, they passed the same spot and found the old woman occupying the pig-sty herself as her cottage had burned down. Kenneth Cameron had a forebear in Ross-shire, known as the Kildey Witch, and there is a suggestion in all this that Kenneth had certain powers himself and ill-wished the old woman whose attitudes did not fit in with traditional country hospitality.[53] If an area was lonely enough, there might be neither inn, kindly house nor even a pig-sty for a traveller as night fell. Areas of Kintail, Ross-shire, fell into this category. Through them ran a route from Skye to Inverness and Dingwall and benighted travellers, often carrying heavy loads, simply made use of shepherds' huts. This was all very well but in bad weather they were not above burning some of them as fuel, which must have caused great hardship to the shepherds and was a breach of respect for the people whose property they were using.[54] As travelling became more common in the Highlands, thanks to Telford's roads and bridges, so inns developed and free hospitality died out although a relic of it remains in the still-accepted Highland custom of 'dropping in', though this is not done at meal times, nor to stay the night.

Going back to the earlier days of inn-keeping, inns were ill-equipped so that
wise travellers carried their own knives and forks in a side pocket of their
clothing and one glass might have to go round a large number of people.[55] Sir
William Brereton wrote in 1636 of a 40-mile journey in Ayrshire at the end
of which all he and his party could find was very wretched accommodation,
and food which only consisted of oatcakes, two eggs and some buttered fish
with nothing to drink but water so that several of their horses, and one of the
travellers 'almost fainted for lack of relief'. But Sir William did not find all
inns bad. At the town of Ayr he stayed in one which had a good, clean hostess,
well-cooked food, good sleeping quarters and entertainment.[56] He was more
fortunate than James Boswell who found himself at a dreadful inn at Glenelg,
Inverness-shire, in 1773. Admittedly, Glenelg is a very out of the way place
and not one that would expect much passing trade but the room shown to
Boswell and his companions was damp and dirty, with bare walls and 'a
variety of bad smells' and furnished with a rough black greasy fir table and
forms of the same kind. As they entered a man started up from his sleep in a
wretched bed. There was nothing to eat or drink and they had to send for
fresh hay to make beds on which they put their own sheets and used their
clothes and greatcoats as coverings.[57] James Hogg, the Ettrick Shepherd, made
a tour of the Highlands at the very beginning of the nineteenth century and,
with his party, got to an inn in the Fort William area of Inverness-shire after
everyone was in bed and had to knock them up. The landlord who let them
in was a 'big, black terrible-looking fellow, stark naked', who lit a candle, tied
on his kilt and asked how far they had come that day. He gave them a meal of
cakes, milk and rum, there being surprisingly no whisky. The room he gave
them for the night was earth-floored and damp; in it were two heather beds,
on one of which a woman and some children were lying. At sight of them, one
of the party flew into a rage and swore he would take shelter in the woods
rather than sleep there, at which the woman and children slunk quietly away.
The beds were made up with clean clothes and they spent the night as best
they might although in the morning one of them complained bitterly of the
'rude engravings' made on his body by the heather roots.[58] Although
accommodation in such inns might be bad, food even in simple ones could be
good enough and about the same time that James Hogg was enduring this
uncomfortable visit, an inn in West or Old Kilpatrick was visited by a group
of travellers and described thus, ' . . . we came to an inn, and were shown into
a room, not very cleanly to be sure, for the floor was of soft dirt which stuck
to our shoes, and the ceiling was boarded and plentifully hung with cobwebs;
the chairs, table and windows not too much accustomed to the pail and cloth.
However, they got us an abundant breakfast, of tea, eggs, milk and bread, all
very good of their kind'.[59] Many inns became very good. Some, indeed, may
have been over-generous with their refreshments which could explain an
entry in the Book of Garth and Fortingall which said, '1561, Feb. 12. James

Campbell of Lawers died at Perth on the twelfth day of Feb. . . . He broke al his bones on the stair of the inn'.[60]

In certain areas inns were a direct follow-on from road construction. These were inns known as King's Houses or just as Kinghouse. They had originally been camps for General Wade's soldiers when working on the military roads and were later transformed into inns.[61] The hotel at Amulree, Perthshire, used to be a King's House and there are others to be found; and at Kinghouse on Rannoch Moor there used to be one, to run which the Government gave the inn-keeper a grant and charged him no rent, in spite of which it managed to be remarkably unwelcoming.[62] Other Government help for inn-building came when the Treasury paid for one at Beattock Summit, Dumfries-shire,[63] and there were other instances of this too. Many inns were built by landed proprietors and often carried the family or estate name, i.e. Balnagown Arms Hotel or Inn. Sometimes a group of gentlemen might join to provide an inn, like the seven Edinburgh heritors who, along with eight in Selkirkshire and Roxburghshire, joined to build Torsonce Inn at Stow, Midlothian. Finished in 1819, it cost £3,000, a large sum, but the result was good and it was 'admired by travellers, as perhaps unequalled by any country inn in Scotland'.[64]

Just as toll-keepers near the border with England learnt to benefit from the marriage trade, so did some inn-keepers. When David Lang or Laing set up as a 'priest' about the 1780s–1790s, in the village of Springfield not far from Gretna Green, in opposition to Joseph Paisley, the 'grand old man of the Gretna marriage business', he made his headquarters in an inn, to his, his clients' and the inn-keeper's mutual advantage. Paisley followed suit and established himself in that village too, but in a different inn. In 1825, John Linton, formerly a valet, leased Gretna Hall and arranged that stage-coaches should make it a halting place for changing horses and turned it into a hotel catering for a good class of guests, with marriage ceremonies available.[65]

As already said, improved roads and the resultant increase in horse-drawn traffic attracted travellers and produced a great number of coaching inns. However, many of them were to be gravely affected in time by the coming of railways. Nevertheless, railways encouraged far more people to travel and created boom conditions for hotels on railway routes, and prices which were described by the Star Hotel in Kingussie, Inverness-shire, in 1896 as 'strictly moderate' seem all the more attractive now: 2s. per night for a bed; 1s. 6d. to 2s. for breakfast; luncheon 1s. 6d. to 2s. 6d.; dinner 2s. and upwards; plain teas 1s. and teas with meat 2s.[66]

13 ALL KINDS OF CARRIERS

Before the country was opened up by modern communications, there were few people more valued than packmen, pedlars and chapmen, in spite of their being described rather unfavourably in some old bye-laws and proclamations as 'hawkers, vendors, petty chapmen and unruly people'.[1] They carried their loads themselves and by using hill paths, byways and church routes could get to virtually wherever they thought some business might be done, however isolated that place might be. They were largely independent of roads and so their role was at its most valuable when there were no roads or, at any rate, not good ones.[2]

It may be because they carried their goods on their own backs, to start with anyway, that they acquired a reputation for cheating on weights. An indication of how commonly they did this appeared at the inspection of weights and measures at just one fair — Sumereve's Fair in Banffshire in 1715, when one pedlar had a plaiden ell for measuring cloth which was not the right length; another had a short English yard; and several others had either stone or iron weights which were too light although, to be fair to them, not by much.[3] In addition to these deceptions, many pedlars would nowadays be guilty of breaching the Trade Descriptions Act by selling goods with faulty designations. Because tradesmen wore woollen cord trousers, these were greatly envied by country folk and packmen found a gullible market for material which looked and felt the same but was really made of cotton and much inferior. Although this was not fair to the buyer, it did at least keep the manufacture of this material booming for some time. Another ploy was to sell cotton table cloths as linen, getting between 5s. and 6s. for something only worth 1s. to 1s. 6d. Certain hawkers took to pledging these cloths at pawn-brokers but, unfortunately for themselves, they did it to such an extent that suspicions were aroused and the trade collapsed.[4]

In spite of all this, packmen and pedlars were welcome wherever they went. Manufactured goods were rare in the country where the few shops that there were, were ill-stocked. To many households, these trading visitors were the only source of news, which lost nothing in the telling, while the excitement of seeing the opening of a pack was almost beyond belief. Where else could a countryman buy shaving requisites or a knife or his wife obtain linen (even if it turned out to be cotton), a bowl or other domestic smallwares? How else could one buy a length of cloth, a shawl, some ribbon to give new life to an old bonnet, or any of the little fairings a young man liked to give to his girl? Even gypsy hawkers were welcome in many households, bringing baskets and besoms, horn spoons, tinware and crockery.

Although these traders, men and women, began by being their own beasts of burden, as roads improved many progressed to having a pack or panniered pony or to riding on their rounds with their goods in saddle-bags. A pedlar mounted like this was sometimes known as 'the rider' or even 'our representative', due, one supposes, to his carrying out commissions for his customers, as did many of his kind.[5] Later still, they might have a pony and trap and a married pedlar often took his wife with him to lend a hand. A gravestone in Bonkle churchyard, Berwickshire, is that of Patrick James, 'pedler of small wares', who died in 1739 aged fifty-seven. On the stone are carvings, not only of the pedlar but also of his wife and his horse, stressing the importance of both of them in a life such as his. Willie 'Bowlie' was a Highland pedlar early this century who had a wife to assist him, a woman who always impressed everyone with the clever knot she used for tying the four corners of the big red blanket which formed their pack, so that it could be quickly and easily opened to display the bowls from which he got his nickname and other kitchen goods.[6] Many pedlars had a real flair for showing off their wares and the best of them never opened a pack at the back door or 'kitchen end' but insisted on going through to the best room to do so, thereby immediately elevating the quality of their goods in the eyes of the family.[7] Although packmen carried their packs on their backs when walking a distance, they sometimes hung them from their necks, down the front, like a cinema usherette's ice-cream tray, when displaying goods at, say, a fair. Even a wooden box could be hung in this way, which sounds most uncomfortable.[8]

Packmen sometimes specialised in certain goods, such as Quill Charlie who sold quill pens to houses, offices and schools until the introduction of steel nibs ruined his trade.[9] Another, unable any longer to carry a heavy pack, took to selling spectacles which needed little outlay and were light to carry although real salesmanship was required to sell them.[10] Many were real characters. There was Thomas Tyre in West Kilbride, a small man who always wore blue knee breeches, a short coat, a blue bonnet or a cocked hat and huggers — coarse footless stockings — on his legs, with bare feet beneath. Although a packman, occupied in selling his own wares, he sometimes acted as a carrier, taking webs for the silk weavers to a nearby town. He was very keen on the Bible and whenever there was a Presbyterial visit to inspect the school, he used to present himself for examination too.[11] Another character was Cobble Davy, a 'broken-down sailor' who became a chapman in the Lammermuir district and was noted for singing to attract attention as he held

40 Gravestone of Patrick James, retailer of small wares, d. 1739, in Bonkle churchyard. Shows him and his wife and below, left to right, scales, crossed bones, loaded horse, and above it a bulk measure.

out bunches of printed ballads for sale.[12] There was Tammy Jenkins in Liddesdale, a neat little man who always carried a cat in his coat front;[13] and there was William Nicholson, the packman-poet of the parish of Borgue, Kirkcudbright, who may well have gleaned on his travels some of the poetry he later published in book form in 1814;[14] and there were many, many more.

A packman's life was a hard and a potentially dangerous one. Not only were the contents of his pack of considerable value but he was usually carrying money too and that made him the target of thieves and so a number of them were murdered. For some reason, the grave of a murdered packman seemed to have had rather uncanny connotations and there are, or were, memories of them in various parts of the country, including that of a packwoman in a glen near the River Don in Aberdeenshire.[15]

The chapman, or 'chapman billie' as he was sometimes called, though a pedlar like the rest, was primarily a seller of chapbooks, those popular and cheap books and pamphlets of no literary merit which were the sole reading matter of the poor, apart from the Bible, and which helped to while away many a dark evening.[16] About the 1820s the term chapman was sometimes dropped in favour of the term Flying or Running Stationer because by then the chapman carried a considerable stock of better goods and would take orders for what he could not supply on the spot.[17] Possibly because of their literary wares, chapmen seem to have regarded themselves as rather special and were often incorporated, by petitioning their burghs, into special groups.[18] Pride in their calling is clear from the fact that when a steeple was being built at Kinross, the principal 'Lord of the Chapmen' appeared and gave half-a-crown to finish it off, which seems to have been for the provision of a weather cock or vane.[19]

Chapmen often acted as agents for goldsmiths, buying old gold and silver for re-use, and the Church found these travelling salesmen useful too. The fact that the parish of Fettercairn received about a third of its Sunday collections in bad coin has already been referred to in the chapter on bridges, and this sort of thing was common throughout Scotland. People did not mean to cheat the Church but bad coin was so common throughout the country that it was all that people had to give in many cases. The particular coin most often found in church plates was the doit or dyte, a copper coin worth about one-twelfth of a penny sterling, and these coins, along with bad brass, had to be disposed of somehow to the best advantage. Some of them were sold by weight as scrap metal, some went to blacksmiths[20] and some were made into bells, jougs or cups for collecting for the poor,[21] but there was a limit to how many bells, cups or jougs were required. Sometimes therefore the parish minister took them with him to sell when he went to the General Assembly in Edinburgh, but not all ministers went to the Assembly and not all can have wanted to burden themselves on the journey with a considerable weight of metal. In 1708 the Kirk Session of Nigg, Ross-shire, had accumulated over 1,100 of these coins and numbers would be similar in other parishes. It was here that chapmen and pedlars were of benefit — some travelled the country regularly with panniered ponies for the specific purpose of buying up worn or bad metal, especially copper, which was generally sold for 7d. per Dutch pound weight.[22] Making the best of a bad job in this way was what lay behind this entry in Nigg's Kirk Session Minutes in November 1787: 'Rev Mr Grant also gave in three shillings and six pence being the price of the bad coper he

had got from George Rainy a travelling chapman and which coper had lain
beside Mr Grant for some time past with an order to dispose of it to any
account that could be got.'

Although 'shouldering a pack' was many a young Scotsman's idea of a
passport to a fortune, the truth is that packmen, pedlars and chapmen tended
to end their lives ill or in poverty. It was said truly that, 'The worst of these
clever and pleasant fellows is that they have a way of dying off as they draw
towards forty. They may see people under the table but people get their
revenge by seeing them under the sod'.[23]

Pedlars and packmen bought goods and carried them around the country
for sale but it was obvious that there was also a demand for the carrying of
other people's goods from place to place. Even before roads were much
improved, many burghs appointed an official town carrier although that did
not preclude other carriers from operating too. The man appointed to this
post in Stirling in 1707 was told that he must 'noeway loss or embasell any
goods, money or effects he shall be entrusted with'.[24] Thirty years later, this
burgh appointed their carrier to travel between there and Edinburgh, for
which responsibility he was given a salary of £48 Scots.[25] It was normal for
these employees to receive a badge of office from their burgh — the Council
of Peebles paid £8 Scots in 1685 for a silver badge for their carrier and some
time before 1872 there was discovered, along with records and charters there,
a silver arm plate engraved with the burgh arms, with a card stating that it had
belonged to the town carrier.[26] These badges were much valued and
sometimes burghs even provided their carriers' horses with bells as well,
something looked on with envy by Thomas Wilson, town carrier in Stirling
in 1745, who asked the Council if his horse might be equipped with bells in
the same way as in several other towns. The Council allowed him to get the
bells himself, to be paid for by the Treasurer, but Thomas was to be held
responsible for them and had to hand them over on demand to the Council
or to any succeeding carrier.[27] Another group of carriers who wore a mark of
office were carriers of lead. In 1597 the Privy Council ordered these men to
wear a 'blason of lead', a badge bearing the royal arms and the mark of the
lessee of the lead mines, so that there should be no mistaking who and what
they were. This was decreed because 'disordered and broken men of the
borders' had been attacking these carriers and stealing not only the lead but
their horses, their clothing and anything else upon which they could lay their
hands.[28]

These were a special class of carriers but there were many others who did
carrying on their own account. At its simplest, carrying could be done by
someone like Maggie Gillanders who, in the first half of the twentieth century,
walked a limited route between a farm and the villages of Hilton and Balintore
in Ross-shire. She was really a farm worker but she also carried out the useful
task of bringing farm produce to the villages and shop groceries home to her

neighbours. As the New Year approached she was an even more kenspeckle figure than usual, like a walking Christmas tree, with butter and eggs in baskets on her arms and hens slung over her shoulders. An early form of the carrying trade involved using barrows but this was only done in towns where barrow-men carried on a regular business.[29]

As roads improved and the Industrial Revolution progressed, so the carts of carriers and carters began to serve the community taking country produce to towns and bringing back goods unobtainable in rural areas, just as Maggie Gillanders was doing many years later. There was also a class of these men known as cadgers who mainly took minerals — silver, tin, copper and especially lead and slates, but who by the end of the nineteenth century had become primarily fish salesmen.[30]

A Dumfries-shire minister, Rev James Fraser, said, ' . . . without carriers, I do not know how people would have secured the necessaries of life. They were an excellent and most useful class of men'.[31] An instance of how useful they were appears in the *New Statistical Account for Smailholm, Roxburghshire*, which said, 'An Earlstown carrier regularly attends at Smailholm on Monday afternoons for the purpose of procuring eggs, butter, poultry for the Edinburgh market, which is a great advantage to the village and neighbourhood'.[32] He gave country people a better market for their produce than they would otherwise have had and townspeople benefitted from a regular supply of fresh food. In cases like this, the carrier acted as a merchant, paying for goods on the spot and taking them to the nearest large town — with the hens in coops with their necks stretched out through the bars, 'to hae the view' as one carrier put it[33] — where he sold them on his own account. Some carriers obtained their produce by their own physical efforts such as mussel-sellers who brought a regular supply to towns from the sea shores nearby.[34] Town and country were interdependent and the carrier and his cart were a vital link between them, as *New Statistical Accounts* from all round the country make very clear.

Charges for carrying goods varied but at the time of the *New Statistical Accounts*, the mid-nineteenth century, the cost of carrying goods approximately 40 miles to Edinburgh was 2s. per cwt. In addition, and very importantly, people travelled by carrier's cart and were doing so well into this century. Even when such a cart was loaded with goods, there was room to pile a few people on top and passengers, usually women, even for a long journey found themselves perched on top of a heavily laden cart.[35] For those unable to afford other public transport or where it was not in any case available, this was the only mode of conveyance and the ordinary people just had to make the best of it. There is a story of a young woman living in Dumfries-shire who had to go to hospital in Edinburgh in 1821 to have a growth removed from her cheek bone. She made the journey by carrier's cart, taking two days for the trip, jolting along the roads in intense pain the whole time but there was no alternative and she survived to a good age and liked to tell this story.[36] More comfort could be available in something like a slate cart. Carriers who did a one-way traffic in specific goods like this were only too glad to carry passengers when returning. This happened between Langholm and Annan Water Foot in Dumfries-shire and passengers made the 20-odd mile journey sitting on a fairly narrow bar along the side of the cart. It was entirely at the whim of the carrier if he chose to provide hay or straw to sit on but at a charge of only 1s. for the whole journey no one could expect too much.[37]

The various customs and dues imposed in burghs have been mentioned already and burgh councils kept a close eye on carriers to prevent any evasions such as the way in which carters brought wine up from Leith to Edinburgh at 'unseasonable hours' and by a variety of routes 'to the great prejudice of the imposition office'. This was in 1667 and as a result the Burgh Council of Edinburgh forbade them to enter the city except within half an hour before sunrise and half an hour after sunset and confined them to a choice of only two routes.[38]

For long journeys it was sometimes inevitable that a carrier was on the road on a Sunday but often there was no need for it apart from commercial enthusiasm. This met with great disapproval from both burgh and Church and in 1752 the Synod of Aberdeen took steps 'to suppress the scandalous custom of carriers travelling on the Lord's Day with loaded carts, wagons and other carriages, to and from Aberdeen, Banff etc.'[39] Travelling on a fast day was another sin, one difficult to avoid as fast days fell during the week. In 1719 four Lanark carriers were called before the Bailies and Council for setting out on a fast day, two to Edinburgh and two to Glasgow, and each fined 20s. Scots and ordered to be kept in ward until the fine was paid.[40]

Although the average speed of a carrier's cart was 4 mph, going slow was not inevitable. In 1673 the Burgh of Edinburgh had to appoint a special committee to consider what to do about the furious driving of carts, and coaches, through the streets.[41] A table in the Notes to the *New Statistical Account for East Lothian* in 1836 shows a total of one hundred and sixty-two minor offences committed by males, covering everything from allowing pigs to stray on streets, deforcing sheriff-officers, fraud and imposition, destroying tombstones, poaching, drunkenness and riot, and others besides. Of these one hundred and sixty-two, there were twenty-seven cases of furious driving, eight of leaving carts unattended and one of not confining a dog to a cart, a surprisingly high figure of some 22 per cent for transport offences.[42] East Lothian was one of the few counties which was zealous in enforcing carting regulations including one which forbade the driver of a cart to lie down in it because of the danger of falling asleep with all the obvious risks that that entailed.[43] In 1803 two carriers appeared in court in Kelso, Roxburghshire, for galloping their carts abreast along a road so that two men in a gig were forced into a field to avoid them. One was fined 30s. because it was his second offence, the other 10s. and both were ordered to spend a month in Bridewell also.[44] One can only assume that they had been having a race, perhaps with a bet on the result to help them on. In other cases, far from being able to race, carriers' horses needed a helping hand and one man in Kilsyth, Stirlingshire, made a living by providing trace horses to get them up a particularly steep hill.[45].

Good though most carters were, they had a tendency to drink too much. On trips taking several days they stayed at inns or whisky houses and on short trips, too, it was unavoidable that they should call at these places to eat and drink with colleagues and rivals, as well as with pedlars and packmen, and press reports have various references to carriers appearing in court charged with being drunk and disorderly. But no carrier's business could have survived successfully with too much of that sort of conduct. A carrier had to be as regular as possible in his goings and comings; he had to call when he said he would at farms and houses where he expected business, and having got to his destination, he had to arrange return loads, carry out any commissions given him by customers and collect goods ordered by them, and once he got home there would be deliveries to be made next day. The lobby of the home of a carrier called John Gowdie, who travelled between the Borders and Edinburgh, was more like a grocer's shop than a private house. It was always stacked with hams, cheeses, barrels of herrings and bundles of dried fish and much else besides, ready for delivery in one direction or the other.[46]

Many carriers were characters, just as packmen were. There was one particularly difficult man, Rab the Carrier, who like John Gowdie lived in the Borders. On one occasion he carried a chest for someone, having first of all suggested that they could perfectly well take it themselves; he then forgot to deliver it but had the nerve to demand double carriage. However, his mean nature was his undoing. He steadfastly refused to repair the ramshackle building in which he lived above and his horse below, with the result that it collapsed in a storm, killing both of them.[47] However, the picture of carriers is, in general, one of kindly men, epitomised in the account by Anne Thomson in the *Border Magazine* of the red-letter day of the week, Saturday, when the carrier's cart paid its weekly visit. This was perhaps more of a travelling shop but in any event, when their mother had finished her transactions the children waited with bated breath to see if the carrier would say, as he always did, 'Would anyone like a hurl up to the Rig?' and they would be up and into the cart before he finished speaking. 'Oh, let him go slow,' they inwardly prayed, 'or it will be over in a minute', and as they ran home from the Rig they longed for the next visit of this good-natured man.[48]

Two other forms of carrier's business were the milk cart, taking milk from farms round villages and towns, and the travelling shop, a horse-drawn van, sent round country districts by town or village shops. Anyone lucky enough to find the account books in which the customers' accounts were kept — and

41   W B Firth's shop van from Stenness, on the Back Road, Stromness. These
     travelling shops served the country districts from the late nineteenth
     century (c.1900–1910). Photograph by R H Robertson. Source: Orkney
                              Library.

everyone ran accounts — will discover a rich source of social history. Those
of Gordon's Stores in Fearn, Ross-shire, for the first decade of this century,
list the names and occupations of virtually everyone in every farm and house
in a wide area and show the different life styles in different categories of
household: baking soda, a little tobacco and snuff for the common people,
and lots of starch and blacklead for the manse, as well as a weekly gigot of
mutton. Such vans might do a little unofficial carrying too, by way of a good
turn, as appears in a letter to the miller at Milton, Ross-shire, about 1904–6:[49]

Barbaraville Delny.

Mr Ross,

Dear Sir,
    If your van won't be coming this way soon would you please give the butcher
1 firlot oat meal as I am quite done. And the first time you come please bring
1 firlot of the cheapest flour, and oblige,
                                        Your Sincerely,
                                        B. Mackay, Brewer.

The carrier's cart was a link between a rural area and a coach service and
when railways opened, it provided a similar service for them and in many

areas carrier and railway co-existed and complemented one another. To give two examples — using the carrier's cart to get to the railway station and then going further by train could greatly increase a fishwife's travelling range, thereby enlarging her market and bringing a supply of fresh fish to places previously without it; and the carrier's cart got plenty of work from the railway delivering coal from station to households. But it was quite different for carriers who operated between towns which came to be served by a railway, giving a much faster daily service than they could. Carriers on such routes found their livelihoods gone, although one from Lilliesleaf, Roxburghshire, fondly thought that he could compete with the railway by increasing his trips to Edinburgh from one a week to two, but he had not appreciated the type of competition he was up against.[50] By the end of the nineteenth century only two carriers waited in a market in Edinburgh's High Street where before the railway opened there would have been thirty.[51] An extreme reaction to the loss of a carrier's business was the case of John Gowdie, the man whose lobby was always full of goods. He thought of trying general carting in connection with the railway but found that the railway company had its own vans and horses for this work and, as life had no more meaning for him, he took to his bed and died within the week.[52] So far as the rural carrier was concerned it was not until motor transport was well established, with country buses and motor vans, that the death-knell was sounded for him.

14 HUMAN BEASTS OF BURDEN

In every district of Scotland where men had neither servants nor animals, their women folk were used in their place. When Thomas Pennant got to Caithness on his Scottish travels in the second half of the eighteenth century, he was appalled to find not a single cart and the women carrying dung out to the fields in creels on their backs. He saw them standing patiently at dunghills for the men to fork in as much as they thought fit and then saw them trudging away with their loads, although these creels did at least have bottoms which opened to let the dung fall out which saved the women having to sling them off their backs on every trip. Pennant said that he blushed for Caithness men that they could let their women work in this way,[1] but from end to end of Scotland this was common practice. Women did the heavy work — in places they also pulled the harrows[2] — and it was often more economical for a crofter to marry than to buy a pony. A wife could carry almost as much as the pony and could use her hands at the same time — knitting, for instance, or spinning on the distaff, and could do all the drudgery of home and croft also; all this saved feeding a beast. Even where there were horses to carry dung, women were still required to lead them although it was said that when the women ultimately stopped doing this work and took up home industries like knitting stockings, presumably inside poor, damp, dark cottages, they seemed less vigorous and healthy.[3] Surely there could have been a happy medium.

There was no standard of design for human-borne creels, just plain common sense applied to what was needed and what materials were available, but there was pride in their making and the *New Statistical Account for Kilmuir, Skye*, particularly mentions the beautiful plaiting of bulrushes to make what were called 'plats'.[4] Carrying home peat in creels was another job for women, especially when nothing but human transport could get to the peat moss. This was very arduous work. The minister of Lochbroom, Ross-shire, felt strongly about it and wished very much that there were some sort of cottage industry which would enable the women to earn enough to buy coal 'instead of degrading their persons and often losing their lives, by carrying peats upon their backs from almost exhausted mosses inaccessible to horses or to carts'.[5]

While a supply of coal could be of great help to women in rural areas, its

42   Peat carriers, Shetland. Photograph C J Williamson.

production was a great burden to those involved in it. Many abuses occurred in coal pits where what went on was not seen by outsiders and in them not only women, but children too, were employed as bearers to carry coal on their backs up from the pit face to the surface. At most pits there were traps or stairs, with a hand rail, to help them, and a 'diligent bearer' could bring up about 6 chalders or 9 tons a week, for which they were paid, in the late eighteenth century, 4d. per chalder of 30 cwts.[6] These human beasts of burden seem to have been not only hard-working but to have taken a pride in how much they could carry and it was said that although 1–2 cwts was the usual load, in a trial of strength some could manage 3 cwts. Even a lame woman is recorded as having carried a single piece of coal weighing 2 cwts up from a pit 12 fathoms deep; and another carried a piece of coal weighing 4 cwts the 400 yards from the pit mouth to the overseer's house.[7] This saved the pit owner the expense of using horse- or water-operated gins to raise the coal although, where the pit was over 18 fathoms (108 feet) deep, these machines had to be used.[8] By about 1810 the practice of using women in coal pits in this way had stopped and the result was a marked improvement in their domestic lives.[9]

About the first half of the eighteenth century, when the demand for vegetables had increased tenfold in Edinburgh, the city was supplied with garden produce from Fisherrow and Musselburgh where the soil suited early crops. This produce, as well as sand for cleaning floors and also salt, was carried there in creels or baskets by women who did not return empty-handed but brought back either messages for neighbours or dirty linen to be washed in the clean water of the River Esk. These women were usually the wives of weavers, shoemakers, tailors or seive-wrights who worked at home and could take charge of the family while the women were occupied in this way. The minister who wrote about this in the *Statistical Account for Inveresk* was one of the few of his contemporaries who seemed concerned that women should work in this way but he made the interesting point that they had a 'free, social and disengaged life' and could mostly earn between 8*d.* and 1*s.* 3*d.* per day which was a greater contribution to the family budget than they could have made in any other way. The most hard-worked of this group were the sand carriers, who also earned the least. They carried not less than 200 lbs every morning into town and returned about midday to spend the afternoon and evening in the quarry digging stone and beating it to sand, for which they earned about 5*d.* a day, working six days a week. Although this report only refers to Edinburgh, inevitably similar work was being done by women to service other towns throughout the country.[10]

'No man can be a fisher and want a wife,' is a well-known and very true statement. Not only did fisher women gather bait and bring it home in creels — and suitable bait might only be found at a distance of several miles — they then, having baited the lines, carried the men out to boats lying off in the sea so that, it was said, they should not get wet at the start of their fishing. But a photograph of the Banff-shire coast shows women carrying men out of the boats too, something which was conveniently attributed to the fact that the men's long leather boots would go crinkly if they got wet. If they carried the men out of the boats, it is obvious that they carried the catch out too. All this carrying was done by hitching up their skirts as high as necessary, decent or not, and explains why the question often asked by a young fisherman's mother about a prospective daughter-in-law was, 'Can she bear my son's weight?' In addition, those fishermen's wives who were also fishwives — preparers and sellers of fish — carried creels of fish home and, having dealt with them, which included smoking a certain amount, carried them for sale round the countryside and into towns. They are remembered as carrying at least 1 cwt on their backs and usually more in hand baskets but it is said that on one occasion at the end of the eighteenth century, three fishwives went the 27 miles from Dunbar to Edinburgh in 5 hours, each carrying 200 lbs of herring, and that it was not unknown for them to carry 250 lbs. Should the boats come in later than usual the women sometimes used a relay system to carry fish in to town so as to catch the morning trade. This was done between

43 Buckie coast — women carrying men from fishing boat to shore.

Inveresk and Edinburgh where three women could carry one basket between them, changing it over every 100 yards, and do the 5-mile journey in under three-quarters of an hour.[11] These were strong, tough women with a desperate determination to earn all they could for their families' sakes; one, Janey Inglis, from Ferryden, Angus, actually fell under the load she insisted on taking because the catch had been so good.[12] This direct selling of fish, the avoidance of middlemen and adding value by smoking some of it, was very worthwhile and so the women did these journeys several days a week, even three or four days after childbirth. They spent the other days smoking fish, doing the washing, tending the potato rig, with never a minute's rest until Sunday. The introduction of the carrier's cart and the railway made a difference to their lives certainly, but they did not reduce the distance they carried their loads, they merely extended the area they could cover. Fishwives were disappointed if they did not bring home a creel as full as when they set out, possibly containing farm produce bartered for fish, firewood gathered on the way or fir cones for smoking. If they knew of anywhere that whins had been burnt by gamekeepers, they went and gathered them using not a creel, but a 'chower' or rope with an iron ring at one end to make a loop to hitch them into a bundle for the journey home.

Gypsies and tinkers were another group where the women did the carrying and selling of family produce. Their menfolk were very indolent but the women hawked their wares from door to door with great determination, although they had the benefit of a cart not far away to carry them between farms and homesteads and the consolation that their wares did not weigh as heavily as wet fish.

Until water was piped into houses, both country women and townswomen had the heavy and constant job of carrying water from the well or standpipe to the house, often using a wooden frame called a gird which they stood inside and used to hold the pails out from their legs so that they did not lose water by splashing. Getting water could involve a long walk and it could also take an inordinate amount of time should the supply of water be reduced for any cause, such as a well filling slowly when too many people came at once.

Carrying a heavy load on dry land or through the sea to land was no light task but what must have been far worse was carrying such loads across rivers, with slippery uneven stones underfoot and water up to the waist. Women used to wade the River Tweed at Kelso to take their washing to bleach on the Anna at the other side, a remarkable example of domestic standards, and in Inverness, where the toll of 1d. to cross the bridge was quite beyond the pockets of the poor, their only way was to take to the river. Before a bridge was built at Annan about 1705, women crossed the river there, at times just carrying loads but when there was a fair they acted as ford women and bore on their backs anyone who wished to cross dry-shod.[13]

What is astonishing is just how much of this work women were prepared

45 Laird of Dundas's henwife, using a gird. Source: Scottish Ethnological Archive, Royal Museum of Scotland.

44 Fishwife from Seaboard Villages, Ross-shire, carrying a creel.

46 Woman using a yoke to carry water barrels. Source: Scottish Ethnological
Archive, Royal Museum of Scotland.

to do to help their families. As pregnancy was virtually a perpetual condition
for married women, their efforts are all the more remarkable and the fact that
they would carry loads for employers too for a pitiful reward is a commentary
on their devotion and courage as well as on the times. It is said that when
Murdo Lowe, an Orkney merchant, brought meal in to a geo near the Smoo
Cave, Durness, in Sutherland, in the 1690s, local women carried it up the cliff
path, a boll of 140 lbs each time, for nothing more than an oatmeal biscuit.[14]
In a very small way, carrying articles in creels still goes on in the north and
west of Scotland but it is now voluntary and for convenience sake, rather than
done by necessity.[15]

Men did not usually carry such burdens although when James Hogg got to
Lochbroom on the west coast of Ross-shire on his travels about 1802, he
wrote that they were received by Dundonnell who had 'the pleasure of
absolute sway. He is even more so in his domains than Bonaparte is in France.
I saw him call two men from their labour a full mile, to carry us through the
water. I told him he must not expect to be served thus by the shepherds if once
he had given them possession'.[16] Highland ghillies were, in fact, about the
only group of men prepared to do such a thing.

There were other aspects of transport that women undertook, apart from
actual carrying. Should necessity arise, they sometimes got involved in
regular ferry work. When a ferryman at Kessock, Inverness, died in the late
nineteenth century, his wife, faced with the prospect of having to give up the
ferry house, undertook to row the ferryboat in his place and did so for years.

These examples of women's work in transport make some other instances seem positively easy. Women became post-runners and in the course of their working lives covered surprising distances, in all weathers, but at least not carrying such excessive weights as those mentioned and with the knowledge that they would be paid a regular wage. Some were notable characters. One such was Jean Elliot, known as Lucie Lass, a post-woman in the Borders. She must have been a conspicuous figure, with a weather-beaten, wrinkled face, small piercing eyes under shaggy brows, her short white hair always uncovered, and dressed in a drugget skirt, a man's coat, shepherd's plaid and Wellington boots. She could neither read nor write and was considered to be not entirely all there but she always expected a seat in the parlour rather than the kitchen and got it too, partly because she was related to some of the better families and partly because of her flair for discovering skeletons in people's cupboards and letting it be known that she would pass on the facts if anyone offended her.[17] One post-woman took on her late husband's job when widowed in 1878, just as the ferry-woman had done, in order to keep the house. For thirty years she walked her route of some 12 miles a day and was only off work sick for fourteen days in all that time.[18] Some post-women had a donkey and cart like old Lizzie Douglas in Rulewater, Roxburghshire.[19] Other women operated a light carrier's business, taking parcels and seeing to people's errands for them in town.[20] As already said, many women who were married to hawkers and pedlars travelled with them and it is likely that their husbands did not take them along for the ride but to do their bit.

A form of human-borne short-distance transport was the carrying of sedan chairs and this was something that did fall to men. The sedan chair was rather like a mobile sentry-box, often covered on the outside with black leather, with a seat inside for one person to sit on in reasonable comfort.[21] It was supported and carried by two long poles, with a bearer at either end, with straps from the shoulders to the poles to help to take the weight. Although not always used in this way, a sedan chair had one particular convenience: it could be taken right into a house where the intending passenger could get in, dressed for any occasion, and then step out at the destination without needing any further attention to his or her appearance. These chairs were carried at a semi-trot, a motion which was said to be not unpleasant.[22] Highlanders were thought to be particularly good bearers, much better than the Irish chairmen of London, and it is said that enough men from the North of Scotland were employed to justify the holding of Gaelic church services for them in Edinburgh. Fares were reasonable and these chairs were in general very popular and particularly well-suited to narrow streets where other vehicles could not go. The first public one became available in the late seventeenth century, and by 1788/9 there were 118 hackney chairs in Edinburgh in addition to about fifty privately owned ones. Ready availability of a chair for hire depended on the type and size of a town; in Edinburgh it was said that a chair could be got at a moment's notice, day or night,[23] whereas in a town like Ayr they had to be booked in good time.[24] Sedan chairs were an accepted and respectable way for a woman on her own to travel short distances but one hazard appeared in the early hours of New Year's Day when the custom of 'kissing for luck' meant that any woman could be kissed by any man, even should she be in a chair or carriage, a tradition which she was expected to submit to with a good grace.[25] Both men and women used sedan chairs although with women, they seem to have been more in demand in large towns than in small ones and when two were bought for Elgin about 1812 'for conveying ladies to evening parties' it was found that they were not much used.[26] They were occasionally found in the country — the dropsical Baron David Ross, last Baron of Balnagown in Ross-shire, who died in the early eighteenth century, was frequently carried in one from Balnagown Castle to Logie Church for Sunday worship. An unusual use of a sedan chair appears in a story told of a Scottish judge, Lord Monboddo, who made use of a chair for only one thing and that was to keep his wig dry in wet weather. It sat in state on the seat and was borne home while he walked alongside in the rain.[27] This somewhat exclusive form of transport had died out by the mid nineteenth century.

15 CHURCH AND SCHOOL ATTENDANCE

One of the Church's major involvements with transport was to do with bridges, which has already been described. A sidelight on water crossings or, rather, lack of them, appeared in complaints made in 1677 to a Presbytery meeting that Rev Robert Munro was not attending properly to his duties in Glenmoriston, Inverness-shire, his excuse being that not only was there no church building there, neither was there a bridge over the river nor a boat to take him across.[1] He had no intention of getting wet in the execution of his duties, yet it was not unknown for parishioners to get soaked crossing rivers to get to church. The *New Statistical Account for Applecross, Ross-shire*, said that some of the congregation living on the far side of an unbridged river often 'wade the water, and sit in church during service with wet feet and clothes which no doubt occasions many serious complaints among them.'[2] When conditions were already so difficult for people, the fact that many lacked suitable or adequate clothing did not help.[3]

Water crossings were only one of the difficulties in the way of church attendance. Others were lack of roads, the impassability of the country in bad weather and sheer distance. Many parishes, especially in the north and west, were very large and no one building could serve them properly. In 1645, for instance, the people of Kells and Dalry, Ayrshire, felt constrained to make a supplication to Parliament saying that the parish church was so remote that not only were they 'defrauded of the comfort of the Word and benefit of the Sacraments' but that many poor people were buried in the fields because they had no one to carry their bodies the 12 miles to the graveyard.[4] In the parish of Rogart, Sutherland, 'Some of the parishioners travel ten miles in coming to hear sermon; which, being doubled before they return to their homes, is a severe exertion, though it be cheerfully made, even in the short days of winter. The distance of parishioners from the manse is also productive of much trouble and inconvenience to them. Having few besides their minister whom they consult, various and often are the occasions which oblige them to travel from their places of residence to his'.[5] In the hilly parish of Creich, Sutherland, the church lay near the sea, 9 miles from the eastern boundary and over 30 from the western. Across the Kyle of Shin from Creich, in the parish of Kincardine,

Ross-shire, the church was also close to the shore and 34 miles from the farthest part. The church at Portree in Skye was 15 miles from the southern boundary which, although a smaller distance than the others quoted, still made it inaccessible to the great part of the people, and at Weem, Perthshire, though the church was convenient for much of the population it was a distance of 20–30 miles for some. Even in a moderately sized parish the church was often badly situated so that the journey to it took far longer than it might have taken. The position of parish churches seems to have originated with the division of the country into parishes by Alexander I (1107–24) and David I (1124–53). Norman and Saxon nobles who came to Scotland with grants of land from these two kings brought with them the custom of dedicating a piece of land for religious purposes and it became common for the laird or lord to build a church or chapel on his property for himself, his household and his people, and to gift it to some religious foundation. Where several of these churches or chapels existed in one parish, ultimately that of the most important landowner became the parish church and churchyard, whether or not this was convenient to the local people. In addition, centres of population could shift and so make a once-convenient church more difficult of access.

The problems of getting to church were partly solved as time went on by bringing the church to the people with the establishment of outlying preaching stations visited by the minister at intervals. In the mid-nineteenth century, in Assynt, Sutherland, the minister in addition to preaching in his own church was required to visit two different stations about 14 miles away. One had a road to it and a General Assembly school building in which to hold services and here he went every three weeks; the other had neither access road nor building, and preaching had to be done in the open air, every six to seven weeks, whatever the weather[6] — no excuses for him such as were given by Rev Robert Munro in Glenmoriston. At Balfron, Stirlingshire, the minister preached every six weeks in a school house 5 miles from the church; in summer he could do this after Sunday worship in the church but in winter it meant that that church could have no service on the days he went to the school house.[7] In the Shetland parish of Walls there were four churches and only one minister and services had to be held in rotation in the different churches — in Walls every fortnight, in Sandness once in four weeks, both of these being on the mainland; in the island of Papa Stour once every four weeks and occasionally in summer every fortnight. The island of Foula was visited once a year, when the minister stayed for a fortnight, preaching frequently during that time, but leaving three empty churches while he was there.[8] At the time described, about the 1840s, this way of filling the pulpit was worthy of mention but with the many linkings and unions of churches in modern times, it would be nothing out of the ordinary.

In some areas, such as North Uist, even outlying preaching stations were not practical. 'It is impossible that one clergyman, however assiduous he may be in the discharge of his duty, can be equal to the task of instructing in the principles of religion, such a multitude of people dispersed over a great tract of country, many of them in situations so discontinuous to the places of worship that they hardly have an opportunity of hearing the Word of God preached once in the twelvemonth.'[9] So said the minister and it was a problem that could only be solved by the appointment of missionaries to serve outlying areas and very difficult their work could be, as the following instances show. In Halkirk, Caithness, there was 'committed to the pastoral superintendence of a missionary a boundary, the extremes of which, by a practical road, are from 40–50 miles from each other. The distance is the least of the obstructions in his way. There are moors, mosses and quaking fens which disjoin one valley from another and which make it impossible, except by circuitous routes, to pass from glen to glen during the winter and spring months'.[10] At Kilmallie, Inverness-shire, there was a missionary for some time but the four stations assigned to him were so far apart and some of them so difficult to get to, as to make his labours not only difficult but of less value than they might have been for the people and in the end the unfortunate man had to give up his work on the ground of ill health.[11]

So much did church-going matter to people that parishioners were prepared to do what they could to help provide churches. In 1836, one hundred and three heads of families in the southern part of the parish of Lonmay, Aberdeenshire, petitioned the Presbytery of Deer about their 'grievous disadvantage of want of opportunities for public worship and of adequate pastoral superintendence, because of their distance from the parish church', and four hundred and sixteen people in Lonmay as well as sixty other families who could not get to their own church co-operated in organizing a subscription to put up a building which, with help from the Church Extension Committee, was ultimately erected.[12] A church was built by subscription at Lybster, Caithness, where heritors and people both in and out of the county joined in 'a favourite measure in which all felt interested'.[13] Chapels of ease were also built by the church authorities and at Kilconquhar, Fife, the people raised a subscription to pay a preacher to live in the district and officiate regularly in the chapel.[14] In the early nineteenth century the Government took a hand and built what were known as Government or Parliamentary churches such as at Croick, Ross-shire; Rannoch and Glenlyon, Perthshire; and Tomintoul, Banffshire; all of which were later erected by the General Assembly into quoad sacra parishes, that is, an ecclesiastical parish within a civil one.

On top of the distances ministers had to travel in connection with parish work, there were Presbytery meetings to attend which, particularly in the Highlands, could involve cross-country journeys on horseback of up to 70 miles. Synod meetings could require even longer journeys, as much as 200 miles both ways, and worst of all were Presbytery visitations to west coast parishes when the travelling time might run into days or even weeks. The Kirk Session of Craig, Angus, met in 1732 to consider 'the many inconveniencys to which the minister and people of this parish are exposed when called to attend the Reverend Presbyterie, by reason of the considerable distance of this place from, as also the badness of the road to Brechin, the place of the Presby's meeting for ordinary; by which several affairs and concerns of this parish which ought to be advised with, or determined by the Presby may come to be neglected'. The records of Presbytery meetings often refer to the brethren being prevented from attending due to weather conditions such as 'spaitts of watter' which are mentioned in Fordyce Presbytery minutes, Banff-shire, in 1629 as well as 'raine and extraordinaire spaitts' there in 1657.[15] One writer on Highland affairs lists some of the excuses for absence produced by ministers unable, or unwilling, to attend Presbytery meetings: 'This is my marriage day'; 'My child is at the point of death'; 'I am tormented with the worm'; 'I have taken physic'; 'I am tender and not able to travel'; 'My horse fell under me and I cannot ride'; 'My horse has been stolen'.[16] In the very first years of the eighteenth century all schoolmasters were required to sign the Confession of Faith and it was as difficult for them to get to the Presbytery seat to do so as it was for ministers and elders to get there, a difficulty which was appreciated by the Church authorities as the following entry from the records of the Presbytery of Strathbogie, Aberdeenshire, show: '1703. The other schoolmasters within the bounds of this Presbyterie pleading the great difficulty in travelling in the winter season to attend the meetings of Presbyterie, the further calling of them was delayed till the summer season.' It was also very hard for delinquents who were delated to appear before Presbyteries to get to their meetings. Even those summoned to appear before the Kirk Session of a parish in which they had offended, might well by then have left it to work elsewhere and could find the journey back almost impossible, although they were often allowed to wait until the May or November terms so as to give them a little more travelling time.

Baptism of children was often very difficult too. In many areas there was no way in which a child could be taken to church and the parents had to wait until the minster came to catechise the family, when he would also baptise all requiring this sacrament. Records show that up to four children in one family might be baptised on the same day, an indication of how infrequently some ministers made rounds of outlying areas. Not only did people fear that an unbaptised child might be taken by the fairies but it was believed that without baptism, there could be no salvation and in the event of the death of an unbaptised child, it was buried hastily and almost secretly, and never inside the churchyard, and the possibility of such a thing happening led to great anxiety in parents. Not all ministers were so obliging as that of the Relief Congregation in Duns, Berwickshire, who, when a coach service began between there and Greenlaw, came by it to Greenlaw and during the changing of the horses, administered baptism to those needing it in the house of one of his flock who lived in that town.[17]

There were other aspects of transport and travel with which the Church of Scotland became involved and a considerable amount of money was spent on them by Kirk Sessions. Their records have many references to help given to travellers and poor strangers, generous help too, which may seem surprising when they had very limited funds but, as parishes were responsible for the poor within their bounds, their one idea was to speed the departure of all those not actually belonging to the parish, by helping them on their way and, if possible, back to their parish of origin where they would be entitled to relief. The Kirk Session of Bonkle and Preston, Berwickshire, gave considerable help in this way:

1669. '6s. given to Cathirin Stewart, a poor distrest travelling woman.'
1673. '6s. 4d. given to a poor travelling stranger.'
1674. '8s. to a poore traveler.'
1688. Money was given to 'a poor lame stranger' recommended by the Archbishop and Synod of Glasgow and to a 'poor distempered stranger'.
1689. 'To four poore people, pretending they had fled from Ireland. . . .'
'To Charles Williamson, a poor blind man come from Galloway. . . .'
'12s. given to Andrew Scott and John Strachan, two honest men from Ireland.'
'To a distrest gentleman from Ireland and his wife and children. . . .'
14s. given 'to an honest gentleman come from Ireland being recommended by the Moderator of the Presbytery'.

The Kirk Session of Lilliesleaf, Roxburghshire, gave 'to four women comed from Ireland and also many children with them, 24s.' in 1650 — this was a time of great distress in Ireland — while in 1610 the Kirk Session of Aberdeen have a minute saying, 'Gewin to ane Dutch woman to helpe hir and hir barneis hameward. . . .' Coldingham Kirk Session, Berwickshire, gave money 'for the relief of a poor passenger on the road to England' and to 'a stranger, recommended to Christian compassion, being upon the road for England, her husband being in Flanders', as well as to 'an honest distressed Englishman, who being upon the road has lost his money'. Alyth Kirk Session, Perthshire, gave money to, among others, 'ane travelling blind man' and to 'Irish fugitives' who got no less than 56 merks. While such financial contributions could enable these strangers to move on, there were also cases where actual transport was provided: Bonkle and Preston, 1686 — 'There was likewise given 8s. Scots to Jean Guthrie, a poor creeple gentlewoman recommended by the Ministers of Edinburgh, and likewise 4s. Scots was given to James Montgomery to transport her on his horse to St. Bothans'. West Kilbride, Ayrshire, Kirk Session records have this entry for 1789, 'To

Robert Scott for taking a poor cripple to Largs, who came here on a carrier's cart from Saltcoats, who had nothing but his knees to walk upon, 1s.'; and in 1791, 'To a carrier to take up a poor, insane person who will not walk to Largs, who came with a carrier to this place from Saltcoats to carry her from one place to another, till she arrived to her parish or to some place where she is known, 3s. 6d.'. Not only was transport provided for this poor woman but an element of care too as 1s. was paid to James Fullarton 'for keeping the poor object above all night, who was sent back from Largs to be sent to Saltcoats, they sat up with her all night. Gave her before she went away some punch, 1s.'. It is not clear if the following entry refers to the same woman but a mere six days later a payment was made to Francis Tarbert 'for taking down the poor dying woman to Saltcoats, but he says he must have more'. In 1802 this church paid a man 'for conveyance for a lame woman to Largs, with horse and cart',[18] while the Angus parish of Auchterhouse paid, 'to Walter Kinnaird, a paralytick supplicant 10d. To horse hire for carrying him to the next parish 4d.', and in Ashkirk, Selkirkshire, 6s. was given 'for hyreing a horse to carry a crople to Roberton' in 1702. Burgh Councils sometimes helped with this sort of transport too — the accounts of Peebles show a charge of 5s. 'for taking away ane crippil boy callit Blackstokis tua several tymes'.[19]

Churches not only gave help with transport to strangers but to their own parishioners too. In 1780, for instance, the parish of Tarbat, Ross-shire, gave £3. 18s. to a woman 'to support the expense of her going to Aberdeen to be cutt of a cancer in her breast', and in 1763 a man in Melrose, Roxburghshire, was given 16s. by his Kirk Session to enable him to carry his wife to Edinburgh Infirmary, while the church in West Kilbride ordered a public collection to pay for a man to go to Moffat Wells in search of a cure for King's Evil.

In their sincere efforts to help the sick poor, Kirk Sessions were responsible for what nowadays sounds a very degrading type of transport but which, if one thinks about it, was really the fore-runner of the wheelchair or even the pram. Ashkirk Kirk Session's records for 1702 show the following, 'Given to buy a barrow to John Veitch, orphan, he now having losed the use of his legs'. It used to be the custom for parishes to give their own poor begging licences and it made good sense to provide the handicapped poor with this simple form of transport so that they could be moved around and solicit alms as they went. This continued into the nineteenth century. The unfortunate person had to find someone to push him to, possibly, a farm house and there he was left in his barrow in the sure knowledge that he would be fed and that someone would make sure that he was pushed along to the next farm as quickly as possible; and so he kept making the rounds of the parish and was self-supporting. The fact that John Veitch died the month after getting his barrow shows that great infirmity was no barrier to this sort of parish care. It seems that poor from other parishes might appear in barrows and in A Thomson's *Lauder and Lauderdale*, it is recorded that there was so much

47 A beggar being transported by wheel-barrow. Drawing by Anne Carrick.

inconvenience in the town of Lauder 'from the frequency of lame beggars being carried about the street in hand-barrows' that the Sheriff Officer was authorised to convey them out of the parish at the expense of the heritors.

Kirk Sessions were nothing if not practical and one way in which they might help a poor man was to buy him a horse so that he might earn a living as a carrier and so not be a burden on the parish. An example of this was at Colinsburgh, Fife, where over the years sums varying from £12 to £18 Scots were spent on this. Here practicality also extended to members of the Session — when an elder lost his horse and could not afford another, the Session bought him one but stipulated that it should remain their property.[20]

A church congregation might be called on to provide money for the repair of a local road, such as the Kirk Street in Dingwall, Ross-shire,[21] but as has already been said, the Church of Scotland was the only national organisation which could be used for large-scale fund-raising and voluntary collections were ordered not only for bridges but for a variety of public works all round the country, continuing a tradition begun by the Roman Catholic Church as when the Abbot of Arbroath and the people of that town joined forces to build a pier or harbour, with the Abbot paying the greater share in return for a yearly tax on every rood of land in the burgh.[22] The Presbyterian Church, however, got nothing in return for the money it co-operated in raising on behalf of causes such as a road over Lochar Moss, Dumfries-shire, and harbours at Anstruther, Burntisland, Dundee, Eyemouth, Roseheartie,

Cullen, Elie, Banff, Aberdeen and St Andrews. There were also appeals for such things as bulwarks at Peterhead, Stonehaven and Dundee, and however remote they might be, they were all supported, and much more besides.

As to schools, although John Knox's idea of a school in every parish was admirable, what he envisaged was one school only, which did not allow for the sheer size of some parishes, nor for their physical characteristics and lack of roads and bridges. The same problems which affected church-going also affected school attendance. The length of the journey to school was a constant difficulty, made clear in this extract from the school log book of Nigg, Ross-shire, in March 1895: 'Strenuous efforts being made to overcome the dullness and drowsiness which pervade a large number of the children. The distance which fully 50% of the children have to travel to school is no doubt a cause of weariness and lack of brightness, as many of the infants seem from time to time to be pretty well exhausted before the close of the day's work and when they arrive at school in the morning are not always in a fit state to receive instruction.' Even in 1926, three children at this school were at the age of five 'not strong enough to walk the distance to school', although this implies that these children could at least get to school. In many other places they could not. In Moy and Dalarossie, Inverness-shire, the parish was 'so extensive that only a very inconsiderable part of them [children] can be accommodated at the parish school'.[23] At the end of the eighteenth century there was no parish school on the island of Unst, Shetland, one reason being that the population was so scattered that very few children could have attended anyway.[24] About the same date, in the parish of Eddrachillis, Sutherland, there was a school but distance and the lack of anywhere that children might board to attend it, made it impossible for it to be of general benefit;[25] in Gairloch, Ross-shire, the parish was so large that although there was a school the 'rising generation suffer much and are wholly neglected, having no access to the benefit of instruction'.[26] In Portree, Skye, two districts of the parish were so remote that education was impossible for the children although there were fifty children in one area and between sixty and one hundred in the other, who might all attend.[27] The difficulties of some children in Glenelg, on the west coast of Inverness-shire, at the same time, were even worse. There was a school at a place where two hundred children could get to it but it was 14 miles from the district of Arnisdale, 18 from Knoydart with a ferry in between and 20 from Morar with two ferries to cross.[28] The *New Statistical Account for Boleskine and Abertarff, Inverness-shire*, said, 'In a parish where the population is thin and scattered over so large an extent, there must be some so distant from school as to be unable to attend, particularly in winter when, being least occupied with their vocations, they are most disposed to attend'.[29]

This reference to the children's 'vocations' is a euphemism for the large amount of work which many rural children had to do at home in the spring, summer and early autumn — planting, hoeing and lifting potatoes; gathering bait and sea ware; helping with the peats and the sheep and going to the sheilings; all work which precluded any thought of attending school. Obviously there were children who did go to school in summer too but for many it was only in the winter months that they were free to do any learning — and those were the months when bad weather made the distance to school a sore trial. It was written of Strathdon, Aberdeenshire, that 'Except in a mild winter, the school is seldom strong owing to the situation of the parish which abounds in hills and rivers or burns so that the children at a distance cannot attend in frost or snow'.[30] In Sandwick, Orkney, there were five hundred children at the north end of the parish which, although only 3 miles from the school was, in that climate, 'sufficient to prevent attendance in the winter when they have most time'.[31] The log book of one west Highland school summed it up in the winter of 1877 thus, 'Snow storms, no attendance from a distance'.[32] Lack of roads meant that children could have to go across country to get to school. In Westray, Orkney, the district of Rapness was at least 5 miles from the parish school and for the greater part of the year the connecting road was almost impassable because an immense tract of peat moss lay on the route, something that was desperately dangerous for all ages, let alone children on their own.[33] Even where there were roads of a sort, their condition combined with distance from school, could cause problems as school log books show: 'November 1875. Weather stormy. Attendance very irregular. Parents complain sadly of the distance and the badness of the roads which cause irregularity of attendance';[34] 'The attendance of infants is now materially affected by the severe weather, many having to come a long distance';[35] 'Bad roads still prevent weaker children from attending';[36] or 'Attendance of boys good, very few girls could come in owing to the very bad condition of the roads'.[37] Even when a school was well within reach of the whole parish, the state of the roads could still affect attendance. In Baldernock, Stirlingshire, there was a perfectly accessible school but what was called 'the ill repair and dangerous state of some of the roads' made it unavailable to many children,[38] while the *Statistical Account for Kilmadock, Perthshire*, said that 'the boys in the country are in great danger of colds from bad roads. Foot paths on the sides of the roads should become general which would be a great ease to the children in bad weather',[39] which indicates how soaked they got, stumbling about in wet potholes and ruts.

Bad roads were one thing, swollen water crossings, with or without bridges, were another, and this too appears in school log books: 'There was a heavy rain this morning so that a good many of the youngsters, afraid of the overflowing of the burns that are without bridges, were detained at home',[40] or 'The Syart children are also absent, probably on account of the bad weather and having a bad bridge to cross'.[41] At Dollar, Clackmannanshire, there was in one place a ruinous wooden bridge which was often impassable, which not only prevented people on the south side of the Devon from going to church but also the children from attending school,[42] and in Orkney, the main road from Kirkwall to Stromness crossed what was not so much a bridge as a causeway, some 150 yards long and built of logs laid on pillars, never properly finished and without railings, so that young children were in real danger of being blown off and drowned which made their school attendance hazardous.[43] To all these people water was a restraint but to some it appears to have been a challenge. Rather than have their children miss school, people are known to have stilted across the River Yarrow in Selkirkshire to take their youngsters over to a little private school at Craig Douglas farm.[44] Even more surprising is an account of the Glenmoriston area of Inverness-shire which said that the river that divided that glen was 'so deep in every part as not to be fordable for man or horse and, from there being no boats on it, every child from 8 years age learnt to swim. This shows the effects of necessity by which many difficult things are rendered easy'.[45] This is a strange report, as ordinary people at that time did not swim, not even fishermen; and the thought of little children swimming a deep river to get to school, which is what is implied, is a horrifying thought although an interesting comment on the desire of people for learning for their children.

To the problems of distance, lack of roads and bridges, and bad weather, there was added that of inadequate clothing, which compounded the miseries of all the others and school log books often describe the wretchedness of ill-clad children. One said in December 1877, 'Snow — most of the children barefooted and not at school', and in November the following year, 'Attendance most irregular this week, chiefly owing to severe weather, children being barefooted and scantily clad'; and yet again in December 1882, 'Weather cold. Bare-footed and bare-legged children of whom there are a number irregular in attendance'.[46] At another school it was the same story: 'November 1875, Heavy frost. Roads impassable. ... Want of shoes and other clothing hinder regular attendance,' and again later that month, 'Want of shoes and warm clothing keeps a considerable number away'.[47] For those children who had boots for the winter but not the summer, there was the difficulty of learning to do without them in the spring and then getting used to them again in autumn, and this also affected their attendance at school.

For those children who had clothing and who managed to get to school in bad weather, the day ahead was a bleak prospect. The log book of Applecross School, Ross-shire, in March 1876 said, 'The weather has been most severe. The attendance is not so much affected, but the comfort of the children has been very small, being wet, many of them, in their shoes all day. Though it has been often urged on them to put off their shoes, if wet, they prefer to stay as they are at the time'. And children who had trailed a long way to school in pouring rain might have to turn right round and trail home again as Nigg School, Ross-shire, logged in September 1895: 'Children arriving drenched were almost immediately dismissed.' At that school in 1907 on a day of wild

48   Pupils and teachers of Geanies School, Ross-shire, c.1880. See the tackety
boots of the children.

wind and rain even though it was the month of May, when twenty-four children appeared, 'their clothing was in a sodden condition and as it was evident that they were feeling very cold they were sent home after exercises were corrected and given out to be worked at home'. All these things militated against regular attendance.

For some parents at a distance from the parish school, one solution was to send their children to board in the school house or in some convenient place nearby but this depended on being able to pay boarding fees in addition to the elementary school fees which were required until they were abolished by the 1872 Education Act. Another way of dealing with the problem of distance from schools was to have what were called ambulatory schools. It was the Society for the Propagation of Christian Knowledge, in particular, that provided these schools which were in fact not so much schools as mobile teachers, who moved from place to place, living with the people and teaching in whatever accommodation was made available to them, be it house, outhouse or barn. In some cases they moved every few months, in others they stayed for several years in one area, before moving on to the next. There were also various little 'adventure' or 'venture' (i.e. private venture) schools started by people who realised there was a need for education in an area and that they could make a living from it; but these schools were always frowned on by Kirk Sessions who, prior to 1872, tried to keep control of what was being taught to youngsters and by whom, as those running venture schools were often woefully lacking in both knowledge and teaching ability.

So greatly did people value education that where there was no access to the parish school, nor to ambulatory or venture ones, nor to the side schools which Parliament authorised in 1803, they realised that it was up to them to do something about it themselves and so, where it was practicable, tacksmen, tenants and even cottagers clubbed together to employ a young man to teach their children, at least during the four or five winter months. They gave him board and lodging by turn in their houses and a small wage — £3–£4 a year for one household or £5–£6 if there were quite a number of families involved, this at a time when the parish schoolmaster received about £8. 6s. 8d. sterling in addition to fees and what came from his almost-certain appointment as Session Clerk and precentor. In some places — Dunoon, Argyllshire, was one — even more economical arrangements were made. The teacher was often just a senior pupil from the parish school, only twelve to fifteen years old, and paid about £1 a year, with board and lodging. Although these boys' educational qualifications cannot have been great, it was apparently surprising how well and successfully they managed.[48] When the summer came, they returned to the parish school for as much time as home duties allowed because those who took winter teaching posts were usually intent on ultimately qualifying as proper teachers. In some cases, parents went even further and did not just employ a youth to teach but erected school buildings too, as happened at Cargill, Perthshire, in 1787 because of the great distance from the parish school.[49]

Before the Education Act made elementary education free in 1872, the poor could apply to have their children's school fees at the parish school paid by the Kirk Session but payment of these could be, and often was, withheld for education at any other school. Thus the really poor were unable to co-operate in private educational efforts as they could not contribute towards a teacher's wage nor provide board and lodging for him and so, if no charity was forthcoming, their children went uneducated unless their parents knew enough to be able to teach them at least to read the Bible and to learn the psalms by heart.

The 1872 Education Act which made elementary education free also made it compulsory. Absenteeism, therefore, became an offence and was also something which could adversely affect the school grant. The grant was essential to the running of the school and many school log books have dejected entries about pupils' absence, such as that of Inverasdale School, Ross-shire, in April 1879 which said, 'Attendance very irregular which is very disheartening', and in January 1880 stated that attendance was so low that 'schoolwork is brought to deadlock'. Other log books say that the irregular attendance of some pupils was a great drawback on classes and told on backward pupils. Rather than risk losing the grant, schoolmasters made efforts to prevent absenteeism or at least to get around it. One way was to strike off the roll for the winter months those children who lived so far away as to be doubtful attenders then, hence this entry in Megget's log book: 'Winterhope children left for the winter months, owing to the great distance from school.'[50] This practice was not approved of in official quarters and was what lay behind an instruction given to schools in 1886 that no child of school age, who had not passed the fifth standard, was to be struck off the register unless they had left the district or were known to be attending another school. It is worth noting that Megget's entry was thirteen years after this ruling. Another way of avoiding a record of absenteeism was simply to falsify the register and not show absentees, in the hope that no one would notice. This was chancy as School Board members regularly visited schools without notice and the records of one school show how a Board member came unexpectedly in 1878, checked the register and found no less than five absentees marked as being present. The result was a deduction of one-fifth of the grant along with the threat that if ever it happened again, the whole grant would be withdrawn and the teacher's certificate suspended, a dire prospect.[51]

To continue with education beyond local school level, it was necessary to have a bursary to cover transport to secondary schools and the fees payable there until secondary education became free in 1918. The free education and school transport of the later twentieth century years is a far cry from conditions two hundred years ago and would have been a great blessing at that time. Surprisingly, one of the earliest examples of school transport, something which was very uncommon at the time, must be that provided in the parish of Tyninghame in the mid-1600s by the Kirk Session who paid the ferryman an annual sum for taking the children over a river to and from school.[52]

16 FUEL, FERTILISERS AND FAIRS

Attendance at rural churches and schools suffered from the problems of distance and lack of transport but another great handicap to rural communities in general was distance from fuel, from manures and from markets, something which could only be improved by the building of good roads.

To take fuel first: for the poor who had neither the time, the transport nor the physical strength to go far, fuel often had to be such fallen wood or cones as they could find in nearby woods — they were not allowed to cut timber — and any bits of heath, broom, whins and dried dung as could be found on uncultivated ground. Turf was also used as fuel but, as agricultural improvements began, what had formerly been common land tended to be divided out between the surrounding proprietors and enclosed, which meant the end of turf-cutting, which resulted in the ordinary people having to seek ever farther afield for their firing.[1] Where there was peat, things were, or could be better but transport was generally difficult. In Bendothy, Perthshire, peats took seven hours to get, going and returning, not counting the cutting and drying of them.[2] There was no peat at all in the parish of Nigg, Ross-shire, and people had to go to another parish for it, crossing over the sands of Nigg Bay at low tide, which meant that this work might have to be done late, early or even at night.[3] In mountainous areas such as Glenshiel, Ross-shire, there was plenty of peat but it was so inaccessible that, even in good conditions, the most industrious people could barely gather enough for the winter.[4] In Clunie, Perthshire, where the two peat mosses in the parish were far off and high in the hills, the *Statistical Account* said that the roads to them were 'fit only for killing the horses and dashing the carts to pieces'.[5] In parts of Sutherland, the basic weakness of underfed horses made peat gathering very difficult and when mosses were far afield, the people often went part of the way one day and lay out all night, ready to load up in the morning, a practice which did not do their health any good when the weather was damp.[6] Island communities had other difficulties. In Westray, Orkney, use of the only peat moss on the island was confined to its owner's tenants. No one else could use it and no peat could be obtained from neighbouring islands either as their

49 Bringing home the peats. Photograph C J Williamson.

50 Loading peats into a horse-drawn sledge. Selkirkshire, pre-1914. Source:
Mrs Kerr, Borchester Bridge.

proprietors feared that their peat would run out if over-exploited.[7] In the islands of Gigha and Cara, Argyllshire, fuel was also very scarce but the proprietors were more merciful than those in Orkney and allowed the people to slice off the surface turf of pasture and even of meadow land, but this was obviously something which could not go on indefinitely,[8] and even where islanders could get peat from elsewhere, there was still the difficulty of ferrying it, and it is heavy stuff, over stretches of the sea.[9]

Summer farm work often had to be neglected because of the labour of gathering peats. It was written of the island of Tiree, that 'We spend the best season of the year, which should otherwise be usefully employed, in providing fuel ... '[10] and of Nigg, Ross-shire, that, 'In cutting and carrying [peats and turf] the farmers and their servants are employed for the whole of the summer season, to the total neglect of everything that might improve and benefit their farms'. Rain there was another hazard. 'If the season be wet, they generally lose their labour, being not able to carry their fuel out of the moss; and what they carry home is so wet, that it will not answer for fire. ... The badness of the roads, and the great distance which they have to go, occasion them great expense in carts and harness.[11] And nothing was more exhausting to horses than carrying peat, especially as summer time was when they should have been out at grass.[12] There were other difficulties to do with peat gathering. In some districts, well into the eighteenth century, as has already been said, services had to be rendered by tenants to their proprietors in addition to paying rent. These services might include casting and bringing to his home what peat he required for the year. In parts of Scotland at the end of the eighteenth century, anyone renting a plough of land — a variable measure — had to bring home for the landlord a 'leet' of peats, that is, a stack of them, 24 foot long, 12 foot broad at the base and 12 foot high. In parts of Aberdeenshire, doing this work brought the benefit of a reduced rent but even under good conditions, it meant at least a week's work for all a tenant's horses and creels or carts, and about 10s. for digging and building.[13] If the weather was bad, the work was delayed but it still had to be done and, all the while, the tenant still had his own fuel to secure.

The effects of lack of fuel were tragic. When it was scarce it frequently could only be used for cooking, not for warmth. The *Statistical Account for Duffus, Morayshire*, said that lack of fuel was often 'attended with loss of health and lives among the poor'[14] while that for Kirkinner, Wigtownshire, said that the greatest barrier to household industry was the scarcity of fuel: 'A human being, pinched with cold, when confined indoors, is always an inactive being. The daylight, during winter, is spent by many of the women and children in gathering "elding" as they call it, that is flicks, furze or broom for fuel, and the evening in warming their shivering limbs before the scanty fire that this produces.'[15] Even worse was reported from the Argyllshire parish of Glenorchy and Inishail, which endured great hardship in this respect: 'The sufferings of the lower classes, with respect to firing in wet years, during the rigour of winter, can only be conceived by such as have felt them. A few years ago, many poor people in the west Highlands were obliged to burn most of their household furniture to repel the cold and prepare their food. Old people and young children, unable to bear the cold, were mostly confined to bed.'[16]

The obvious solution to the difficulties of using peat was to use coal but it was more expensive and for a considerable time was subject to what seem to have been most unreasonable taxes. Although there was no alternative fuel in Eyemouth, Berwickshire, at the end of the eighteenth century people there were almost prohibited from using Scottish coal because it bore a tax of 3s. 4d. per ton,[17] and this applied to other areas too while people living much further north also suffered because all coal carried by sea north of the Red Head, which lay between Arbroath and Montrose in Angus, was taxed. Fortunately these taxes were lifted about the 1790s which was a tremendous benefit to those with access to coal because its availability did not depend on the weather, and they no longer had to spend virtually the whole summer trying to secure peat for the winter. Of course, for those not near to a coal pit, or after they were built in the eighteenth and ninteenth centuries, to a canal giving access to coal, or to the coast, the transport of coal was not without difficulties, and even danger. The people of the Berwickshire parish of Swinton and Simprim could get coal from Northumberland but in the late eighteenth century, before there were proper roads and bridges, it had to come across a ford which was tricky and there was never a year when horses were not lost there due to the river rising suddenly and the rashness of the men when this happened.[18]

Those with no transport of their own had to rely on others for fuel, and supplying peat, and later coal, became a worthwhile occupation. In Inverness, where coal was unknown until 1770, in which year one cargo was sold, the townspeople were supplied certainly until 1810 with peats and wood, brought by small tenants who came in every Tuesday and Friday with small home-made carts and lined them up in a long row for people to come and buy.[19] It was the same elsewhere and those who came first had the choice of the best. When coal began to be used regularly in towns, not only horses but donkeys too were used to bring it there.

The following figures give an idea of costs, showing in certain cases, how transport added to expense:

Peat/Turf	Source	
Garrot load of curbans	SA Wick	1 penny. Each horse carries 10–12 peats. 10/12 of these loads will barely fill a cart
Cart load of peat	SA Fordice	1s. 3d.
Cart load of turf	Banffshire	8d.

Peat/Turf	Source	
Leet of peats in town	SA Fraserburgh Aberdeenshire	£5
Cart load of peat in town 1800–12	Co. of Caithness Horne	3s. 6d. per cart load
Peats per creel	SA Roseneath, Dumbarton	6d.
Peat	SA Sorbie	3d. the horse load at the mosses, double when cart to consumer
Peat sold in H/K	SA Roberton, Roxb.	3s. to 4s. per single cart. 1s. 3d. to 1s. 6d. per back load.
Peats per cart load	NSA Holnam Roxburgh	3s.

Coal

Donkey carts for poor	NSA Hamilton, Lanarkshire	10–12 cwts for 2s. 3d. to 2s. 6d.
Coal at K/brt port	SA Kelton, K/brtsh	£1. 8s. per ton. Carriage to p of Kelton makes it £2. 2s.
Coal at Newburgh (Ad/sh)	SA Ellon, Aberdeenshire	4s. to 4s. 6d. per boll, plus carriage to any destination
English coal	NSA Newburgh, Fife	7d. per bushel
Scots coal		4s. 6d. per boll of 40 stones
Coal	NSA Abercrombie, Fife	1s. 3d. per 22 stones (1s. 4d. if toll incl.)
English coal, 1800–1812	Co. of Caithness Horne	21s. to 30s. per ton in towns
Scots coal, 1800–1812		18s. to 21s. per ton in towns
Cart of 1200 weight	SA Roseneath, Dumbarton	5s. per cart
Single cart at coalhill	NSA Roxburgh	6s. to 7s. including tolls; for 16 cwt; those without carting have to pay 11s. 6d.
Coal	NSA Waterston	8d. to 1s. per cwt
Coal (28/30 miles from North/land from B/ksh via Kelso)	NSA Wilton, Roxburgh	10 cwt at 13s. to 14s. av. 14d. per cwt. After harvest and occ at other times 11d. to 1s. per cwt
Coal delivered	NSA Holman, Roxburgh	8d. per cwt

When ships were of shallow draught, the 'harbours' at which they off-loaded coal were nothing more than suitable parts of the shore where they could beach and load directly on to carts which came out to them; or else they dumped the coal overboard for collection off the sands at low tide. Two entries from the school log book of Nigg, Ross-shire, throw a sidelight on these days: '1888. Two vessels are discharging coals on the beach and the children are employed gathering coals that fall from the ships and carts'; and in 1892, '... two ships on shore discharging coals and the children watch the emptying of the barrels into the carts to pick up any coals that miss the carts and claim them as their own'. Just occasionally a coastal village might get coal free. No one in the Ross-shire village of Hilton who was alive at the time, has forgotten how the coal boat 'Elm' was wrecked about 30 yards from the little harbour there in 1917 and proved a godsend to the villagers for years as they could go out with creels after every storm to gather what had been washed up. As harbours developed, unloading was much easier and many people remember the sight of lines of carts from each farm waiting their turn to take in coal from the boats and, when railways were built, also at the railway stations.

Not only did the land suffer in years gone by from the enforced neglect due to the summer work of fuel-gathering, it also suffered from the lack of

51   Coal carts at Portmahomack, Ross-shire.

fertilisers and this too was largely due to lack of transport. Few farms could make enough dung for their needs and had to seek it elsewhere. Everyone who could, husbanded dung, whether animal or human. It was so highly prized that it was often kept at the doors of houses so as to be under the owners' eyes, a practice that led to a great deal of ill health and which did nothing to help matters during the cholera outbreak of 1832. Townsfolk could find a ready market for all they could provide but its carriage was very costly. For instance, although a quarter of the farms in the parish of New or East Kilpatrick, Dunbartonshire were supplied with dung from Glasgow, Port Glasgow and Greenock, carriage costs put it beyond the means of the rest of the parish and even when the Forth–Clyde Canal was opened, the heavy duty made it as dear as when it came by cart.[20] This rural need for town dung is a good example of town and country inter-dependence and was particularly useful to towns in the days before there was a cleansing service.

Lime was greatly valued but access to it and transport were problems. Time and again, *Statistical Accounts* refer to the desperate problem of obtaining it but as roads improved so did supplies of it even though turnpike tolls, albeit reduced for lime as for coal, added to its cost. People living on the coast were as fortunate in regard to lime as to other goods. Not only could it be brought in by sea but, with any luck, the shores might provide a supply of suitable sea-shells which could be used as an alternative and which, at the end of the eighteenth century, were available at about 2*d*. per cart load from fisher towns.[21] These shells were spread on the land like any fertiliser and left to the influence of the weather although, for a slight extra charge, they could be burnt to produce lime. Marl, a limey clay, was also obtainable on the coast and occasionally it was found in inland lochs which could be drained to allow it to be collected. Seaware — seaweed — was yet another fertiliser available to those on the coast and large-scale maps of estates with a sea-frontage often show what were called 'ware roads' down the cliffs to give access to it; and fish guts were yet another source of enrichment for the soil available to those living near the sea.

Rural economy was affected in yet another way by lack of communications. 'Every article of merchant goods is here very dear on account of the great inland carriage,' said the *Statistical Account for Dalry, Kirkcudbright*,[22] and in some cases, lack of access to markets meant that it was simply not worth bothering to grow produce above subsistence level, badly though extra food was needed. This happened in Blair Atholl and Strowan, Perthshire, which was so far from market towns that many articles were not sent there which otherwise could have been profitable;[23] and it applied even more in island communities, such as Gigha and Cara, Argyllshire, of which it was said, 'There is no market at hand and therefore no incitement to raise a greater amount of produce than serves for the family — this is one reason for the apparent laziness'.[24]

The height of travelling and trading ambition for many country people was to go to the fairs held at intervals throughout the year. As they were holidays, there was a time when people got married on fair days but this practice was ultimately prohibited. Those going to Saturday fairs might have to return on the Sunday and this was something which fell foul of Kirk Sessions, which did not consider such travel a proper occupation for the Lord's Day.[25] Fairs and markets were the only opportunity some had to sell stock and other produce, and very chancy it could be too, and had it not been for the introduction of the droving trade when drovers advanced money on beasts they took south, with more to come if they sold well, stock rearing in the north of Scotland would for many years not have been worthwhile. Equally, of course, farmers in out of the way areas were at the mercy of drovers when it was a matter of accepting what they offered or driving beasts many miles themselves to market.[26] What was needed was good, regular markets and access to them;

52   Roundabout, St Boswells Fair. Source: Miss S. Lowe.

and this was only achieved by the improvements in travel of the eighteenth and nineteenth centuries, so that the *New Statistical Account for Glenelg, Inverness-shire*, was able to say that although the parish was about 70 miles from Inverness which was the market town, the communication with it was good because the Parliamentary road went part of the way.[27] Elsewhere, the 'signal benefit' of turnpike roads meant that instead of markets being inaccessible at certain times because of the weather, roads could carry the heaviest of goods at all times of the year and people from distant parts no longer had to sell their produce in less good markets in 'inferior towns' just because they were nearer.[28]

What were called 'the superior means of communication which the age affords'[29] included sea transport. Better shipping allowed stock to be taken directly to markets in the south which meant that they could be fattened at home, which better farming allowed and which brought more profit; it also led to the end of the droving trade. When roads had become 'of the very best description' in the eastern part of Ross-shire in the mid-nineteenth century, there were also regular steam boats to Edinburgh and a recently started service to London, which all had a marked influence on farming by opening up new markets.[30] Steam boats also helped salmon fishing by taking the salmon, packed in ice, direct to the London markets.[31] Fir wood for pit props left many a small pier by sea for the south; and so did eggs for consumption in towns, and goods of all sorts. Where rents in kind had previously been eaten by the proprietor's family, they could now be exported, often from the girnals (storehouses) still to be seen at strategic points on the coast. However, with the best will in the world, not everywhere could have such benefits and North Uist was one place which suffered greatly from the lack of shipping for the agricultural trade. Attempts to provide it had failed because ships were not designed for the trade suitable to the district, which was cattle, but instead were 'splendidly fitted up for passengers'.[32] Canals too had their part to play. To mention one example, the parish of Anstruther-Wester rejoiced in the great prices available in the Glasgow market which opened to them about the 1780s to 1790s with the completion of the Forth–Clyde Canal.[33] Well-planned canals, in addition to carrying goods reasonably cheaply and efficiently and giving easy transport for passengers, also provided a good deal of employment. There were in the mid nineteenth century, on the Glasgow, Paisley and Ardrossan Canal alone, fifty-two men and seventeen boys, as well as sixty-four horses for gig-boats and fourteen for luggage-boats.[34] Canals became extremely popular, so much so that many districts wanted to have them, almost for the sake of it. There was one example of this, about the turn of the nineteenth century — a suggestion for a canal through the Mearns and Strathmore to join the River Tay about 4 miles above Perth. It would have been easy to build and would have required few locks and there was nothing against it 'but that it would be of no use', because no one was going to carry goods 40–50 miles by water when they could get them to market, as they could there, quite easily in a quarter of the time and distance by going overland.[35]

Access to the wider world and what it had to offer had a bad as well as a good effect on rural life. Shops opened in towns and villages, filled with goods made elsewhere and brought within the reach of all by means of improved communications. Poor, simple, homespun materials were no longer acceptable and neither was the sometimes indifferent workmanship of the local craftsman. Low quality produce, such as butter, which had always sold readily before, found a less ready market and higher standards made things difficult for those who could only produce to a certain level. Thus many skills died out and access to towns farther afield meant the death of many fairs. William Aiton, who wrote the *General View of the Agriculture of Bute* in 1816, would have approved of this, believing that only those who needed to go to fairs should do so once goods were available in local shops. His concern was due to the drinking that took place at them, especially on an empty stomach, and the dangers that people risked on the way home, when they were intoxicated themselves or accompanying people who were in that state.[36]

Increased market prices for farm produce in large towns meant increased costs for the local consumer but this was partly offset by a rise in wages about the end of the eighteenth century. Where men servants had formerly received about £6 a year they now got £8, and women's pay rose from £2. 10s. to

£3 due to the Industrial Revolution and to road-making which employed a large number of people and pushed up wages generally.[37] The cutting and floating of wood, which did such damage to bridges, was a form of transport which also pushed up wages in areas where it went on, at a 'most alarming rate',[38] but it gave work to every available man between sixteen and sixty years of age, and all this was good news for the working man.

17 THE POSTAL SERVICE

The earliest 'posts' were royal messengers sent hurrying through the country to deliver information or orders which were usually to do with threatened invasions or national emergencies. A little further down the scale were the hired messengers or servants who carried communications for people of power and influence; but as time went on and burghs developed, so did the need for better means of keeping in touch and even by the end of the sixteenth century, some towns had what they called a 'post'. Dumfries employed one in the late 1500s and Aberdeen is said to have had a foot post to Edinburgh by 1590[1] and certainly had one in 1595 as records for that year show that he was supplied with a livery. His role seems to have been to deliver official communications rather than to serve the general public: in 1610 he carried letters on two occasions direct to the Privy Council for a payment of £3 Scots the first time and £3. 6s. 4d. Scots the second. It does not seem, however, as if it was always the 'post' who was used as two years previously, in 1608, 'a boy' was employed and paid 5s. Scots to take a letter to Maryculter, in the county of Aberdeenshire, 'to desyr the Laird to cum doon and tak ordour for his men in Torry', and neither is there any mention of the 'post' when in 1612 a letter had to be sent to Alford, not too far away, at the cost of £1 Scots, 'to know if there was ony infectioune of the pest, as wes bruited'.[2]

Although there were public posts of a sort in the early seventeenth century, because roads were few and far between and because the majority of the population were not letter-writers anyway, the early service was very limited and confined initially to the Edinburgh–Berwick route. In 1695 the Act anent the Post Office was passed, providing among other things that single letters to Berwick or any place within 50 miles of Edinburgh would cost 2s; double letters 4s; and so on proportionately and that packet boats would carry letters from Portpatrick over to Donaghadee in Ireland.[3] In 1710 another Act amended the Post Office establishment and under it regular posts were to be sent to all parts of the country — at least that was the intention, but it certainly did not work out that way. Lack of roads prevented the development of the mail service and even when this position improved, there was still a lack of 'cross posts' connecting with mail routes and so other methods had to be found to send and deliver letters.

The Act of 1695 which gave the Post Office in Scotland the right to carry letters, allowed for certain exceptions and, to complement such service as there was, carriers were authorised to carry letters to and from the nearest postal centre, something that fitted in well with their usual business and brought them in an extra income. It became the custom for many burghs to pay a carrier a few pounds a year — it was £4 in Jedburgh, Roxburghshire, in the late eighteenth century —[4] to go weekly to the nearest large town and to bring back all the letters, what the parish minister of Jedburgh called 'conveying epistolary correspondence',[5] as well as fetching newspapers. It is said that about 1740, before the nearby town of Hawick had a Post Office, letters were brought there once a month from Jedburgh by a hawker and laid out on a stall in the street on market day, like so many cakes of ginger bread, arousing the most intense interest and speculation from the general public.[6]

For many years, much of Scotland's mail was carried on foot, apart from horse-transport on the Edinburgh-Berwick route. Early post-masters on this route were required to keep horses to provide the mail service and were given a monopoly of horse hire in addition, although this did not in fact amount to much.[7] Even after roads improved sufficiently for mail coaches to be used, these coaches took mail only to the various towns on their route and from there it was foot-posts and runners who carried it onwards and outwards, something that was still happening in many parts of the country into the mid-nineteenth century. In the Highlands especially, the life of a post-runner was particularly arduous. A bag of mail could weigh up to 2 stones and the routes were long and often dangerous with bogs, mountains and near-precipices to negotiate and always there was the weather to contend with. Runners were not well paid either, certainly not as much as could be earned in various public works being done in the nineteenth century. Why did they do it? Could it have been that they preferred regular low-paid work than better-paid temporary jobs?

A few years ago, television recreated the journey of a Highland post runner, Ian Mor am Posda, Big John the Post, who ran between Dingwall and Poolewe in Ross-shire, taking three days each way over incredibly rough country, until the building of the destitution roads allowed horses to be used instead and Big John, finding himself out of a job, emigrated to Australia in 1848.[8]

Like many men who worked on their own, rural post-runners were often a law unto themselves. They knew that they were welcome whenever they appeared, on time or late, and any little peccadilloes that held them up were looked on sympathetically and excused and some runners took advantage of this. It is said that Tom Robson who ran between Langholm in Dumfries-shire and Hawick in Roxburghshire, would fish his way up Ewes Water and down the River Teviot and if the trout were taking, the mail was late. One old

runner's mail bag was nothing more than 'the croon o' his hat' and if he
indulged too much at an inn, the mail was soon in total confusion. In another
case, a postman was so very late that people really did get worried and
someone was sent out to look for him, only to find him sleeping happily on
a bank with the letters scattered around him.[9] These three instances all come
from one small area, Langholm in Dumfries-shire, and presumably the
picture was repeated around the country. The troubles of these men were
mostly self-inflicted but one old post-runner in Peebles-shire in the
nineteenth century always took the precaution of wearing a sprig of rowan in
his hat to ward off evil spirits.[10]

As time went on, foot-posts on suitable routes progressed to having a cart
drawn by a pony, donkey or mule, although Joseph Macgregor who carried
the mail between Selkirk and Lilliesleaf thought his own two feet were far
better than any four, and on one occasion refused a lift because he was in a
hurry.[11] A man who carried the mail from Prestonkirk to Stenton in East
Lothian had a donkey until some well-meaning farmers gave him a pony
instead. This was bad luck on the pony because whenever its new owner met
the mail coach he liked to gallop along with it and the wretched beast died of
rough usage.[12] Soon it dawned on more enterprising postmen that the use of
a light cart would allow them to carry a passenger too with consequent
financial benefit and post gigs served many a district very well.

Where a public service could not be provided because of distance and cost,
self-help came into play. Towards the end of the eighteenth century in places
like Kilmorack, Inverness-shire, the local gentry employed a runner
themselves to go to Inverness three times a week for their mail and
newspapers.[13] About the same time, in Eddrachillis, Sutherland, a few
parishioners paid a runner to go once a fortnight the wild and long route to
Tongue to collect mail which arrived there once a week from Thurso.[14] In the
very early 1800s, gentlemen in the Kinlochewe area of Ross-shire sent a
runner to Loch Carron to fetch the mail from the foot-post there and in 1820
several gentlemen in Lerwick, Shetland, provided a more general service by
employing a man to travel from Lerwick to Unst, calling at various places on
the way, and country people used either friends or agents in Lerwick to collect
their mail from the Post Office and pass it on to this runner for rural
delivery.[15] A more surprising instance of this sort of thing was the case of
Tibbie (or Luckie) Walker who carried letters once a week between the parish
of Daviot, Aberdeenshire, and the town of Aberdeen for the Laird of Glack
and the parish minister. This she did until shortly before her death in 1774
— at the age of 111.[16] In some cases, self-help along with a generous dose of
public spirit took the form of guaranteeing the costs if a Post Office were to
be established in a particular area. In the late 1700s, Colonel Fraser of
Belladrum, Inverness-shire, became surety in this way for a Post Office at
Beauly, a genuinely philanthropic deed as he got his own letters direct from

Inverness. It was not thought that this office could ever become profitable but correspondence so increased that it was able to send in regularly a clear profit of £90 to the GPO.[17] In the 63-mile long parish of Lismore and Appin, Argyllshire, a land-owner named Mr Seaton managed, after a lot of trouble, to get a Post Office established at Appin, by guaranteeing any deficiency. To start with, the income barely paid the runner's wage, but once again, business increased so rapidly that by the end of the eighteenth century this small office was able to send £74 a year to the GPO.[18] From many parts of the country, *Statistical Accounts* tell of the underwriting of Post Office costs or the employment of private runners, while in the various small islands off the west coast, even at the time of the *New Statistical Account*, self-help meant using one's own boat.

Very often, letter-carrying depended on the goodwill of neighbours. Anyone going to the local market town, which was the usual destination of country correspondence, would take letters without charge, or else a pedlar or carrier might take them for about a penny. It was on these grounds that the communities of Morebattle and Mow, Roxburghshire, refused to have a 'side-post' about the 1830s, because sending a letter by official postal channels would cost the much larger sum of 3d to 4d.[19] That being so, it is very understandable that in the case of a letter destined for somewhere like London, with a considerably higher postal charge, every effort was always made to find a private bearer. But however letters went, before the days of street names and numbers, finding town addresses was no easy task and some very detailed directions appeared on mail, such as:

> 1702. 'ffor
> Mr Archibald Dunbar of Thundertoune to be left at Captain Dunbar's writing Chamber at the Iron revell third storie below the Cross near the end of the close at Edinburgh';
> 1703. 'For
> Captain Philip Anstruther off Newgrange att his lodgeing a litle above the fountain-well south side of the street, Edenbrough.'
> 1704. 'ffor
> Mrs Mary Stowell at Whiteakers in St Andrew Street next door save one to the blew balcony near the sun dyall near long aiker London.'[20]

Delivery of letters to houses in towns was done entirely at the discretion of the local postmaster and when it was done, he was entitled to charge for the service, usually $\frac{1}{2}d$. a time within the town and possibly a penny if it was necessary to go out into the country. It must have been a charming sight in Haddington, East Lothian, in the days when the postmaster's daughter, a Mrs Bell, went round delivering letters which she carried in her large snow white apron.[21] In rural areas, mail was carried to a 'receiving-house', which was sometimes dignified with the title of Post Office, although 'receiving house' was, in many cases, only too literal a description. Letters were indeed received but as there was no responsibility for delivery, no special care was taken of them while waiting collection. Receiving houses might be village shops or inns or wherever was central and someone could be found to undertake the task. This system must have led to mislaid mail and unfortunate consequences such as what is said to have happened at Dalbeattie, Kirkcudbright, where the Post Office was nothing more than a little closet in or off the bar of an inn, where letters lay all jumbled up with lots of other things. A man just out of prison and planning a new start on the other side of the Atlantic, missed notification of his passage because it lay unnoticed in the muddle of the cupboard but the story had a happy ending as the shipping company heard what had happened and gave him a later sailing.[22]

In many cases, this last lap of getting one's mail from the Post Office or receiving house could produce great problems. The Post Office for the parish of Blair Atholl and Strowan in Perthshire was Dunkeld, at least 19 miles away. In many cases letters lying there for collection had to be returned to the GPO because people at a distance simply could not spare the time to go to Dunkeld on the off chance of there being mail for them. Certainly, there were always people prepared to collect mail for others but unless they were known and reliable, no one wished to entrust to them the money to pay for letters, which had to be produced on receipt, not on posting.[23] Outlying places were always

53   Postman on donkey-drawn postal cart outside the post office, Culbokie, Ross-shire.

worse served than anywhere else and letters for them were often just left at cottages by the way. Toll-houses also became depositories for mail which made them splendid centres for getting and passing on news and gossip. 'An evening in a "bar" was equal to reading a well-stocked newspaper and a deal more entertaining', said one writer.[24] There was no obligation on the part of cottager or toll-keeper to deliver letters and, just as in regular receiving houses, they could lie for days or until someone 'took a chance' of getting them sent on.

Some foot-posts enlisted unofficial auxiliaries. One such was Jamie Nichol who travelled a route by the Liddel and Hermitage rivers, Roxburghshire, on alternate days but did not need to travel anything like the full distance as he passed the letters on to the pupils of the various little schools and the children took them on the final lap, or at least part of it.[25] Occasionally it was the schoolmaster who was the postmaster,[26] and doubtless he did the same. Even church-going could be put to use in letter-carrying. In the early nineteenth century, letters for Gordon and Westruther, Berwickshire, were left at Greenlaw to be collected each Sunday by members of the Seceeder congregation who came from these places, and to be delivered by them.[27] Obviously there was no inter-denominational friction there. One very unusual receiving and delivery point was devised by a Border shepherd — a water-tight tin box which could be sunk into the ground at the top of a hill where his hirsel adjoined another one on the more frequented side of the hill. Whenever he wanted to send a letter, into the box it went, with a pole stuck in the ground alongside and a big bunch of broom tied to it to attract his friend's attention. He knew what was required and did the same thing for any incoming mail too.[28] Well-read and intelligent men appeared in surprising places in Scotland and it would be interesting to know why such a man at that time needed a mail service of this sort.

Not only were people prepared on occasion to pay for their own post-runners, they sometimes joined together to provide a local Post Office. This happened at Ormiston, East Lothian, for one, where the mail came to the village by official means but the Post Office was established and kept up by each family subscribing a small annual sum or else paying something for every letter and newspaper received.[29] In time, many small cottage homes, although unsuitable as public offices, were designated Post Offices rather than receiving houses and served their turn well enough. One such was described in the 1872 Ordnance Survey details as 'part of a small house used for the receipt and despatch of letters' although not for other postal transactions. This house was in fact a tiny two-roomed cottage with a family living in it,[30] and there are still cottages and houses with a room entirely given over for service as the local Post Office.

The introduction of the national penny post in January 1840 really set the Post Office system on its way. No longer did people pay for letters on

54   Mail bus, Campbeltown and Tarbert. Source: Scottish Ethnological
Archive, Royal Museum of Scotland.

THE MAIL TRAIN.

SWELL. *"Haw!—He—ar! What's-your-Name! What Time do we Arrive at Aberdeen?"*
GUARD (snappishly). *"7·10."*
SWELL (making himself quite at home). *"7·10? Haw!—Well then, let me have my Boots, and Call Me at—Haw—6·45."*

55   The Mail Train. Cartoon from *Punch*, 1861.

collection. Stamps were bought and put on letters by the sender, although at the outset the penny post confused some people who put the letter and the penny into the post box together. By the mid nineteenth century railways did much to speed mail on its way all round the country. Foot-posts and postmen with carts became a thing of the past as bicycles and then vans took over, and a parcel service was developed. The telegraph system was a great boon when introduced about the 1870s but for many households the arrival of a boy with a telegram threw the family into a panic. A telegram usually meant bad news rather than good and it is said that it was not until betting by telegram began, that this attitude changed. Delivery of telegrams, as of mail, could be a little unorthodox. Although the telegraph office for Nigg, Ross-shire, was Nigg Station Post Office in the 1960s, at least one elderly resident of the parish could remember when telegrams for the Nigg Ferry end of the parish, were sent by sailing boat from Cromarty. The boat did not land but the message was simply wrapped round a stone and flung ashore in the certainty that someone would be looking out and would pick it up and deliver it, possibly causing less alarm than had it come by normal channels.[31] Nowadays, a telegram is only used for greetings and it is a moot point whether the postal service of the 1980s is better than it was, say, fifty years ago.

For the more official side of the Scottish postal service, no one can do better than to read A R B Haldane's *Three Centuries of Scottish Posts*.

18 PLEASURE SEEKERS

The early travellers who visited Scotland in the sixteenth, seventeenth and early part of the eighteenth centuries can hardly be called tourists, yet they were fore-runners of the many who came to see the beauties of Scotland as soon as roads, and later on railways and steam-ships, made travelling attractive.

James Hogg, the Ettrick Shepherd, who has already been mentioned, has left good accounts of his tours of the Highlands and Western Isles during the years 1802–4 but in 1800, as turnpike roads were developing, one of the first tourists in the real sense of the word, made one of several visits to Scotland. This was the Hon Mrs Murray who left her home in London and headed north to Perth, where she stayed in the Salutation Hotel for some days. Leaving there, she visited the Trossachs and went on via Glen Ogle and Glen Dochart, past Tyndrum and through the Pass of Brander to Oban, and later on through the Pass of Awe, a route of which she said, 'To have a steady horse and a careful driver on such occasions are a great comfort to a traveller's mind'. In Oban itself, all she could find to hire for expeditions was 'Gibraltar's small cart', Gibraltar being a Chelsea out-pensioner, commonly known by the name of the place where he had been wounded in 1799. Mrs Murray was not content to remain on the mainland and decided to visit the island of Staffa. There was a good, regular ferry by that time from Oban to the island of Mull from which Staffa could be reached, but going that way meant crossing the whole of Mull on foot or on a pony, over rough going, so that it was often neither advisable nor practical. It was quicker and easier to hire a boat or go by the revenue cutter — so long as one did not mind if one had to change direction and go after smugglers — up the north-east coast of Mull to Aros, from where one walked or rode across a neck of land to the west coast of Mull. Mrs Murray rode on a pony 'led by an honest Highlander' over a very rough track which at one point was so steep that going up she 'was obliged to lie on the horse's back and in descending almost on its tail'.[1] A trip of this sort was not cheap. From Oban to Aros, the boatman charged 1 guinea, the guide from Aros to the west coast was 5s., the boat to Staffa was 15s. and a further 15s. was added if Iona was included in the trip;[2] and on arrival at

Iona, tourists had to scramble ashore through rocks and pools, the quay being nothing more than 'sundry misshapen rocks'.[3] On such a trip everything depended on the weather and visitors could be storm-stayed anywhere on the way — in 1799 some visitors had to spend three days on the island of Staffa which was uninhabited, but what a tale they would have had to tell afterwards.[4]

In spite of the fact that there seems to have been no particular difficulty in visiting these places, anyone wanting a chaise in Oban at the time Mrs Murray was there, had to send to Perth for it and it took ten days to arrive.[5] There was a distinct shortage of suitable transport for tourists at that time and for a good many years afterwards and a travelling guide, describing a tour from Dunkeld, Perthshire, westwards by Killin, said in 1823, 'Travellers will do well to furnish themselves for this tour with horses and carriages at Perth for they will find but a scanty supply of even tolerable horses upon the road, and no chaises beyond Dunkeld'.[6]

In 1740, a journey from Edinburgh to Inverness took at least five days,[7] and a writer to the *Inverness Courier* recalled the experience of travelling at the very beginning of the nineteenth century by post chaise on that route. The first day the party dined at Kinross and supped at Perth; next day, they breakfasted at Inver, near Dunkeld; and so they went on, by Moulinearn, Blair, Dalwhinnie to the north, 'husbanding the poor horses till, on the fifth morning, if the vehicles held good, the party was safely deposited in Inverness'.[8] By 1809 things had improved and the tourist heading to or from the capital of the north was being better catered for. The proprietors of the Duchess of Gordon coach announced that from 4 September that year the coach would run twice a week between Edinburgh and Inverness and 'as the days are shortening considerably, the passengers both going and coming will have an opportunity of sleeping on the road ... Dalwhinnie the first night, Dunkeld the second and Edinburgh the third ... which arrangement will give ladies and gentlemen visiting the North an opportunity of passing through the beautiful country between Dunkeld and Blair by daylight'.[9] In the summer there was no need for such consideration; speed mattered more and in June 1811 the Caledonian Coaching Company in Inverness announced that they would run their coaches 'with such expedition that a person leaving Inverness at six o'clock in the morning can with comfort and ease get to Edinburgh next day to dinner; and in like manner from Edinburgh to Inverness'.[10]

During this time, one coach on the Edinburgh–Inverness route provided a service which must have been a tourist's dream. Some years before 1836 this coach was regarded as 'a truly accommodating vehicle. The driver did not hesitate to give his passengers "a blink of the afternoon" to discuss a bottle of port or an extra tumbler of whisky punch, or to drive the vehicle a few miles off the road to oblige a lady or an inquisitive tourist, who might happen to be a bit of an antiquary or a lover of the picturesque'. Sadly, however, more down-to-earth rules were ultimately imposed and the coach had to conform to 'the usual plodding regularity and expedition of a long or heavy coach in any other part of the kingdom'.[11]

All in all, such coach services, accommodating or swift as they might be, appealed to pleasure seekers and the *Inverness Journal* reported in August 1811 that the town had 'for some days back been the resort of an immense number of persons of rank and fashion, who at this season of the year generally visit the North for the purpose of viewing its beautiful and romantic scenery'.[12] The lure of sporting activities in the Highlands also drew people to the north and the *Inverness Courier* reported in 1836 that the town was crowded during summer and autumn with 'tourists and their baggage, a motley collection of guns, fishing rods, pointers, creels and baskets'.[13] By the middle of that century, many more tourists were using Inverness as a base for touring in the area, including parties of French and Germans. Eight steamers were constantly arriving and departing, three on the Caledonian Canal, three on the east coast line to the Forth, one north to Sutherland and one to London, and in addition, eight coaches arrived and left daily.[14] The opening of the Caledonian Canal in 1822, with a steamer service, provided an easy and scenic link for anyone visiting the west coast and wishing to go on to see the north as well, and it also provided day trips for those holidaying in the area.

Passenger and pleasure traffic on canals began in a fairly attractive way, like a trip on the Forth–Clyde canal in the 'Hoolet', a big, decked, roofed scow, pulled by a horse at 4 mph and providing its patrons not only with refreshments but with a fiddler too.[15] Such a trip was very exciting and although a canal boat heeled over and eighty-five people were lost on the Glasgow, Paisley and Ardrossan Canal a few days after it was opened in 1810,[16] this did nothing to put people off canal travel.

Steam ships were, of course, a great boon to tourists and a great source of excitement when they first appeared in any waters. The arrival of the 'Comet', a paddle steamer of 25 tons with a 3 hp engine and capable of 5 mph, off Oban in 1812 was considered a remarkable sight;[17] and when a steam ship first anchored off Thurso, Caithness, in 1829, people flocked from far and near to see it, especially as they were sure it was on fire.[18] Little wonder that it was written in *Duncan's Itinerary of Scotland* 1823, 'The application of the steam engine to the purposes of navigation has been productive of the most important advantages to the traveller who can now enjoy the pleasures of a water excursion with all the expedition and certainty of a mail coach ride'.[19] Describing boats on the river Clyde, the same source went on to say that they were 'fitted up with great elegance; a library of books in the cabin supplies food for the mind; and the stewards can furnish the hungry tourist with the more substantial refreshment of a comfortable meal. He may thus, at a small expense, visit all the western coast from Liverpool to Tobermory, or the eastern coast from London to Inverness, without entering a stage coach or walking a mile. . . . In order to direct and inform travellers of the beauties, antiquities etc. of these places, an interesting work to which we have often referred is "The Steam Boat Companion and Guide to the Highlands and Western Islands".'[20] This implies that not to walk was a pleasure but, to many people, combining a day trip on a pleasure steamer with a walk was very pleasant and a book about Greenock, Renfrewshire, suggested a 'delightful excursion' from there to Helensburgh by boat, getting off and walking part of the way up the loch to see scenery 'of the most sublime description combining as it does, many beautiful scenes of high cultivation; all of which are bounded with a ridge of finely-marked hills'.[21]

But improvements always bring problems with them and just as roads had encouraged the movement of undesirables, and railways threatened increased Sunday travel, so with steam boats: those intent on enjoying their time off work at the weekend, in Monifieth, Angus, found that, 'Steam boats, during the summer months, bring down an inundation of the worst population of Dundee on the Sabbath Day. Hence drunkenness and riot, in spite of moral exertions to put a stop to the evil, are too common on a day set apart for holy rest'.[22] In tourism, one man's meat is another's poison.

In spite of the advantages of rail and steam ships, a vital part was still played in the tourist business by coaches and other forms of horse-drawn transport. The west coast has always appealed to tourists and those who holidayed there in the late nineteenth century stayed longer and needed far more luggage than

MR. BRIGGS, feeling that his Heart is in the Highlands a-chasing the Deer, starts for the North.

56   Mr Briggs starts for the North. Cartoon from *Punch*, 1861.

would be usual today and a coaching business, operating for them between Oban and Fort William, used specifically designed coaches to carry passengers and the mass of baggage they had with them. The seats beside the driver were always reckoned the best for sight-seeing and in consequence cost that much extra but, often enough passengers perched themselves up amongst the luggage on the roof to see better, in a way rather reminiscent of those who were obliged , rather than chose, to perch on top of the goods in the carrier's cart. This west coast service was busy enough in the season to require one hundred horses. Two Oban–Fort William coaches were named the 'Glencoe' and the 'Glenorchy' and so became widely known to travellers as the 'G and G' coaches; and there were also specially designed 'excursion coaches' in tourist centres to take people for day trips.[23]

The importance of inns and hotels for the coaching and railway trade has already been mentioned but the flood of tourism resulting from these, as well as steamer sailings, helped the establishment of hotels purely for a holiday market. An advertisement in 1864 for the Royal Hotel in Ullapool, Ross-shire, stated that 'By the munificence of Sir James Matheson Bt. of Lews, MP, this hotel has been expressly built for the convenience of tourists and others visiting the west coast'.[24] Elsewhere hotels were enlarging the number of their rooms, the West End Hotel in Fort William actually doubling its accommodation in 1896.[25]

Just as guide books were produced for rail travellers and steam boat passengers, so they were for general tourists. One of the best was the improved 1823 edition of Duncan's *Itinerary of Scotland* which has already been mentioned, produced at a cost of 7s. 6d., bound in green leather and of a convenient size for slipping into a breast pocket or bag, $3\frac{1}{2}"\times 8"$. It gave the names of inns which kept post horses and listed a whole range of journeys, giving all sorts of information about what to see along the route — houses and their owners' names, lochs, tolls, ancient buildings, villages, churches and manses, Roman remains, the dates of fairs, very abbreviated historical notes, and times of connecting steamers. An example of its style is the description of the run from Dunkeld to Killin, the one requiring travellers to arrange about horses themselves: 'The road on the S. side of Tay from Kenmore to Killin is generally considered the best for tourists. The views are grand beyond description. About 2 miles from Kenmore by this road is the Fall of Acharn. The ascent is from a small public-house on the roadside where a guide can be procured, and the fall is about $\frac{1}{4}$ mile distant. ... It will amply repay the curiosity of the traveller for the trouble and time he may consume in inspecting it.' *Carey's Roads* was another useful guide, giving the routes of all mail and stage coaches in Great Britain, along with the population of towns, distances between them and from them to London, the names of rivers crossed and so on. A good deal later, maps for tourists were introduced and proved exceedingly popular.

Although travellers were able to get to Inverness and much of the Highlands quite easily by the 1820s, travel to the far north of the mainland at that time was still difficult in parts, so that *Duncan's Itinerary* said of the north coast, 'There is no made road farther than 2 miles beyond Reay Kirk. Travellers going in the direction of Tongue and Durness should endeavour to procure a guide, as they may otherwise deviate from the path, which is what Highlanders call a Bridle Road and there are few houses to be met with. The Traveller will also do well to fill his flask and supply his scrip [bag or satchel] at Reay Inn as he may rest assured he will require their aid before he reaches Tongue. This has become more necessary since the country has been depopulated [by the Clearances].'[26]

Many pleasure-seekers found their enjoyment in the bicycle. Cycling became a great pastime as the many old photographs of cycling and picnic parties show. As with tourist guides, special cycling guides were produced for this market, including one in 1901 which was described thus, 'So many go awheel nowadays that every addition to the list of pocket maps is gladly welcome for cyclists and pedestrians alike'.[27] Before bicycles were accepted as a pleasurable and practical form of transport, they were greeted with amazement and sometimes derision, but never without curiosity. It was in the early decades of the nineteenth century that press reports from around the country began to mention that there was considerable interest in the construction of velocipedes, the earliest form of bone-shaking bicycle. One was made in Inverness in 1819, by a cartwright under the direction of a writing master in the town who was soon making daily excursions on it in the neighbourhood and becoming ever more skilful until he could ultimately 'travel with great velocity',[28] but in spite of the reports said to come from all around the country, not everyone knew about the invention of bicycles and there were various claims about who made the first one. As late as 1839 there was an assertion that the first pedal cycle was built by Kirkpatrick MacMillan, the blacksmith at Courthill Smithy in the parish of Keir, Dumfries-shire. It may or may not have been his own invention; some say that it was that of a friend, Sandy Anderson, improved upon by MacMillan. Either way, although MacMillan was a well-respected man who also acted as the local dentist by drawing teeth at the smithy, he acquired the name of Daft Pate from all those who scoffed at his attempts to ride his strange contraption. Unlike the town of Inverness, where the appearance of a man on a velocipede appears to have aroused interest certainly but no special astonishment, when Daft Pate rode his bicycle people made a point of coming to watch and some came a long way for a view of this novel sight. He is reported to have cycled to Glasgow to sell his invention and there are differing accounts of what happened — that the sight of him and his machine did nothing more than cause an obstruction; that he knocked down a child and was fined 5s.; or that when he stopped at Lesmahagow en route, such a great crowd gathered about

57   Tain cycling club, 1889, with a tricycle on the left and penny-farthings.
Source: Tain & District Museum.

58   St Duthus Cycle Works, Tain. Source: Tain & District Museum.

him that he was arrested for causing a breach of the peace, taken to prison and his precious bicycle thrown on a scrap heap. Fortunately, he managed to find it again after his release and went on to Glasgow where he is said to have sold it for not very much.[29]

Bicycles which were first of all ridden for pleasure and the interest of inventing them, soon became a virtual necessity for every working household in rural areas. In one Highland parish, the first bicycle seen there was acquired by a family locally known for some reason as the 'Porridgies' and it was so highly prized by its owner that he kept it at his bedside. For many families, a bicycle was their only private transport until after the Second World War, when cars became common in all walks of life; but even so, bicycles were still used by many people and had a commercial use too, as message boys carried orders on them to customers' houses. A motor cycle was a great luxury and one with a side-car to take a wife and even a child or two as well, was a great boon in the country.

It is very easy to think that tourism in all its forms has only got going through the efforts of Tourist Boards, yet it has been developing steadily, without any outside bodies to help it along, for many, many years.

19 BACKWARDS AND ONWARDS

In former days, people travelled because they had to but things are very different now. As systems of travel have developed and overtaken their predecessors, so old forms of transport are being revived for pleasure.

The mail coach has been superseded in some areas by the mail bus and although coaching has long since died out, carriage driving is now a recognised sport, both for competition and for pleasure, and riding side-saddle, which declined greatly, is now making a certain come-back, even among young people, at smart horse-shows. Traction engines which did a limited amount of heavy draught work before falling out of favour, now take pride of place at shows of vintage machinery. Steam trains, which overtook

59　An early steam traction lorry, belonging to Alexander Robertson of Kintore, restricted by the Highways and Locomotives Acts of the 1860s to a speed of 5 miles an hour. Source: GWW Special Collection, University of Aberdeen.

coaching, died out in the face of electrification and diesel engines, yet there are now societies dedicated to their preservation and a few sections of old railway lines where enthusiasts run them as a tourist attraction. At the time of writing, negotiations are going on to see whether the National Trust for Scotland can take over the Leaderfoot Railway Viaduct in Roxburghshire — the one that was admired by Queen Victoria and shunned by Lady John Scott — because of its fine construction, striking appearance and its place in transport history. Just as people in former days longed for accessible schools, proposed closures of small schools are still today vigorously opposed, often on transport grounds, although the closure of churches does not arouse the same hostility.

Fairs, which were such an important feature of commercial and social life, have largely died out but the few that still exist, such as St Boswell's Fair held annually in July, give great pleasure, and the Inverness Wool Fair still exists in name, although it is now simply a sale, although an important one. At least one fair has been revived — the St Boniface Fair, in Fortrose, Ross-shire, which is a great day for the community and is put to charitable use as well, with £200 given in 1985 to the Save the Children Fund. Tolls which were so unpopular when they were introduced, are still found to be a good way of financing large new bridges. The Dumfries-shire minister who wondered whether human legs would be as serviceable in a hundred years' time as they were when he said this in 1898, might be pleasantly surprised by the pleasure people take in walking. The form of walking known as 'back-packing' is reminiscent of the days of the old packmen carrying their loads on their backs; and people are concerned to establish and use long distance walkways and to keep rights of way open for rambling. A number of military roads are now used by walkers and provide, instead of a repressive role, one of enjoyment and healthy exercise. Opening a restored Wade bridge at Melgarve on the Ruthven Barracks to Fort Augustus military road in 1985, the Chairman of the Countryside Commission for Scotland, Mr David Nickson, said, 'General Wade could not have foreseen the value of his roads to twentieth-century users, nor the much more peaceful purposes they now so happily serve for recreation'. General Wade's roads are so highly regarded that the Association for the Preservation of Rural Scotland organised voluntary work parties in 1985 to save the 'Eye of the Window', a bridge built by Wade in 1728 to span a gorge near Calvine, Perthshire. That an organisation of this sort should be prepared to spend £6,500 on something that does not belong to it is due to its being, in the words of a press report, a 'historic and lovely structure'. Many of Telford's bridges still give good service and great pleasure to the eye, as well as a feeling of history, as do some earlier bridges which can still be found. The destitution roads survive in Highland folk memory, along with the Clearances, in a way which it might be better to forget.

Although canals were busy commercial thoroughfares when they opened,

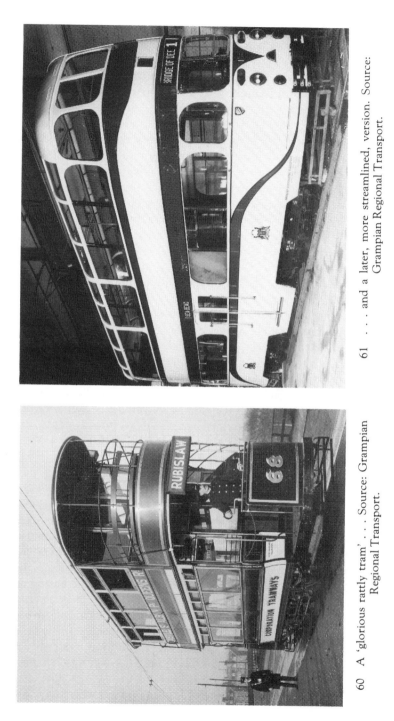

61   . . . and a later, more streamlined, version. Source: Grampian Regional Transport.

60   A 'glorious rattly tram'. . . Source: Grampian Regional Transport.

they are now little used for their original purpose of carrying heavy goods but their value for recreation and wild life has been recognised and efforts are going on to make them places of enjoyment. The Union Canal, linking Edinburgh and Glasgow, which has three of the finest aqueducts in Britain, has been cleaned up in many parts to allow boating and the British Waterways Board, who manage canals, are anxious to see its, and other canals' use widened and increased. A 'Workship' group from the Society for the Interpretation of Scotland's Heritage visited the canal in 1985 and *The Scotsman* gave coverage to their report which said, among other things, that there was considerable scope for involving local people and that a ranger service might be expanded to organise a range of activities for local residents, particularly children, youth groups and schools, to encourage them to enjoy the canal's wildlife and to find out about its history. It was also suggested that there could be a boat service, more paths and signposting and information available about the canal in general. This would be a splendid thing for all similar waterways.

Many people remember with nostalgic affection the glorious rattly trams which ran in Scottish cities for most of the first half of the twentieth century. They were powered by electricity from overhead cables which did nothing for the scenic appearance of somewhere like Edinburgh's Princes Street. Because this power supply ran down the centre of the street, so did the trams and anyone wishing to board one did so from an island in the middle of the street, with traffic moving on either side, so that running for a tram was a hazardous business which could mean dodging through traffic and risking a twisted ankle on the stone setts in which the tram rails were laid. Trams had two decks and a very upright and rather prim appearance but this impression was offset by the electric sparks which flashed from the overhead wires as they passed below them.

Trolley buses, more sedate than the noisy, bumpy trams, originated in France in 1901 and became a feature of Glasgow and its environs; like trams they reached their peak during the next forty years. They too were run by overhead cables, but this form of motivation — with the additional disadvantages of rails in the case of trams — confined them to specific routes. Thus, although investment was high, because of the impossibility of varying the journeys both these forms of city transport fell out of favour, becoming instead much-admired museum exhibits while their public service role was taken over by buses.

Everyone knows about the gradual introduction of motor cars and one can imagine how astonished people in the north of Scotland must have been in the 1880s to see the Earl of Caithness driving with his wife on the Inverness–Wick road at a speed of 7–8 mph in the steam carriage which he is said to have invented.[1] Soon cars were no longer such a startling innovation and by the 1920s to 1930s every well-to-do person owned one and probably also had a

62   Trolley Bus. Drawing by J McDonald, Grampian Regional Transport.

chauffeur to go with it. After the Second World War the ownership of cars increased and the number of chauffeurs declined; women learned to drive as a matter of course, where previously this had been largely the preserve of the menfolk. Nowadays two and even three-car households are common, and instead of having to get permission to use a parent's car, young people buy one for themselves as soon as they possibly can.

In country areas, of course, it was the motor bus, descendant of the horse-drawn omnibus, that really mattered in the first half of the twentieth century. Surprisingly, Orkney is said to have had its first motor bus as early as 1905 on the Kirkwall–Stromness road,[2] and a number of buses began to run on certain days of the week on the mainland of Scotland before the First World War. However it was not until immediately after the war that the rural bus service

63   Mr J H Paterson, manager of Caledonian Motor Co., Aberdeen, and family
in 1894 touring car. Source: Aberdeen City Libraries.

64   On holiday in a fairly old crock — but not so old as the Reg. No. — AD 50
— suggests. Source: Aberdeen City Libraries.

65   An early open-topped omnibus, lovely on a fine summer day, but there is an essential hood for wet weather, c.1929.

66   A slightly later closed omnibus — max speed 12 mph!

really developed, very possibly because at that time free secondary education began and it was necessary to have transport to take children to whatever town housed the nearest school. These buses were frequently known as 'the scholars' bus'. And if buses were needed for one purpose, it made sense to widen their use and availability for other purposes. Day trips by bus began to replace those provided in earlier days by the railways, and this has expanded to the point where holidays by coach are a major part of the tourist industry. Some no-smoking seats are provided in buses nowadays, but segregation of smokers and non-smokers is not new. Many non-smokers would gladly go back to the style of one of the first buses in Ross-shire which had a partition with a sliding door completely dividing the bus, allowing two-thirds for non-smokers and one-third for smokers.[3] Was this an early awareness of the dangers of smoking or simply because the bulk of the people could not afford to smoke much anyway?

Just as motor buses superseded trolley buses and trams in cities, so cars caused a decline in the rural bus services. Over the past few years, however, bus services, with the closure of so many lines and stations in Scotland, are once more providing a reasonable alternative to railways, but the wheel may once again turn full circle as there are suggestions afoot to reopen or start building underground railways to ease traffic congestion amd transport problems in the cities.

Cycling, so popular for many years, also went into decline as motor cars, which made travel so much easier, increased in popularity, but the desire for a healthier lifestyle has once more pushed the bicycle to the forefront of fashion. Cycling clubs abound and most youngsters yearn for the latest model or craze in bikes.

Every transport development has been founded on, or caused the decline of another. One wonders what will happen in the future to flying and to what further new uses old ways may be put.

NOTES

Abbreviations

APS   Acts of the Parliament of Scotland
OSA   *Old Statistical Account of Scotland*
NSA   *New Statistical Account of Scotland*
PSAS   *Proceedings of the Society of Antiquaries of Scotland*
GVA   *General View of the Agriculture of . . .*
SN & Q   *Scottish Notes and Queries*
Dumfries Antiquarian Society   Transactions of the Dumfries-shire and Galloway
Natural History and Antiquarian Society

1 *The Early Highways of Scotland*

1   Moir, *Scottish Hill Tracks*, p. 5.
2   Fenton and Stell, *Loads and Roads in Scotland and Beyond*, pp. 49–63. (Article by Prof G W S Barrow, 'Land routes: The medieval evidence'.)
3   Moir, *Scottish Hill Tracks*, p. 6.
4   APS, 1555, II, 498.
5   Munro, *Tain through the Centuries*, pp. 28–29.
6   OSA, Campsie, Stirlingshire, XV, p. 353.
7   Mitchell, *Reminiscences of my Life in the Highlands*, I, p. 6.
8   Munro, *Tain through the Centuries*, p. 29.
9   Rankin, *Cockburnspath*, p. 44.
10   Fenton and Stell, *Loads and Roads in Scotland and Beyond*, p. 60. (Article by Prof G W S Barrow, 'Land routes: The medieval evidence'.)
11   Brown, *Early Travellers in Scotland*, p. 119.
12   APS, 1617, IV, 536.
13   APS, 1641, V, 702.a.
14   APS, 1655, VI, 832.b.
15   OSA, Craig, II, p. 498.
16   NSA, Dalry, Ayrshire, V (Ayrshire), p. 234.
17   Somerville, *My Own Life and Times*, p. 355.
18   Fenton and Stell, *Loads and Roads in Scotland and Beyond*, p. 67. (Article by Ted Ruddock, 'Bridges and Roads in Scotland 1400–1750'.)
19   Haldane, *Drove Roads of Scotland*, p. 31.
20   Ibid.
21   Pennant, *Tour in Scotland in 1769*, p. 166.
22   Horne, *The County of Caithness*, p. 140.
23   Pococke, *Tour of Dr Richard Pococke in 1760*, p. 50.
24   OSA, Delting, Shetland, I, p. 405.

25 NSA, Sandsting and Aithsting, XV (Shetland), p. 134.
26 NSA, Westray, XV (Orkney), p. 130.
27 NSA, Fetlar and North Yell, XV (Shetland), p. 32.
28 NSA, Tiree, VII (Argyllshire), p. 218.
29 OSA, North Uist, XIII, p. 321.
30 Munro, *Tain through the Centuries*, p. 60.
31 Weir, *History of Greenock*, p. 46.
32 Hall, *History of Galashiels*, p. 61.
33 OSA, Swinton and Simprim, Berwickshire, VI, p. 323.
34 Smith, *The Turnpike Age*, p. 1.
35 Robertson, *GVA, Inverness* (1808), p. 296.
36 Ibid., p. 290.

2 Roadways of the Highlands

1 Baker, *A Walker's Companion to the Wade Roads*, pp. 15, 19, 20.
2 Mitchell, *Reminiscences of my Life in the Highlands*, vol. I, p. 7.
3 OSA, Urr, Kirkcudbright, XI, p. 79.
4 Baker, *A Walker's Companion to the Wade Roads*, p. 97.
5 Mitchell, *Reminiscences of my Life in the Highlands*, vol. I, p. 9.
6 OSA, Kintail, Ross-shire, VI, p. 244.
7 Mitchell, *Reminiscences of my Life in the Highlands*, vol. I, p. 9.
8 PSAS, 46, p. 172. (H R G Inglis, 'Ancient Bridges of Scotland'.)
9 OSA, Lochgoilhead and Kilmorlich, Argyll, III, p. 192; and OSA, Weem, Perthshire, XII, pp. 131, 132.
10 OSA, Sorbie, Wigtownshire, I, p. 256.
11 OSA, Blairgowrie, Perthshire, XVII, p. 205.
12 OSA, Glenshiel, Ross-shire, VII, p. 130.
13 Aiton, *GVA, Bute* (1816), p. 328.
14 Mitchell, *Reminiscences of my Life in the Highlands*, vol. I, pp. 20, 21.
15 Ibid., pp. 21, 22.
16 Ibid., p. 31.
17 Barron, *Northern Highlands in the Nineteenth Century*, II, p. 64.
18 NSA, Dalserf, VI (Lanarkshire), p. 749.
19 Barron, *Northern Highlands in the Nineteenth Century*, II, p. 52.
20 Ibid., III, pp. 121, 124.
21 Ibid., III, pp. xxvi, xxvii.
22 Ibid., III, pp. 149, 150.
23 Ibid., III, pp. 157, 158.
24 Ibid., III, p. xxvii.
25 Ibid., III, p. 245.
26 Mitchell, *Reminiscences of my Life in the Highlands*, vol. I, p. 33.

3 Statute Labour

1 APS, 1669, VII, 574.
2 Whetstone, *Scottish County Government in the Eighteenth and Nineteenth Centuries*, p. 27.

3   APS, 1669, VII, 574.
4   Whetstone, *Scottish County Government in the Eighteenth and Nineteenth Centuries*, pp. 83, 84.
5   Ibid., p. 61.
6   APS, 1670, VIII; 18.
7   OSA, Leochel, Aberdeenshire, VI, p. 218 and OSA, New Machar, Aberdeenshire, VI, p. 474.
8   OSA, New Machar, Aberdeenshire, VI, p. 474.
9   APS, 1686, VIII, 590.
10 Headrick, *GVA, Angus* (1813), p. 222.
11 Ure, *GVA, Kinross* (1797), p. 20.
12 OSA, Grange, Banffshire, IX, pp. 571, 572.
13 Baker, *Companion to the Wade Roads*, p. 8, quoting John Knox, 'A tour through the Highlands of Scotland in 1786'.
14 OSA, Blackford, Perthshire, III, p. 212.
15 OSA, Auchtermuchty, VI, p. 347.
16 OSA, Kirkwall and St Ola, VII, p. 558.
17 OSA, Crimond, Aberdeenshire, XI, p. 418.
18 OSA, Little Dunkeld, VI, p. 374.
19 OSA, Mortlach, Banffshire, XVII, p. 436.
20 Hilson, *Jedburgh a Hundred Years Ago*, p. 18.
21 Robertson, *GVA, Perth* (1799), p. 362.
22 OSA, Mortlach, Banffshire, XVII, p. 436.
23 OSA, Crimond, Aberdeenshire, XI, p. 418.
24 Whetstone, *Scottish County Government in the Eighteenth and Nineteenth Centuries*, p. 85.
25 Robertson, *GVA, Perth* (1799), pp. 361–3.
26 OSA, Rogart, Sutherland, III, pp. 566, 567.
27 OSA, Keith, Banffshire, V, p. 426.
28 OSA, Gargunnock, Stirlingshire, XVIII, p. 103.
29 OSA, Peterculter, Aberdeenshire, XVI, p. 376.
30 Henderson, *GVA, Caithness* (1815), p. 235.
31 Headrick, *GVA, Angus* (1813), p. 514.
32 OSA, St Fergus, Aberdeenshire, XV, p. 145.
33 OSA, Lumphanan, Aberdeenshire, VI, p. 389.
34 OSA, Avoch, Ross-shire, XV, p. 631.
35 OSA, Peterculter, Aberdeenshire, XVI, p. 376.
36 Napier, *Survey of Selkirkshire or Ettrick Forest 1829*, pp. 8, 9.
37 OSA, Lochgoilhead and Kilmorlich, Argyllshire, III, p. 189.
38 OSA, Avoch, Ross-shire, XV, pp. 631, 632.
39 OSA, Logie and Pert, Angus, IX, p. 53.
40 Douglas, *GVA, Selkirkshire and Roxburghshire* (1798), p. 201.
41 OSA, Duffus, Morayshire, VIII, note to p. 394.
42 Headrick, *GVA, Angus* (1813), pp. 521, 522.
43 Barron, *Northern Highlands in the Nineteenth Century*, vol. III, p. 7.
44 Headrick, *GVA, Angus* (1813), pp. 521, 522.
45 Hilson, *Jedburgh a Hundred Years Ago*, p. 18.
46 OSA, Irvine, Ayrshire, VII, p. 172.
47 NSA, Berwickshire (Notes), II, p. 371.
48 Robertson, *GVA, Kincardineshire*, pp. 401, 402.
49 *Kelso Mail*, 29 September 1803.
50 Smith, *The Turnpike Age*, p. 1.

51 Dumfries Antiquarian Society, vol. 14–17, p. 76. (Mrs Brown, 'Moral and social conditions of Dumfries and Galloway a century ago — 1898–9'.)
52 Erskine, GVA, Clackmannanshire (1795), pp. 77, 79.
53 Johnston, GVA, Dumfries (1794), p. 73.
54 APS, 1669, VII, 574.
55 OSA, Inveresk, Edinburgh, XVI, p. 47.
56 OSA, Coldingham, Berwickshire, XII, p. 59.
57 Minutes of Ross-shire 1st District Roads Committee, 1816 and 1818.
58 Minutes of Trustees for the Statute Labour Conversion District of Melrose, 1825.
59 OSA, Barrie, Angus, IV, p. 244.
60 OSA, Arbirlot, Angus, III, p. 472.
61 OSA, Crimond, Aberdeenshire, XI, p. 418.
62 OSA, Peterculter, Aberdeenshire, XVI, p. 376.
63 NSA, Nigg, XIV (Ross-shire), p. 35.
64 NSA, Glenshiel, XIV (Ross-shire), p. 209.
65 Maxwell, Iona and the Ionians, p. 31.
66 OSA, Kirkden, Angus, II, p. 513.
67 OSA, Kilchrenan and Dalavich, VI, p. 270.
68 NSA, Crimond, XII (Aberdeenshire), p. 713.
69 Leslie, GVA, Nairn and Moray (1813), p. 379.
70 Headrick, GVA, Angus (1813), pp. 527, 528.
71 NSA, West Kilbride, V (Ayrshire), p. 268.
72 Johnston, GVA, Dumfries (1794), p. 68.
73 NSA, Kirkmichael and Cullicudden, XIV (Ross-shire), pp. 49, 50.
74 Minutes of Ross-shire 1st District Roads Committee, 1816, 1819, 1820.
75 Tain Museum papers.
76 Minutes of Ross-shire 1st District Roads Committee, 1820.
77 OSA, Baldernock, Stirlingshire, XV, p. 276.
78 APS, 1661, VII, 263.
79 APS, 1607, IV, 388.
80 APS, 1645, VI, 473.
81 APS, 1661, VII, 276.
82 Minutes of Ross-shire 1st District Roads Committee, 1821.
83 Kirk Session records of Nigg, Ross-shire, 1831; Martin, Church Chronicles of Nigg, pp. 38, 39, 40.
84 Maclennan, Ferindonald Papers, p. 43.
85 OSA, Kiltearn, Ross-shire, I, p. 284.
86 NSA, Broughton, Glenholm and Kilbucho, III (Peebles-shire), p. 92.
87 Whetstone, Scottish County Government in the Eighteenth and Nineteenth Centuries, pp. 56, 57.
88 Minutes of Trustees for the Statute Labour Conversion District of Melrose, 1812.
89 NSA, Buittle, IV (Kirkcudbright), p. 214.
90 NSA, Borgue, IV (Kirkcudbright), p. 60.
91 OSA, Inveravon, Banffshire, XIII, pp. 41, 42.
92 NSA, Canonbie, IV (Dumfries-shire), pp. 493, 494.
93 OSA, Langholm, Dumfries-shire, XIII, note to pp. 613, 614.
94 Barron, Northern Highlands in the Nineteenth Century, vol. I, pp. 21, 22.
95 OSA, Tough, Aberdeenshire, VIII, p. 268.
96 NSA, Knapdale, VII (Argyllshire), p. 274.
97 OSA, Humbie, East Lothian, VI, p. 159.

4 Turnpike Roads

1 OSA, Alloa, Clackmannanshire, VIII, p. 640.
2 OSA, Ormiston, East Lothian, IV, p, 171.
3 APS, 1669, VII, 574.
4 Haldane, *Drove Roads of Scotland*, p. 209.
5 Graham, *GVA, Kinross and Clackmannanshire* (1814), p. 342.
6 Erskine, *GVA, Clackmannanshire* (1795), p. 79.
7 Said by Mrs Rosemary Mackenzie, Tain.
8 *Kelso Mail*, 12 August 1847.
9 Leslie, *GVA, Nairn and Moray* (1813), pp. 380, 381.
10 OSA, West Linton, I, p. 456.
11 Henderson, *GVA, Caithness* (1815), p. 237.
12 Minutes of Ross-shire 1st District Roads Committee, 1816, 1819.
13 OSA, Foulis Wester, Perthshire, XV, p. 607.
14 *Kelso Mail*, 1803.
15 *Kelso Mail*, 3 April 1854.
16 Sederunt Book, Lauder–Kelso Road, 1824.
17 Ibid., 1823.
18 Smith, *The Turnpike Age*, p. 1.
19 *Kelso Mail*, 1 October 1855.
20 Johnston, *GVA, Dumfries-shire* (1794), p. 72.
21 Logue, *Popular Disturbances in Scotland 1780–1815*, p. 177.
22 OSA, Skene, Aberdeenshire, IV, p. 62.
23 OSA, Tealing, Angus, IV, p. 102.
24 OSA, Dallas, Morayshire, IV, p. 110.
25 OSA, Kirkconnel, Dumfries-shire, X, p. 456.
26 OSA, Crossmichael, Kirkcudbright, I, p. 181.
27 OSA, Kilspindie, Perth, IV, p. 208.
28 Logue, *Popular Disturbances in Scotland 1780–1815*, pp. 181, 182.
29 Sederunt Book, Lauder–Kelso Road, 1811.
30 Johnston, *GVA, Dumfries-shire* (1794), p. 72.
31 *Kelso Mail*, 3 April 1854.
32 Ibid., 29 May 1854.
33 Hyslop, *Langholm as it Was*, p. 666.
34 Ibid., pp. 672, 673.
35 Mackenzie, *Guide to Inverness and the Highlands*, p. 21.
36 *Kelso Mail*, 23 August 1847.
37 Ibid., 10 September 1855.
38 Barron, *Northern Highlands in the Nineteenth Century*, II, p. 180.
39 Ibid., II, p. 226.
40 Ibid., I, p. 119.
41 *Kelso Mail*, 13 September 1855.
42 Minutes of Turnpike Road Trustees, Kelso Union Turnpike, 1793.
43 *Kelso Mail*, 10 November 1803.
44 Johnston, *GVA, Dumfries-shire* (1794), pp. 72, 73.
45 *Kelso Mail*, 7 June 1847.
46 NSA, Biggar, VI (Lanarkshire), note to p. 371.
47 NSA, Carnwath, VI (Lanarkshire), p. 92.
48 NSA, Galashiels, III (Selkirkshire), p. 27.
49 *Border Magazine*, XII, p. 152. ('Reminiscences of old Liddesdale in pre-railway days', by Jock Elliot.)

50   OSA, Cleish, Kinross, III, p. 560.
51   NSA, St Cyrus, XI (Kincardine), p. 296.
52   NSA, Hobkirk, III (Roxburghshire), p. 217.
53   NSA, Tinwald and Trailflat, IV (Dumfries), p. 50.
54   NSA, Hobkirk, III (Roxburghshire), p. 217.
55   NSA, Wandell and Lamingtoune, VI (Lanarkshire), p. 844.
56   NSA, Biggar, VI (Lanarkshire), note to p. 371.
57   *Kelso Mail*, 11 November 1847.
58   *Kelso Mail*, 8 August 1842.
59   Lochinvar, *Romances of Gretna Green and its Runaway Marriages*, pp. 4, 5, 36, 37.
60   Haldane, *Drove Roads of Scotland*, p. 11.
61   NSA, Oxnam, III (Roxburghshire), p. 265.
62   *Kelso Mail*, 6 November 1848.
63   NSA, Duirinish, Skye, XIV (Inverness-shire), p. 357.
64   NSA, Sandsting and Aithsting, XV (Shetland), p. 134.
65   NSA, Strath (Skye), XIV (Inverness-shire), p. 313.
66   NSA, Pettie, XIV (Inverness-shire), p. 415.
67   OSA, Scoonie, Fife, V, p. 117.
68   OSA, Cupar, Fife, XVII, p. 151.
69   OSA, Symington, Ayrshire, V, p. 403.
70   OSA, Sanquhar, Dumfries-shire, VI, p. 461.
71   NSA, Killean and Kilchenzie, VII (Argyllshire), p. 379.
72   NSA, Moulin, X (Perthshire), p. 666.
73   OSA, Laurencekirk, Kincardine, V, p. 180.
74   OSA, Dunlop, Ayrshire, IX, p. 535.
75   Hood, *Melrose 1826*, p. 25.
76   Porteous, *History of Crieff*, p. 292.
77   Wordsworth, *Recollections of a Tour in Scotland in 1803*, p. 317.

5 *Travel on Two Feet*

1   Diary is in the possession of Miss Robb, Stenhouse, Newtown St Boswells.
2   Inglis, *An Angus Parish in the Eighteenth Century*, p. 18.
3   Barron, *Northern Highlands in the Nineteenth Century*, II, p. 144.
4   Brown, *Early Travellers in Scotland*, p. 273.
5   Inglis, *An Angus Parish in the Eighteenth Century*, p. 17.
6   *Dumfries Antiquarian Society*, 1894–5, vol. 9–13 ('Thirty years residence in Tynron', by James Shaw), p. 102.
7   *Border Magazine*, vol. 40, p. 10. ('The Kirk Bannie', by Harry Fraser.)
8   Ibid., vol. 13, pp. 208, 209. ('Yarrow Blanket Preaching'.)
9   Watson, *Place Names of Ross and Cromarty*, p. 57.
10   Moir, *Scottish Hill Tracks*, p. 34.
11   NSA, Sandsting and Aithsting, XV (Shetland), p. 134.
12   Young, *Annals of Elgin*, p. 55.
13   PSAS, vol. 47, pp. 210, 211. ('Fords, ferries and bridges near Lanark', by Thomas Reid.)
14   OSA, Urquhart and Loggie, Ross-shire, V, p. 215.
15   OSA, Loth, Sutherland, VI, p. 313.
16   Somerville, *My own Life and Times*, pp. 355, 356.
17   NSA, II (Berwickshire), notes to p. 372.
18   OSA, Bendochy, Perthshire, XIX, p. 358.

19 Maclennan, *Ferindonald Papers*, p. 43.
20 NSA, Crailing, III (Roxburghshire), pp. 183, 184.
21 Fenton and Stell, *Loads and Roads in Scotland and Beyond*, p. 59. (Article by Prof G W S Barrow, 'Land routes: The medieval evidence'.)
22 NSA, Nigg, XIV (Ross-shire), p. 20.
23 Scott and Gordon, *The Parish of Nigg*, p. 35.
24 Told by Mr P E Durham, Scotsburn, Kildary.
25 W G Blackie, *Descriptive Atlas of the World and General Geography*.
26 NSA, Dunipace (Stirlingshire), pp. 385, 386.
27 Kennedy, *Ancrum Remembered*, p. 23.
28 OSA, Dollar, Clackmannanshire, XV, p. 157 and note to p. 157.
29 Bathgate, *Aunt Janet's Legacy*, pp. 55, 62.
30 *Border Magazine*, vol. 15, p. 168. ('The Kelso Convoy', by G Watson.)
31 *Dumfries-shire Antiquarian Society's Transactions*, 1897–8, vol. 14–17 (Rev Thomas Rain, 'A century's changes'), p. 58.
32 Maclachlan, *The Story of Helensburgh*, pp. 216, 217.

6 *Ferries*

1   Fenton and Stell, *Loads and Roads in Scotland and Beyond*, p. 60. (Article by Prof G W S Barrow, 'Land routes: The medieval evidence'.)
2   Hogg, *Highland Tours*, p. 91.
3   APS, 1478, II, 119; APS, 1485, II, 172; APS, 1489, II, 221.
4   OSA, Ferry Port-on-Craig, VIII, note to p. 457.
5   APS, 1551, II, 486.
6   Fenton and Stell, *Loads and Roads in Scotland and Beyond*, p. 55. (Article by Prof G W S Barrow, 'Land routes: The medieval evidence'.)
7   OSA, South Queensferry, XVII, p. 494.
8   OSA, Tulliallan, Fife, XI, p. 550.
9   NSA, South Queensferry, II (Linlithgow), pp. 9–12.
10 Mercer, *History of Dunfermline*, p. 242.
11 Bailey, *Orkney*, p. 116.
12 Faichney, *Oban and the District Around*, p. 78.
13 OSA, Inveravon, Banffshire, XIII, p. 43.
14 APS, 1639, V, 606a.
15 Irving, *History of Dunbartonshire*, p. 507.
16 NSA, South Queensferry, II (Linlithgow), p. 12.
17 Barron, *Northern Highlands in the Nineteenth Century*, I, p. 23.
18 NSA, Galashiels, III (Selkirkshire), p. 18.
19 Barron, *Northern Highlands in the Nineteenth Century*, I, pp. 24, 25.
20 APS, 1425, II, 10.
21 APS, 1467, II, 87; APS, 1469, II, 97; APS, 1474, II, 107.
22 OSA, Ferry Port-on-Craig, Fife, VIII, pp. 457, 458.
23 APS, 1655, VI, 832b.
24 OSA, Ferry Port-on-Craig, Fife, VIII, pp. 457, 458.
25 Brown, *Early Travellers in Scotland*, p. 158.
26 Barron, *Northern Highlands in the Nineteenth Century*, III, p. 106.
27 OSA, Torosay, Argyllshire, III, p. 267.
28 OSA, Creich, Sutherland, VIII, p. 372.
29 Leslie, *GVA, Nairn and Moray* (1813), p. 68.
30 Haldane, *Drove Roads of Scotland*, p. 114.

31   Barron, *Northern Highlands in the Nineteenth Century*, III, p. 178.
32   NSA, Carnwath, VI (Lanarkshire), p. 88; NSA, Pettinain, VI (Lanarkshire), p. 544.
33   NSA, Caputh, X (Perthshire), pp. 681, 682; NSA, Logierait, X (Perthshire), pp. 697, 698.
34   NSA, Carnwath, VI (Lanarkshire), p. 88.
35   OSA, Airth, Stirlingshire, III, p. 489.
36   OSA, Craig, Angus, II, p. 499.
37   NSA, Falkirk (Stirlingshire), p. 30.
38   Faichney, *Oban and the District Around*, p. 64.
39   Barron, *Northern Highlands in the Nineteenth Century*, I, p. 245.
40   NSA, Kirkcudbright, IV (Kirkcudbright) note to p. 31.
41   Barron, *Northern Highlands in the Nineteenth Century*, I, p. 73.
42   NSA, Inverkeithing, IX (Fife), p. 238.
43   Leslie, GVA, *Nairn and Moray* (1813), p. 383.
44   *Inverness Courier*, 4 June 1864.
45   Mercer, *History of Dunfermline*, p. 242.
46   Ibid., p. 242.
47   *Duncan's Itinerary of Scotland*, App. pp. 11, 12.
48   Tain (Ross-shire), Museum papers.

7 Bridges

1   Robertson, GVA, *Inverness* (1808), p. 292.
2   OSA, Saddell and Skipness, Argyllshire, XII, p. 480.
3   PSAS, 46, p. 159. (H R G Inglis, 'Ancient Bridges of Scotland'.)
4   Brown, *Early Travellers in Scotland*, p. 152.
5   PSAS, 46, p. 158. (H R G Inglis, 'Ancient Bridges of Scotland'.)
6   Brown, *Early Travellers in Scotland*, p. 152.
7   PSAS, 46, p. 158. (H R G Inglis, 'Ancient Bridges of Scotland'.)
8   Ibid., p. 160.
9   Fenton and Stell, *Loads and Roads in Scotland and Beyond*, p. 87. (Article by Ted Ruddock, 'Bridges and Roads in Scotland 1400–1750'.)
10   OSA, St Andrews, Fife, XIII, p. 218.
11   PSAS, 46, p. 160. (H R G Inglis, 'Ancient Bridges of Scotland'.)
12   Ibid., p. 158.
13   OSA, Aberdeen, XIX, p. 153.
14   OSA, North Leith, VI, p. 574.
15   OSA, Cambuslang, Lanarkshire, V, p. 259.
16   OSA, Dunkeld, XX, pp. 441, 442.
17   Fenton and Stell, *Loads and Roads in Scotland and Beyond*, p. 60. (Article by Prof G W S Barrow, 'Land routes: The medieval evidence'.)
18   NSA, Boharm, XIII (Banffshire), pp. 365, 366.
19   OSA, Hamilton, Lanarkshire, II, note, to p. 180.
20   Fenton and Stell, *Loads and Roads in Scotland and Beyond*, pp. 69, 70. (Article by Ted Ruddock, 'Bridges and Roads in Scotland, 1400–1750'.)
21   *Transactions of Hawick Archaeological Society*, August 1877, p. 1. (Article by Alex Michie, 'Old local bridges'.)
22   OSA, Strathmartin, Angus, XIII, p. 97.
23   OSA, Duthil, Inverness-shire, IV, p. 314.
24   OSA, Kilmacolm (Renfrewshire), IV, p. 278.

25 OSA, Edinkillie, Morayshire, VII, note to p. 555.
26 Calder, *Civil and Traditional History of Caithness*, p. 315.
27 *SN & Q*, 3rd series, 1934, XII, p. 75.
28 Gourlay, *Anstruther, or Illustrations of Scottish Burgh Life*, p. 32.
29 Gordon, *Book of the Chronicles of Keith*, p. 50.
30 OSA, Kells, Kirkcudbright, IV, p. 271.
31 OSA, Kilmadock, Perthshire, XX, p. 50.
32 OSA, Logie and Pert, Angus, IX, p. 54.
33 Waddell, *An Old Kirk Chronicle*, pp. 48, 49.
34 NSA, Ayton II (Berwickshire), p. 143.
35 Gibson, *An Old Berwickshire Town*, pp. 231, 232.
36 *SN & Q*, XII, p. 59. (Kirk Session records of Alyth, by W Cramond.)
37 OSA, Edinkillie, Morayshire, VII, note to pp. 554, 555.
38 Kirk Session records of Ashkirk, Selkirkshire.
39 *The Scotsman* (Property Section), October 1984.
40 Gibson, *An Old Bewickshire Town*, pp. 123–5.
41 Mackintosh, *History of the Valley of the Dee*, pp. 30, 31.
42 NSA, Banchory-Devenick, XI (Kincardine), pp. 184, 185.
43 OSA, Fettercairn, Kincardine, V, pp. 333, 334.
44 Kirk Session records of Hownam, Roxburghshire.
45 Kirk Session records of Fettercairn, Kincardine.
46 Inglis, *An Angus Parish in the Eighteenth Century*, p. 101.
47 PSAS, 46, p. 172. (H R G Inglis, 'Ancient Bridges of Scotland'.)
48 Fenton and Stell, *Loads and Roads in Scotland and Beyond*, p. 71. (Article by Ted Ruddock, 'Bridges and Roads in Scotland 1400–1750'.)
49 Ibid., p. 85.
50 PSAS, 47, p. 212. ('Fords, ferries and bridges near Lanark', by Thomas Reid.)
51 Ibid.
52 Gordon, *Book of the Chronicles of Keith*, p. 88; PSAS, 28, p. 44.
53 APS, 1661, VII, 54.
54 Macdonald, *Bowden Kirk*, p. 24.
55 APS, 1685, VIII, 474.
56 Peebles-shire, *An Inventory of the Ancient Monuments*, II (1967), pp. 340, 341.
57 *Dumfries Antiquarian Society*, vol. 14–17, p. 320. (Article by James Barbour, FSA(Scot), 'How Annan got a bridge'.)
58 Burgh of Lanark, *Extracts from Records, 1150–1722* (1893), p. 189.
59 Ibid., p. 193.
60 OSA, North Leith, VI, p. 574.
61 Mackintosh, *History of the Valley of the Dee*, pp. 23, 24.
62 *Charters and Documents Relating to the Burgh of Peebles 1165–1710* (1872), p. 157.
63 Ibid., p. 328.
64 Burgh of Stirling, *Extracts from the Records 1667–1752*, p. 91.
65 NSA, Dalry, V (Ayrshire), p. 235.
66 Burgh of Stirling, *Extracts from the Records 1667–1752*, p. 126.
67 Haldane, *Drove Roads of Scotland*, p. 39.
68 Irving, *History of Dunbartonshire*, pp. 488, 491, 543, 544.
69 Young, *Parish of Spynie*, p. 154.
70 APS, Frag. Coll. C. 29, I, p. 753.
71 *Transactions of Hawick Archaeological Society*, August 1877, p. 4. (Article by Alex Michie, 'Old local bridges'.)
72 Whetstone, *Scottish County Government in the Eighteenth and Nineteenth Centuries*, p. 81.

73 Ibid., p. 82.
74 *PSAS*, 46, pp. 161, 162. (H R G Inglis, 'Ancient Bridges of Scotland'.)
75 Irving, *History of Dunbartonshire*, p. 551.
76 Ibid., p. 556.
77 OSA, Inverurie, Aberdeenshire, VII, p. 332.
78 *PSAS*, 46, pp. 162, 163. (H R G Inglis, 'Ancient Bridges of Scotland'.)
79 MacGeorge, *Old Glasgow*, p. 221.
80 *Dumfries Antiquarian Society*, vol. 14–17, pp. 320–6. (Article by James Barbour, FSA(Scot), 'How Annan got a bridge'.)
81 OSA, Rutherglen, Lanarkshire, IX, pp. 10, 11.
82 APS, 1661.
83 Burgh of Lanark, *Extracts from the Records, 1150–1722* (1893), p. 272.
84 *Dumfries Antiquarian Society*, vol 14–17, pp. 325, 326. (Article by James Barbour, FSA(Scot), 'How Annan got a bridge'.)
85 Burgh of Stirling, *Extracts from the Records, 1667–1752*, p. 123.
86 APS, 1670, VII, Ap. 5. ab.
87 APS, 1594, IV, 85.
88 APS, 1695, IX, 458.
89 APS, 1700, X, 231 a.
90 APS, 1669, VII, 574.
91 Burgh of Stirling, *Extracts from the Records, 1667–1752* (1889), p. 234.
92 *Transactions of Hawick Archaeological Society*, August 1877, p. 3. (Article by Alex Michie, 'Old local bridges'.)
93 Cramond, *Annals of Cullen*, p. 91.
94 *PSAS*, 46, p. 172. (H R G Inglis, 'Ancient Bridges of Scotland'.)
95 Ibid.
96 NSA, Alvah, XIII (Banffshire), p. 175.
97 OSA, Edinkillie, Morayshire, VII, p. 555.
98 OSA, Castletown, Roxburghshire, XVI, pp. 73, 74.
99 OSA, Dalry, Kirkcudbright, XIII, pp. 64, 65.
100 OSA, Dornoch, Sutherland, VIII, p. 10.
101 OSA, Rogart, Sutherland, III, p. 567.
102 OSA, Nesting, Shetland, XVII, p. 500.
103 Fenton and Stell, *Loads and Roads in Scotland and Beyond*, p. 70. (Article by Ted Ruddock, 'Bridges and Roads in Scotland 1400–1750'.)
104 Hyslop, *Langholm as it Was*, pp. 682, 683.
105 NSA, Moy and Dalarossie, XIV (Inverness-shire), p. 11.
106 OSA, Bonkle and Preston, Berwickshire, III, p. 154.
107 OSA, Nairn, XII, p. 389.
108 Haig, *History of Kelso*, pp. 140–2.
109 Mitchell, *Reminiscences of my Life in the Highlands*, I (1883), pp. 159, 160.
110 OSA, Abernethy and Kinchardine, Moray and Inverness, XIII, pp. 133–6.
111 Barron, *Northern Highlands in the Nineteenth Century*, I, p. 73.
112 Haldane, *Drove Roads of Scotland*, note to p. 124.
113 Mackintosh, *History of the Valley of the Dee*, p. 89.

8 The Responsibilities of the Burghs

1 M'Naught, *Kilmaurs Parish and Burgh*, pp. 264, 265.
2 Burgh of Stirling, *Extracts from the Records, 1667–1752* (1889), p. 292.
3 Cranna, *Fraserburgh Past and Present*, p. 61.

4   *Inverness Courier*, 18 August 1864.
5   Burgh of Lanark, *Extracts from Records, 1150–1722* (1893), p. 177.
6   Ibid.
7   Burgh of Stirling, *Extracts from the Records, 1667–1752* (1889), p. 295.
8   Cranna, *Fraserburgh Past and Present*, p. 39.
9   Irving, *History of Dunbartonshire*, p. 504.
10 Cramond, *Annals of Cullen*, pp. 105, 106.
11 Cunningham, *Dysart Past and Present*, p. 93.
12 *SN & Q*, XII, p. 43.
13 *Extracts from the Records of the Burgh of Edinburgh* (1940), vol. 1665–80, p. 149.
14 Burgh of Lanark, *Extracts from Records, 1150–1722* (1893), p. 156.
15 Ibid., p. 32.
16 Ibid., p. 180.
17 APS, 1661, VII, 41.
18 APS, 1669, VII, 574.
19 APS, 1686, VIII, 590.
20 *Extracts from the Records of the Burgh of Edinburgh* (1940), vol. 1665–80, p. 107.
21 Ibid., pp. 197, 198.
22 Ibid., pp. 270.
23 Ibid., vol. 1689–1701, p. 170.
24 Ibid., vol. 1665–80, p. 360.
25 OSA, Aberdour, Fife, IV, p. 329.
26 OSA, Inveresk, Edinburgh, XVI, p. 47.
27 OSA, Coupar Angus, XVII, p. 5.
28 Macdonald and Gordon, *Down to the Sea*, p. 38.
29 Barron, *Northern Highlands in the Nineteenth Century*, vol. III, pp. 50, 51, 55.

9 *Travel on Four Feet*

1   *SN & Q*, XII, p. 43.
2   Headrick, GVA, *Angus* (1813), p. 511.
3   *SN & Q*, XII, p. 43.
4   Calder, *Civil and Traditional History of Caithness*, p. 282.
5   Macdonald, *Bowden Kirk*, pp. 8, 9.
6   OSA, Kinnettles, Angus, IX, p. 214.
7   OSA, Keith, Banffshire, V, p. 423.
8   OSA, Kinnettles, Angus, IX, p. 214.
9   Dunbar, *Social Life in Former Days*, pp. 87–9.
10 OSA, Dumbarton, Dunbartonshire, IV, p. 26.
11 *SN & Q*, XII, p. 43.
12 Dawson, *Abridged Statistical History of Scotland*, note to p. 121.
13 Leslie, GVA, *Nairn and Moray*, p. 122.
14 OSA, Wick, Caithness, X, p. 25.
15 Ibid., p. 23.
16 OSA, Kildrummy, Aberdeenshire, XVIII, p. 413.
17 OSA, Kirkwall and St Ola, Orkney, VII, pp. 543, 544.
18 *Kelso Mail*, 11 August 1803.
19 Brand, *Description of Orkney, Zetland and Pightland Firth and Caithness in 1701*, pp. 117, 118.
20 OSA, South Uist, Inverness-shire, XIII, p. 295.
21 Ibid.

22   OSA, Foulis Wester, Perthshire, XV, p. 603.
23   OSA, Kirkwall and St Ola, Orkney, VII, p. 544.
24   *SN & Q*, IV, 2nd series (1903), p. 175.
25   Buchan, *History of Peebles-shire*, II, p. 128.
26   Headrick, *GVA, Angus* (1813), p. 511.
27   OSA, North Uist, Inverness-shire, XIII, p. 325.
28   Fenton and Stell, *Loads and Roads in Scotland and Beyond*, pp. 116, 119. (Article by Alexander Fenton, 'Wheelless transport in Northern Scotland'.)
29   NSA, Kilmorie, Arran, V (Buteshire), p. 62.
30   OSA, Auldearn, Nairnshire, XIX, p. 623.
31   OSA, Kiltarlity, Inverness-shire, XIII, p. 519.
32   OSA, Auldearn, Nairnshire, XIX, p. 623.
33   Headrick, *GVA, Angus* (1813), p. 511.
34   *Extracts from the Records of the Burgh of Edinburgh* (1940), vol. 1665–80, p. 34.
35   Headrick, *GVA, Angus* (1813), p. 512.
36   NSA, Haddingtonshire, p. 375 (remarks on the county).
37   OSA, Campsie, Stirlingshire, XV, pp. 383, 384.
38   Headrick, *GVA, Angus* (1813), p. 512.
39   *SN & Q*, XII, p. 43. (History of Transport in Scotland.)
40   *SN & Q*, II, 2nd series, p. 95.
41   Henderson, *GVA, Caithness* (1815), pp. 64, 65.
42   *Ross-shire Journal*, 11 Sept. 1986 ('Easter Ross memories', author unknown).
43   *Border Magazine*, VIII, pp. 19, 20. ('Memories of Border picnics', by Margaret Fletcher.)
44   *Dumfries Antiquarian Society*, vol. 9–13, p. 102 (1894–5). ('30 years residence in Tynron', by James Shaw.)
45   *Border Magazine*, XXI, p. 120.
46   Brown, *Early Travellers in Scotland*, p. 27 and note 2 to that page.
47   OSA, Tongland, Kirkcudbright, IX, p. 327.
48   *Border Magazine*, XVII, p. 177.

10   Coaching Days

1   *Border Magazine*, XXXI, p. 61. (Victor de Spiganovicz, 'Coaching days in Scotland'.)
2   *Transactions of Hawick Archaeological Society*, 1904, p. 6. (William Murray, 'Reminiscences of old coaching days'.)
3   Smith, *The Turnpike Age*, notes to Plate 1.
4   *Border Magazine*, XXXI, p. 61. (Victor de Spiganovicz, 'Coaching days in Scotland'.)
5   Smith, *The Turnpike Age*, notes to Plate 1.
6   *Transactions of Hawick Archaeological Society*, 1904, p. 32. (William Murray 'Reminiscences'.)
7   Ibid.
8   Ibid., p. 33.
9   Ibid.
10   Ibid.
11   Ibid.
12   *Border Magazine*, XXXI, p. 61. (Victor de Spiganovicz, 'Coaching days in Scotland.')
13   Ibid.
14   Ibid.

15 Brown, *Early Travellers in Scotland*, p. 278.
16 *Transactions of Hawick Archaeological Society*, 1904, p. 33. (William Murray, 'Reminiscences'.)
17 Brown, *Early Travellers in Scotland*, p. 278.
18 *Transactions of Hawick Archaeological Society*, 1904, p. 33. (William Murray, 'Reminiscences'.)
19 *Border Magazine*, XXXI, p. 63. (Victor de Spiganovicz, 'Coaching days in Scotland'.)
20 Porteous, *History of Crieff*, pp. 287, 288.
21 *Transactions of Hawick Archaeological Society*, 1904, pp. 33, 34. (William Murray, 'Reminiscences'.)
22 Ibid., p. 34.
23 *Extracts from the Records of the Burgh of Glasgow* (1895), III, p. 253.
24 *Transactions of Hawick Archaeological Society*, 1904, p. 34. (William Murray, 'Reminiscences'.)
25 Hood, *Melrose 1826*, p. 26.
26 *Transactions of Hawick Archaeological Society*, 1904, pp. 34, 35. (William Murray, 'Reminiscences'.)
27 Haldane, *Three Centuries of Scottish Posts*, p. 77.
28 Hood, *Melrose 1826*, p. 26.
29 Barron, *Northern Highlands in the Nineteenth Century*, I, pp. 23, 24.
30 *Transactions of Hawick Archaeological Society*, 1904, p. 34. (William Murray, 'Reminiscences'.)
31 Ibid.
32 *Inverness Courier*, 21 July 1864.
33 *Transactions of Hawick Archaeological Society*, 1904, p. 39. (William Murray, 'Reminiscences'.)
34 Miss Robb, Newtown St Boswells.
35 *Border Magazine*, XXXI, p. 62. (Victor de Spiganovicz, 'Coaching days in Scotland'.)
36 *Transactions of Hawick Archaeological Society*, 1904, p. 37. (William Murray, 'Reminiscences'.)
37 Smith, *The Turnpike Age*, notes on Stage-coaches.
38 *Border Magazine*, XXXI, p. 61. (Victor de Spiganovicz, 'Coaching days in Scotland'); Gray, *Auld Toon of Ayr*, p. 12.
39 Gregor, *An Echo of the Olden Time from the North of Scotland*, p. 32.
40 *Border Magazine*, XXXI, p. 61. (Victor de Spiganovicz, 'Coaching days in Scotland'.)
41 *SN & Q*, VIII, 3rd series, p. 59.
42 *Kelso Mail*, 23 June 1803.
43 Ibid., 13 February 1854.
44 *Inverness Courier*, 21 July 1864.
45 Smith, *The Turnpike Age*, notes to post chaises.
46 Haldane, *Three Centuries of Scottish Posts*, pp. 1–16.
47 Ibid., p. 79.
48 Ibid., p. 58.
49 *Transactions of Hawick Archaeological Society*, 1904, p. 37. (William Murray, 'Reminiscences'.)
50 *SN & Q*, VI, 3rd series, p. 218.
51 Headrick, *GVA, Angus* (1813), pp. 515, 516.
52 *Transactions of Hawick Archaeological Society*, 1904, p. 41. (William Murray, 'Reminiscences'.)

53   NSA, Kinross, IX (Kinross-shire), p. 20.
54   *Transactions of Hawick Archaeological Society*, 1904, p. 37. (William Murray, 'Reminiscences'.)
55   Barron, *Northern Highlands in the Nineteenth Century*, II, p. 218.
56   Ibid., p. 117.
57   *Transactions of Hawick Archaeological Society*, 1874, pp. 229, 230. (Walter Wilson, 'Reminiscences of Hawick — Locomotion in former days'.)
58   Young, *Annals of Elgin*, p. 58.
59   *Transactions of Hawick Archaeological Society*, 1904, p. 40. (William Murray, 'Reminiscences'.)
60   NSA, Garvald and Bara (Haddingtonshire), p. 98.
61   NSA, Morham (Haddingtonshire), p. 269.
62   NSA, Dollar (Clackmannanshire), pp. 115, 116.
63   *Transactions of Hawick Archaeological Society*, 1904, p. 37. (William Murray, 'Reminiscences.')
64   Ibid., p. 39; *Border Magazine*, vol. 40, pp. 149–50 (Edward Barton, 'Last journey of the mail coach'.)
65   Hyslop, *Langholm as it Was*, pp. 664, 665.
66   *SN & Q*, X, p. 47.
67   Miss Robb, Stenhouse, Newtown St Boswells.

11 *The Age of the Train*

1   NSA, Dalkeith, I, p. 512.
2   *Transactions of Hawick Archaeological Society*, 1904, p. 37. (William Murray, 'Reminiscences.')
3   NSA, Dundee, XI (Forfarshire), p. 41.
4   NSA, General Observations, vol. VII (Renfrewshire), p. 562.
5   NSA, Neilston, VII (Renfrewshire), p. 340.
6   NSA, Erskine, VII (Renfrewshire), p. 526.
7   *Kelso Mail*, 20 September 1847.
8   Ibid., 12 August 1847. (This is wrongly referred to in the press report as St John's Fair.)
9   *Kelso Mail*, 23 July 1849.
10   Lawrie, *Old St Boswells*, p. 15.
11   *Kelso Mail*, 30 July 1849.
12   Ibid., 7 June 1847.
13   Ibid., 14 June 1847.
14   Lawrie, *Old St Boswells*, p. 23.
15   Rankin, *Cockburnspath*, p. 34.
16   *Border Magazine*, XII, p. 133. ('Reminiscences of Liddesdale in pre-railway days'.)
17   *Kelso Mail*, 16 September 1847.
18   Barron, *Northern Highlands in the Nineteenth Century*, III, p. 339.
19   JEC, The Iron Track through the Highlands, pp. 16, 17. (This reference says the ceremony was performed by Lady Seaforth but contemporary press reports say it was by Lady Seafield.)
20   *Border Magazine*, vol. 38, p. 6.
21   *Kelso Mail*, 9 August 1849.
22   Cranna, *Fraserburgh Past and Present*, pp. 467, 468.
23   *Kelso Mail*, 16 January 1854.
24   *Border Magazine*, vol. 32, p. 66. ('Making of the Border Union Railway'.)
25   *Inverness Courier*, 21 July 1864.

26 *Transactions of Hawick Archaeological Society*, 1904, p. 36. (William Murray, 'Reminiscences'.)
27 *Kelso Mail*, 30 August 1849.
28 Ibid., 30 July 1849.
29 Ibid.
30 Ibid., 3 September 1855.
31 Ibid., 27 August 1849.
32 Lochinvar, *Romances of Gretna Green and its Runaway Marriages*, p. 44.
33 Gibson, *An Old Berwickshire Town*, pp. 224, 225.
34 *Kelso Mail*, 30 March 1854.
35 Ibid., 16 August 1849.
36 *Inverness Courier*, 4 and 11 August 1864.
37 *Kelso Mail*, 9 February 1854.
38 *Inverness Courier*, 30 June 1864.
39 *Border Magazine*, vol. 40, p. 47.
40 Ibid., vol. 38, p. 6. ('Making of the Berwickshire Railway', by T G in *Edinburgh Evening News*.)
41 NSA, Erskine, VII (Renfrewshire), p. 521.
42 Thomson, *Tracts*, pp. 1–8 of Tract 18, 'The Sabbath and the railway'.
43 Pendleton, *Our Railways*, II, pp. 72–4.
44 Barron, *Northern Highlands in the Nineteenth Century*, II, p. 248.
45 Young, *Annals of Elgin*, pp. 602, 603.
46 *Border Magazine*, vol. 32, p. 67. ('Making of the Border Union Railway'.)

12 Rest for the Traveller

1   APS 1336, I, 499.b.
2   APS, 1424, II, 6.
3   APS, 1427, II, 14.
4   APS, 1496, II, 238.
5   APS, 1503, II, 243.
6   APS, 1535, II, 346.
7   APS, 1551, II, 487.
8   APS, 1567, III, 41.
9   APS, 1425, II, 10.
10 APS, 1493, II, 234.
11 APS, 1436, II, 24.
12 APS, 1621, IV, 613.
13 SN & Q, V, p. 8.
14 *Extracts from the Records of the Burgh of Edinburgh* (1940), vol. 1689–1701, p. 171.
15 NSA, North Berwick, Haddingtonshire, p. 343.
16 M'Naught, *Kilmaurs Parish and Burgh*, p. 168.
17 MacGeorge, *Old Glasgow*, p. 234.
18 APS, 1656, VI, ii, 865a–865b.
19 NSA, Hamilton, VI (Lanarkshire), p. 293.
20 Inglis, *An Angus Parish in the Eighteenth Century*, p. 36.
21 OSA, Carnock, Fife, XI, p. 494.
22 OSA, Neilston, Renfrewshire, II, p. 158.
23 NSA, Nigg, XIV (Ross-shire), p. 37.
24 NSA, Ardersier, XIV (Inverness-shire), p. 482.
25 OSA, Canisbay, Caithness, VIII, p. 161.

26 OSA, Port Patrick, Wigtownshire, XXI, pp. 8, 9.
27 NSA, North Berwick, Haddingtonshire, p. 343.
28 NSA, Kirkintilloch, VIII (Dunbartonshire), p. 210.
29 NSA, Liberton (Edinburgh), I, pp. 27, 28.
30 NSA, Yarrow, III (Selkirkshire), p. 56.
31 NSA, Auchtergaven, X (Perthshire), pp. 449, 450.
32 OSA, Assynt, Sutherland, XVI, p. 210.
33 OSA, Clatt, Aberdeenshire, VIII, p. 541.
34 NSA, Ormiston, Haddingtonshire, p. 152.
35 OSA, Dingwall, Ross-shire, III, p. 18,
36 OSA, Closeburn, Dumfries-shire, XIII, p. 247.
37 OSA, Inverbervie, Kincardineshire, XIII, p. 5.
38 OSA, Moffat, II, pp. 295, 296.
39 NSA, Portpatrick, IV (Wigtownshire), p. 160. (A hand-written note in the margin of this volume, in the National Library, says of this inn 'because the only one, and miserable'.)
40 Dinnie, *History of Kincardine O'Neil*, p. 55.
41 Douglas, *History of the Village of Ferryden*, p. 8.
42 OSA, Cromdale, Moray and Inverness, VIII, p. 259.
43 OSA, Kirkhill, Inverness-shire, IV, p. 122.
44 Dinnie, *History of Kincardine O'Neil*, pp. 81, 82.
45 SN & Q, vol. VI, p. 106.
46 Brown, *Early Travellers in Scotland*, pp. 127, 128.
47 Ibid., p. 89.
48 OSA, Reay, Caithness, VII, p. 579.
49 OSA, Assynt, Sutherland, XVI, p. 198.
50 SN & Q, vol. VI, 3rd series, p. 92.
51 SN & Q, vol. I, 3rd series, p. 11.
52 OSA, Kildonan, Sutherland, III, p. 411.
53 Maclennan, *Ferindonald Papers*, p. 94.
54 OSA, Kintail, Ross-shire, VI, p. 245.
55 Somerville, *My own Life and Times*, pp. 356, 357.
56 Brown, *Early Travellers in Scotland*, pp. 156, 157.
57 Boswell, *Journal of a Tour to the Hebrides in 1773*, p. 253.
58 Hogg, *Highland Tours*, p. 151.
59 Bruce, *History of the Parish of West or Old Kilpatrick*, pp. 148, 149.
60 Campbell, *Book of Garth and Fortingall*, p. 311.
61 Baker, *A Walker's Companion to the Wade Roads*, note to p. 34.
62 Haldane, *Drove Roads of Scotland*, p. 42.
63 NSA, Kirkpatrick-Juxta, IV (Dumfries-shire), p. 131.
64 NSA, Stow, I (Midlothian), p. 429.
65 Lochinvar, *Romances of Gretna Green and its Runaway Marriages*, p. 15.
66 Mackenzie, *Guide to Inverness and the Highlands*.

13 *All Kinds of Carriers*

1 Ashton, *Chap Books of the Eighteenth Century*, Introduction, p. viii.
2 *Border Magazine*, vol. 36, p. 94. ('The Old Scots Packman', by Charles Menmuir.)
3 SN & Q, vol. VI, 3rd series, p. 244.
4 Cook, *Old Time Traders and their Ways*, pp. 29–31.
5 Gourlay, *Anstruther, or Illustrations of Scottish Burgh Life*, p. 22.

6   Scott and Gordon, *The Parish of Nigg*, p. 23.
7   Thomson, *Recollections of a Speyside Parish Fifty Years Ago*, p. 97.
8   Cook, *Old Time Traders and their Ways*, p. 107.
9   Ibid., p. 105.
10 Ibid., p. 34.
11 Lamb, *West Kilbride*, pp. 240, 241.
12 Browne, *Glimpses into the Past in Lammermuir*, pp. 59, 60.
13 *Border Magazine*, XII, p. 153. ('Reminiscences of Liddesdale in pre-railway days', by Jock Elliot.)
14 Macleod, *Discovering Galloway*, p. 178.
15 SN & Q, XI, p. 89. ('Packmen's Graves', by Jeannie M Laing.)
16 Ashton, *Chap Books of the Eighteenth Century*, Introduction, p. viii.
17 Horne, *The County of Caithness*, pp. 147, 148.
18 OSA, Little Dunkeld, Perthshire, XX, p. 432, has a good description of the Chapman Society, a kind of trade guild, and there is a reference to 'The King of the Travelling Merchants' in 1834 — S N & Q, VI, 3rd series, p. 169.
19 NSA, Kinross, IX (Kinross-shire), p. 19.
20 Inglis, *An Angus Parish in the Eighteenth Century*, p. 47.
21 Allardyce, *Bygone Days in Aberdeenshire*, p. 108.
22 Inglis, *An Angus Parish in the Eighteenth Century*, p. 47.
23 Cook, *Old Time Traders and their Ways*, p. 32.
24 Burgh of Stirling, *Extracts from the Records, 1667–1752* (1889), p. 111.
25 Ibid., p. 241.
26 *Charters and Documents Relating to the Burgh of Peebles, 1165–1710*, p. 400 and note.
27 Burgh of Stirling, *Extracts from the Records 1667–1752* (1889), p. 271.
28 SN & Q, XII, p. 43.
29 SN & Q, XII, p. 42.
30 Ibid., p. 43.
31 *Dumfries Antiquarian Society*, 1894–5, p. 51. ('Colvend as it was', by Rev James Fraser, DD.)
32 NSA, Smailholm, III (Roxburghshire), pp. 142, 143.
33 *Border Magazine*, XXI, p. 135. ('Drumtorland', by Gilbert Rae.)
34 Cook, *Old Time Traders and their Ways*, pp. 106, 107.
35 Hyslop, *Langholm as it Was*, p. 665.
36 *Dumfries Antiquarian Society*, vol. 14–17, 1898–9, p. 76. ('The moral and social conditions of Dumfries and Galloway a century ago', by Mrs Brown.)
37 Hyslop, *Langholm as it Was*, p. 665.
38 *Extracts from the Records of the Burgh of Edinburgh* (1940), 1665–80, p. 34.
39 Cramond, *Presbytery of Fordyce*, p. 71.
40 Burgh of Lanark, *Extracts from Records, 1150–1722* (1893), pp. 300, 301.
41 *Extracts from the Records of the Burgh of Edinburgh* (1940), 1665–80, p. 149.
42 NSA, Haddingtonshire, Notes, p. 380.
43 Whetstone, *Scottish County Government in the Eighteenth and Nineteenth Centuries*, p. 57.
44 *Kelso Mail*, 7 July 1803.
45 Anderson, *A History of Kilsyth*, p. 10.
46 *Border Magazine*, II, p. 19.
47 Ibid., VIII, pp. 135, 136. ('Rab the carrier', by W F C.)
48 Ibid., XXXIX, p. 166.
49 Loose note in Ledger, 1904–6, of Milton Mill, Kildary, Ross-shire.
50 Pollok, *The Parish of Lilliesleaf*, pp. 26, 27.

51 *Border Magazine*, VI, p. 2.
52 Ibid., II, p. 19.
Note: 'Stouriefeet' or 'dustiefoot' were names given to those, usually pedlars or travelling merchants, who had no regular home where they could get the dust off their feet.

14 *Human Beasts of Burden*

1 Pennant, *Tour in Scotland in 1769*, p. 168. Note — OSA, Tongland, Kircudbright, IX, p. 327, also refers to women carrying dung.
2 NSA, Kilmuir, Skye, XIV (Inverness-shire), p. 279.
3 OSA, Keith-Hall and Kinkell, Aberdeenshire, II, p. 540.
4 NSA, Kilmuir, Skye, XIV (Inverness-shire), p. 279.
5 NSA, Lochbroom, XIV (Ross-shire), p. 89.
6 OSA, Alloa, Clackmannanshire, VIII, p. 615.
7 Ibid., pp. 615, 616.
8 Ibid., p. 615.
9 NSA, Alloa (Clackmannanshire), p. 29.
10 OSA, Inveresk (Edinburgh), XVI, pp. 15–17.
11 Ibid., pp. 17, 18, and note to p. 18.
12 Douglas, *History of the Village of Ferryden*, pp. 7, 8.
13 *Dumfries Antiquarian Society*, vol 14–17, p. 320. ('How Annan got a bridge', by James Barbour.)
14 This is said by Mr Jim Johnston, Bettyhill, Sutherland.
15 Fenton and Stell, *Loads and Roads in Scotland and Beyond*, p. 106. ('Wheelless transport in Northern Scotland', by Alexander Fenton.)
16 Hogg, *Highland Tours*, pp. 102, 103.
17 *Border Magazine*, XII, p. 132. ('Reminiscences of Liddesdale in pre-railway days'.)
18 *Border Magazine*, XIV, p. 9.
19 Tancred, *Rulewater and its People*, p. 307.
20 NSA, Wemyss, IX (Fife), p. 398.
21 *Dumfries Antiquarian Society*, vol. 9–13, 1894–5, p. 24. ('Recollections of Dumfries', by Dr Robert Taylor.)
22 *Border Magazine*, XXXI, p. 62. (Victor de Spiganovicz, 'Coaching Days in Scotland.')
23 *SN & Q*, XII, p. 43.
24 Gray, *Auld Toon of Ayr*, p. 21.
25 McNeill, *The Silver Bough*, III, p. 100.
26 Young, *Annals of Elgin*, p. 601.
27 *Scottish Home and Country*, October 1983, p. 344. ('In the days of the sedan chair', by John Mackay.)

15 *Church and School Attendance*

1 Mackay, *Urquhart and Glenmoriston*, p. 362.
2 NSA, Applecross, XIV (Ross-shire), p. 104.
3 NSA, Kirkcolm, IV (Wigtownshire), p. 120.
4 APS, 1645, VI, i, 397.b.
5 NSA, Rogart, XV (Sutherland), p. 54.
6 NSA, Assynt, XV (Sutherland), p. 115.

7   NSA, Balfron, Stirlingshire, p. 298.
8   NSA, Walls, XV (Shetland), pp. 21, 22.
9   OSA, North Uist, XIII, p. 322, 323.
10 NSA, Halkirk, XV (Caithness), pp. 79, 80.
11 NSA, Kilmalle, XIV (Inverness-shire), pp. 125, 126.
12 NSA, Lonmay, Aberdeenshire, XII, pp. 231, 232.
13 NSA, Latheron, XV (Caithness), pp. 107, 108.
14 NSA, Kilconquhar, IX (Fife), pp. 333, 334.
15 Cramond, *Presbytery of Fordyce*, pp. 11, 27.
16 Mackay, *Sidelights of Highland History*, p. 50.
17 Gibson, *An Old Berwickshire Town*, note at foot of p. 225.
18 Lamb, *West Kilbride*, p. 214.
19 *Charters and Documents relating to the Burgh of Peebles, 1165–1710*, p. 414.
20 Dick, *Annals of Colinsburgh*, p. 101.
21 Mackay, *Sidelights of Highland History*, p. 73.
22 OSA, Arbroath, VII, pp. 343, 344.
23 OSA, Moy and Dalarossie, Inverness-shire, VIII, p. 508.
24 OSA, Unst, Shetland, V, note to p. 198.
25 OSA, Eddrachillis, Sutherland, VI, p. 304.
26 OSA, Gairloch, Ross-shire, III, p. 92.
27 NSA, Portree, Skye, XIV (Inverness-shire), p. 233.
28 NSA, Glenelg, XIV (Inverness-shire), p. 142.
Note: A man presently living in Berwickshire remembers his school days in
Kirkcudbright when he, and his brothers and sisters walked 4 miles to school each day
and jogged home, one of them setting the pace and the rest falling in with it. The only
thing that stopped them was an adder on the path — if possible, they killed it and then
carried on jogging.
29 NSA, Boleskine and Abertarff, XIV (Inverness-shire), p. 62.
30 OSA, Srathdon, Aberdenshire, XIII, note to p. 179.
31 NSA, Sandwick, XV (Orkney), p. 65.
32 *Log Book of Arinacrinachd School, Ross-shire, December 1877.*
33 NSA, Westray, XV (Orkney) p. 131.
34 *Log Book of Arinacrinachd School, Ross-shire, November 1875.*
35 *Log Book of Inverasdale School, Ross-shire, December 1877.*
36 *Log Book of Tullich School, Ross-shire, March 1897.*
37 Ibid., March 1906.
38 NSA, Baldernock, Stirlingshire, p. 174.
39 OSA, Kilmadock, Perthshire, XX, p. 83.
40 *Log Book of Arinacrinachd School, Ross-shire, November 1877.*
41 *Log Book of Megget School, Selkirkshire, 1911.*
42 NSA, Dollar, Clackmannanshire, p. 116.
43 Bailey, Orkney, p. 116.
44 There still exists in the Ettrick Valley area a pair of stilts, made last century.
45 Mackay, *Urquhart and Glenmoriston*, p. 456.
46 *Log Book of Inverasdale School, Ross-shire, December 1877; November 1878;* and
    December 1882.
47 *Log Book of Arinacrinachd School, Ross-shire, November 1875.*
48 Murray, *Life in Scotland a Hundred Years Ago*, pp. 228, 229.
49 OSA, Cargill, Perthshire, XIII, p. 545.
50 *Log Book of Megget School, Selkirkshire, November 1899.*
51 *Log Book of Tullich School, Ross-shire, 1878.*
52 Waddell, *An Old Kirk Chronicle*, p. 49.

16 *Fuel, Fertilisers and Fairs*

1   OSA, Fernell, Angus, III, pp. 229, 230.
2   OSA, Bendothy, Perthshire, XIX, p. 358.
3   OSA, Nigg, Ross-shire, XIII, p. 22.
4   OSA, Glenshiel, Ross-shire, VII, p. 130.
5   OSA, Clunie, Perthshire, IX, p. 276.
6   Bentinck, *Dornoch Cathedral and Parish*, p. 475.
7   OSA, Westray, Orkney, XVI, p. 264.
8   OSA, Gigha and Cara, Argyllshire, VIII, p. 44.
9   OSA, Kintail, Ross-shire, VI, p. 249.
10 OSA, Tiree, Argyllshire, X, p. 418.
11 OSA, Nigg, Ross-shire, XIII, p. 22.
12 OSA, Urray, Ross-shire, VII, pp. 250, 251.
13 OSA, Kennethmont, Aberdeenshire, XIII, pp. 71, 72.
14 OSA, Duffus, Morayshire, VIII, p. 397.
15 OSA, Kirkinner, Wigtownshire, IV, p. 147.
16 OSA, Glenorchy and Inishail, Argyllshire, VIII, p. 358.
17 OSA, Eyemouth, Berwickshire, III, p. 116.
18 OSA, Swinton and Simprim, Berwickshire, VI, p. 328.
19 Mitchell, *Reminiscences of my Life in the Highlands*, vol. I, p. 46.
20 OSA, New or East Kilpatrick, Dunbartonshire, VII, p. 108. NSA, New
    Kilpatrick, VIII (Dunbartonshire), p. 59.
21 OSA, Rathven, Banffshire, XIII, p. 396.
22 OSA, Dalry, Kirkcudbright, XIII, p. 64.
23 OSA, Blair Atholl and Strowan, Perthshire, II, p. 481.
24 OSA, Gigha and Cara, Argyllshire, VIII, pp. 67, 68.
25 Kirk Session records of Kirk Yetholm, Roxburghshire, 1710.
26 *Ross-shire Journal*, 11 September 1986 ('Easter Ross Memories' — no author.)
27 NSA, Glenelg, XIV (Inverness-shire), p. 139.
28 OSA, Dundee, Angus, VIII, p. 243.
29 NSA, Muiravonside, Stirlingshire, p. 214.
30 NSA, Dingwall, XIV (Ross-shire), pp. 234, 235.
31 NSA, Rosemarkie, XIV (Ross-shire), p. 365.
32 NSA, North Uist, XIV (Inverness-shire), p. 181.
33 OSA, Anstruther-Wester, Fife, III, p. 88.
34 NSA, Paisley, VII (Renfrewshire), pp. 278, 279.
35 Robertson, *GVA, Kincardine*, pp. 402, 403.
36 Aiton, *GVA, Bute* (1816), pp. 329, 330.
37 OSA, Auchtertool, Fife, VIII, p. 119.
38 OSA, Cromdale, Morayshire, VIII, p. 259.
Note: The parish of Kennethmont, Aberdeenshire, had far more women than men because so many widows and old maids came there because peat mosses were convenient. (OSA, Kennethmont, XIII, p. 75.)

17 *The Postal Service*

1   SN & Q, vol. VI, p. 34. (W Cramond — 'Old time mail arrangements'.)
2   Allardyce, *Bygone Days in Aberdeenshire*, pp. 23, 24.
3   APS, 1695, IX, 417.
4   Somerville, *My Own Life & Times*, p. 355.

5   Ibid.
6   *NSA*, Hawick, III (Roxburghshire), pp. 406, 407.
7   Haldane, *Three Centuries of Scottish Posts*, p. 9.
8   Channel 4 Television, 9 December 1984.
9   Hyslop, *Langholm as it Was*, pp. 696, 697, 698.
10 Buchan, *History of Peebles-shire*, II, pp. 127–8.
11 Pollok, *The Parish of Lilliesleaf*, p. 29.
12 Martine, *Reminiscences of the Royal Burgh of Haddington*, p. 229.
13 OSA, Kilmorack, Inverness-shire, XX, p. 408.
14 OSA, Eddrachillis, Sutherland, VI, p. 305.
15 *NSA*, Unst, XV (Shetland), pp. 47, 48.
16 *SN & Q*, VI, 3rd series, p. 203. (Note — until 1855, when proper registration of births etc. began, there could be confusion about age, so Tibbie Walker may have been younger — or older — than 111.)
17 OSA, Kilmorack, Inverness-shire, XX, p. 408.
18 OSA, Lismore and Appin, Argyllshire, I, p. 497.
19 *NSA*, Morebattle and Mow, III (Roxburghshire), p. 454.
20 Dunbar, *Social Life and Former Days* (1865), pp. 33, 34.
21 Martine, *Reminiscences of the Royal Burgh of Haddington*, p. 231.
22 *Dumfries Antiquarian Society*, vol. 9–13, 1894–5, p. 48. (Rev James Fraser — 'Colvend as it was 50 years ago and is now'.)
23 OSA, Blair Atholl and Strowan, II, p. 481.
24 Hyslop, *Langholm as it Was*, p. 698.
25 *Border Magazine*, XII, p. 132. 'Reminiscences of Liddesdale in pre-railway days'.)
26 Macleod, *Reminiscences of a Highland Parish*, p. 63.
27 Gibson, *An Old Berwickshire Town*, p. 226.
28 *Border Magazine*, XII, p. 132. ('Reminiscences of Liddesdale in pre-railway days').
29 *NSA*, Ormiston, Haddingtonshire, p. 146.
30 Old Post Office, Nigg, Ross-shire, now demolished.
31 Scott and Gordon, *The Parish of Nigg*, p. 18.

18 *Pleasure Seekers*

1   Faichney, *Oban and the District Around*, pp. 64, 65.
2   Ibid., p. 67.
3   Maxwell, *Iona and the Ionians*, pp. 29, 30.
4   Faichney, *Oban and the District Around*, p. 67.
5   Ibid., p. 63.
6   *Duncan's Itinerary of Scotland 1823*, p. 71.
7   *SN & Q*, VI, p. 34. (W Cramond — 'Old time mail arrangements'.)
8   Barron, *Northern Highlands in the Nineteenth Century*, II, p. 186.
9   Ibid., I, p. 26.
10 Ibid., I, p. 42.
11 Ibid., II, p. 186.
12 Ibid., I, p. 43.
13 Ibid., II, p. 187.
14 Ibid., III, p. 185.
15 Anderson, History of Kilsyth, pp. 24, 25.
16 *NSA*, Paisley, VII (Renfrewshire), note to p. 278.
17 Faichney, *Oban and the District Around*, p. 67.
18 Horne, *The County of Caithness*, p. 178.

19 Duncan's *Itinerary of Scotland 1823*, p. 28 of Appendix.
20 Ibid., p. 1 of Appendix.
21 Weir, *History of Greenock*, p. 121.
22 NSA, Monifieth, XI (Forfarshire), p. 553.
23 Faichney, *Oban and the District Around*, pp. 68, 69.
24 *Inverness Courier*, 21 July 1864.
25 Mackenzie, *Guide to Inverness and the Highlands*.
26 Duncan's *Itinerary of Scotland 1823*, p. 77.
27 *Border Magazine*, VI, p. 89.
28 Barron, *Northern Highlands in the Nineteenth Century*, I, pp. 164, 165.
29 *Border Magazine*, XLIV, p. 15.

19 *Backwards and Onwards*

1 Calder, *Civil and Traditional History of Caithness*, p. 307.
2 Bailey, *Orkney*, p. 123.
3 *Ross-shire Journal*, 11 September 1986. ('Easter Ross memories' — no author given.)

BIBLIOGRAPHY

Allardyce, John *Bygone Days in Aberdeenshire* (Aberdeen 1913).

Anderson, Rev Robert *A History of Kilsyth* (Edinburgh and Glasgow 1901).

Ashton, John *Chap Books in the Eighteenth Century* (London 1882).

Bailey, Patrick *Orkney* (Newton Abbot 1971).

Baird, J G A *Muirkirk (Ayrshire) in Bygone Days*.

Baker, Joan and Arthur *A Walker's Companion to the Wade Roads* (Perth 1982).

Barron, James *Northern Highlands in the Nineteenth Century* (Inverness 1907).

Bathgate, Janet *Aunt Janet's Legacy* (Selkirk and Edinburgh 1901).

Beaton, Rev D *Ecclesiastical History of Caithness and Annals of Caithness Parishes* (Wick 1909).

Bentinck, R v G D *Dornoch Cathedral and Parish* (Inverness 1926).

Boswell, James *Journal of a Tour to the Hebrides in 1773* (Oxford 1924).

Brand, Rev John *A Brief Description of Orkney, Zetland and Pightland (sic) Firth and Caithness in 1701* (Wick 1883).

Brown, Hume *Early Travellers in Scotland* (Edinburgh 1978).

Browne, John Hutton *Glimpses into the Past in Lammermuir* (Edinburgh 1892).

Bruce, John *History of the Parish of West or Old Kilpatrick*.

Buchan, J W *History of Peebles-shire* (Glasgow 1925).

Butler, Rev D *Lindean and Galashiels* (Galashiels 1915).

Calder *Civil and Traditional History of Caithness* (Wick 1887).

Campbell, Duncan *Book of Garth and Fortingall* (Inverness 1888).

Cook, A S *Old Time Traders and Their Ways* (Aberdeen 1904).

Cramond, W *Annals of Cullen* (Buckie 1888).

Cramond, W *Pamphlets — Presbytery of Fordyce* (Banff 1885).

Cranna, John *Fraserburgh Past and Present* (Aberdeen 1914).

Crockett, W S *Berwickshire and Roxburghshire* (1926).

Cruickshank, James *Newhills, Annals of a Parish* (Spalding Club 1934).

Cunningham, A S *Dysart, Past and Present* (1912).

Dawson, J H D *An Abbreviated Statistical History of Scotland* (Edinburgh 1853).

Dick, Rev Robert *Annals of Colinsburgh* (Edinburgh 1896).

Dinnie, Robert *History of Kincardine O'Neil* (Aberdeen 1885).

Dobson, Thomas *Reminiscences of Innerleithen and Traquair* (Innerleithen 1896).

Douglas *A History of the Village of Ferryden* (1855).

Dunbar, E *Dunbar, Social Life in Former Days* (Edinburgh 1865).

Faichney, Alexander M *Oban and the District Around* (Oban 1902).

Fenton, Alexander and Stell, Geoffrey *Loads and Roads in Scotland and Beyond* (Edinburgh 1984).

Gibson, Robert *An Old Berwickshire Town* (Edinburgh and London 1905).

Gordon, Rev J F S *Book of the Chronicles of Keith, Grange, Ruthven, Cairney and Botriphnie* (Glasgow 1880).

Gourlay, George   *Anstruther, or Illustrations of Scottish Burgh Life* (Anstruther and Coupar-Fife 1888).

Gray, Henry C   *The Auld Toon of Ayr* (Ayr 1872).

Gregor, Rev Walter   *An Echo of the Olden Time from the North of Scotland* (Edinburgh and Peterhead 1874).

Haig, James   *History of Kelso* (Edinburgh and London 1825).

Haldane, A R B   *Drove Roads in Scotland* (Edinburgh 1968).

Haldane, A R B   *Three Centuries of Scottish Posts* (Edinburgh 1971).

Hall, Robert   *History of Galashiels* (Galashiels 1898).

Henderson, John A   *History of Banchory-Devenick* (Aberdeen 1890).

Henderson, John A   *Annals of Lower Deeside* (Aberdeen 1892).

Hilson, George   *Jedburgh a Hundred Years Ago* (Reprints from *Kelso Mail* 1897).

Hilson, J Lindsay   *Yesterdays in a Royal Burgh* (*Jedburgh Gazette* reprints).

Hogg, James   *Highland Tours* (Byways Books, Hawick 1983).

Hood, D M (ed.)   *Melrose 1826* (Galashiels 1978).

Horne, John   *The County of Caithness* (Wick 1907).

Hyslop, John and Robert   *Langholm as it Was* (Sunderland 1912).

Inglis, Rev W M   *An Angus Parish in the Eighteenth Century* (Dundee 1904).

Irving, Joseph   *History of Dunbartonshire* (Dumbarton 1860).

JEC   *The Iron Track Through the Highlands* (1914).

Johnson, Samuel   *Journey to the Western Isles of Scotland* (Oxford 1924).

Kennedy, Margaret   *Ancrum Remembered* (1980/1).

Knox, John   *A Tour through the Highlands of Scotland and the Hebride Islands in 1786.*

Lamb, Rev John   *West Kilbride* (Glasgow 1896).

Lawrie, Jean S   *Old St Boswells* (1974).

Lawson, Rev Alexander   *The Book of the Parish of Deir* (Aberdeen 1896).

Lochinvar   *Romances of Gretna Green and its Runaway Marriages* (Carlisle 1909).

Logue, Kenneth   *Popular Disturbances in Scotland, 1780–1815* (Edinburgh 1979).

Macdonald, J S M   *Bowden Kirk* (Kelso 1978).

Macdonald, Jessie and Gordon, Anne   *Down to the Sea* (1970).

Macdonald, Mairi   *Historic Hill Routes of Lorn and Lochaber* (Oban 1982).

MacGeorge, Andrew   *Old Glasgow* (Glasgow 1880).

Mackay, William   *Sidelights of Highland History* (1925).

Mackay, William   *Urquhart and Glenmoriston* (1925).

Mackenzie, Alexander   *Guide to Inverness and the Highlands* (Inverness 1893 and 1896).

Mackenzie, W M   *Book of Arran* (Glasgow 1914).

Mackie, J D   *History of Scotland* (Penguin Books, Harmondsworth 1964).

Mackintosh, John   *History of the Valley of the Dee* (Aberdeen 1895).

Maclachlan, G   *The Story of Helensburgh* (Helensburgh 1896).

Maclennan, Frank   *Ferindonald Papers* (Thurso).

Macleod, Donald   *A Nonagenarian's Reminiscences of Garelochside and Helensburgh* (Helensburgh 1883).

Macleod, Innes   *Discovering Galloway* (Edinburgh 1986).

Macleod, Norman   *Reminiscences of a Highland Parish* (London 1891).

Martin, Rev J R   *Church Chronicles of Nigg* (London).

Martine, J   *Reminiscences of the Royal Burgh of Haddington* (Edinburgh and Glasgow 1883).

Maxwell, W   *Iona and the Ionians with a Few Remarks on Mull, Staffa and Tyree* (sic) (Glasgow 1857).

McNeill, F Marion   *The Silver Bough* (Glasgow 1961).

Mercer, A   *History of Dunfermline* (Dunfermline 1828).

Mitchell, Joseph   *Reminiscences of my Life in the Highlands* (1883, reprint David and Charles 1971).

M'Michael, Archibald   *Notes by the Way* (Roxburghshire etc.) (Ayr).

M'Naught, D   *Kilmaurs Parish and Burgh* (Paisley 1912).

Moir, D G   *Scottish Hill Tracks* (Edinburgh 1975).

Munro, R W and Jean   *Tain Through the Centuries* (Inverness 1966).

Murray, James   *Life in Scotland a Hundred Years Ago* (Paisley 1907).

Murray, William   *Reminiscences of Old Coaching Days* (Hawick Archaeological Society, Hawick 1904).

Napier, Lord   *Survey of Selkirkshire or Ettrick Forest 1829.*

Paxton, Ronald and Ruddock, Tim   *A Heritage of Bridges between Edinburgh, Kelso and Berwick* (Edinburgh).

Peacock, Bill   *Waverley Route Reflections* (Hawick 1983).

Peake, F G   *Change at St Boswells* (Galashiels 1961).

Pendleton, John   *Our Railways* (London 1894).

Pennant, Thomas   *Tour in Scotland in 1769* (London 1772).

Pococke, Dr Richard   *Tour of Dr Richard Pococke in 1760* (Edinburgh 1888).

Pollok, Rev Arthur   *The Parish of Lilliesleaf* (Selkirk 1913).

Porteous, Alexander   *Annals of St Fillans* (1912).

Porteous, Alexander   *History of Crieff* (Edinburgh and London 1912).

Rankin, Eric   *Cockburnspath: A Documentary History of a Border Parish* (Edinburgh 1981).

Reid, Alan   *Royal Burgh of Forfar* (Paisley, London, Edinburgh, Glasgow, 1902).

Reid, Alexander G   *Annals of Auchterarder and Memorials of Strathearn* (Crieff 1899).

Sanderson, Margaret H B   *The Mauchline Account Books of Melrose Abbey 1527–8* (Ayrshire Collections, XI, 1976).

Scott, Barbara and Gordon, Anne   *The Parish of Nigg* (1966).

Smith, Peter   *The Turnpike Age* (Luton 1970).

Somerville, Thomas   *My Own Life and Times* (Edinburgh).

Strawhorn, John   'On an Ayrshire Farm' (from *Ayrshire Collections*).

Tancred, George   *Rulewater and its People* (Edinburgh 1907).

Thomson, Rev Andrew   *The Sabbath and the Railway.*

Thomson, James   *Recollections of a Speyside Parish Fifty Years Ago* (1887).

Waddell, Rev P H   *An Old Kirk Chronicle* (Edinburgh and London 1893).

Watson, W J   *Place Names of Ross and Cromarty* (1904).

Weir, Daniel   *History of Greenock* (Greenock 1829).

Whetstone, Ann E   *Scottish County Government in the Eighteenth and Nineteenth Centuries* (Edinburgh 1981).

Wordsworth, Dorothy   *Recollections of a Tour in Scotland in 1803* (Edinburgh 1874).

Young, Robert   *Parish of Spynie* (Elgin 1871).

Young, Robert   *Annals of Elgin* (Elgin 1879).

Also consulted: Acts of the Scottish Parliament; Ayrshire Collections; Balnagown Estate Rent Book 1833; *Border Magazine*; Burgh Records of Glasgow, Edinburgh, Lanark, Peebles, Stirling; *Charters and Documents Relating to the Burgh of Peebles 1165–1710* edited for the Scottish Record Society; *Duncan's Itinerary of Scotland 1823*; *General Views of the Agriculture of . . .*; Kirk Session records; Milton Mill, Ross-shire, Ledgers 1904–6; Minutes of Ross-shire 1st District Roads Trustees; Minutes of the Trustees for the Statute Labour Conversion District of Melrose 1812; Minutes of the Turnpike Road Trustees, Kelso Union Turnpike, 1793–1842; Presbytery records; *Proceedings of the Society of Antiquaries of Scotland*; *Kelso Mail*,

Ross-shire Journal, The Scotsman, The Inverness Courier, The North Star and Farmers' Chronicle, Scottish Home and Country; Inventory of the Royal Commission of the Ancient Monuments in Scotland; *Statistical Accounts*; School log books; Sederunt Book Lauder–Kelso Road 1808; *Scottish Notes and Queries*; *Scottish Topography*, Mitchel and Cash; Tain Museum Papers; *Transactions of Hawick Archaeological Society*; *Transactions of the Dumfries-shire and Galloway Natural History and Antiquarian Society*.